From Power Politics to Conflict Resolution

From Power Politics to Conflict Resolution

The Work of John W. Burton

David J. Dunn

Research Fellow in International Relations
Keele University, UK

First published 2004 by
PALGRAVE MACMILLAN
Houndmills, Basingstoke, Hampshire RG21 6XS and
175 Fifth Avenue, New York, N.Y. 10010
Companies and representatives throughout the world

PALGRAVE MACMILLAN is the global academic imprint of the Palgrave Macmillan division of St Martin's Press, LLC and of Palgrave Macmillan Ltd. Macmillan® is a registered trademark in the United States, United Kingdom and other countries. Palgrave is a registered trademark in the European Union and other countries.

ISBN 0–333–66605–4

This book is printed on paper suitable for recycling and made from fully managed and sustained forest sources.

A catalogue record for this book is available from the British Library.

Library of Congress Cataloging-in-Publication Data
Dunn, David J., 1946–
    From power politics to conflict resolution : the work of John W. Burton / David J. Dunn.
        p.   cm.
    Includes bibliographical references and index.
    ISBN 0–333–66605–4
    1. Conflict management   2. Pacific settlement of international disputes.   3. Burton, John W. (John Wear), 1915–   I. Title.
    JZ6368.D86 2003
        327.1′7—dc21   2003048285

10   9   8   7   6   5   4   3   2
13   12   11   10   09   08   07   06   05   04

Printed and bound in Great Britain by
Antony Rowe Ltd, Chippenham and Eastbourne

To Gill

The Problem

'International Politics has nothing to do with the real world.'

(John W. Burton, in conversation with Fred Northedge)

The Solution

'The key to the understanding of international relations consists of ideas, not facts.'

(Michael Banks, *Conflict in World Society*)

The Process

'Progress in social science lies through controversy, which should be sharpened not veiled.'

(Gunnar Myrdal, quoted by Michael Lipton in his Obituary for Myrdal, *The Independent*, 18 May 1987)

The Promise

'We know enough to be able to do better.'

(Sir Peter Medawar, quoted by his wife in the London *Evening Standard*, 2 April 1986)

Contents

Preface and Acknowledgements

The idea of this book goes back a long way, and my own first encounter with John Burton even further. That first encounter was indirect. I had left school, was working in industry in Manchester, and applied to go to university 'off my own bat', as it were. I was interviewed at University College London (UCL) and accepted, to read for the degree of B.Sc. in Economics. By way of preparation, I went along to my local municipal library and had a look around the social sciences section, and there it was that I first encountered John Burton. More specifically, I saw a brand new (that is, unread) copy of *International Relations: A General Theory*. I had encountered international politics only indirectly at school and my knowledge of history (at that time, I might add) pretty much stopped when I had an idea of how to make a Roman road. I did not understand much of what Burton was on about but I still went back to it.

At University College in London, Burton was among those who taught me International Relations, and within a few weeks I had switched to a Joint Honours degree in International Relations and Economics, just at the point when the Centre for the Analysis of Conflict was in its heyday. Michael Banks, John Groom and Bram Oppenheim were around, so too were Tony de Reuck and Chris Mitchell, combining teaching and innovative work in the conflict workshops. I graduated, left London and went to Graduate School in Pennsylvania (where Professor Carey Joynt was a wise counsel indeed), returning to London to do graduate work at the London School of Economics in an intellectual environment quite different from that encountered at UCL. I then went on to North Staffordshire Polytechnic, as it then was, to join a growing department of International Relations and Politics, with a big teaching load, but finding scope to introduce the work of Burton in the context of courses on 'Contemporary Theory in International Relations'.

I was impressed by Burton. I liked the way he taught and was attracted to what he was saying, even though I did not always understand the deeper nuances. In the 1980s, I had blithely assumed that, surely, there was a vast army of people involved with and writing about Burton's work, so significant was it. To my surprise, there was not, apart from the collection of essays edited by Michael Banks, which involved many of Burton's associates, and it occurred to me that I might even do it myself. A searching, hesitant, letter or two prompted encouragement and I set out to complete the task. I met John Burton (and his partner, Betty) at the joint convention of the International Studies Association and the British International Studies Association in London in 1989 – the first time I had seen him in twenty years. I next met him in 1994, when my wife Gill and I spent three weeks in his (and Betty's) company, in Canberra. They were perfect hosts and I had the opportunity to ask him questions and clarify a few issues in my mind, usually after five o'clock, with a glass of wine in hand. I gave him an early draft of an article that sought to locate his work. He read it and said, 'Sound's allright. Get on with it.' That was the sum total of his involvement in the book, together with our informal conversations, apart from for his final, passive role, when he received a substantially complete manuscript in December 2000, in Canberra.

The book has not been approved by him, and it does not rest on any access to papers, systematic interviews and the like. I have not read every word he has written and I have no stock of interview tapes. As is evident from what follows, I have concentrated on his ideas as these have appeared in the book literature, primarily, but with one or two exceptions where I have found an article of special interest to my argument. Generally speaking, what Burton has written in article form has gone on to form parts of longer book-length treatments. I have tried to set the development of the work in context, but I have not found it necessary to draw attention to reviews of his work as they appeared over the years. Those interested in this process of reception and critique will know where to look, but they may be less enlightened or entertained than they might expect, since Burton's work has often been misunderstood and sometimes over-simplified.

I met John again at the 1996 Brisbane Conference of the International Peace Research Association, where I gave an assessment of his work, with Kevin Clements, at that time of Australian National University. John was quick to remind us all – in the face of a persistent use of the past tense – that he was still alive and was listening! I hope he will find this approach to his work fair, useful and interesting. For others, I hope that it will serve as a useful interpretation – and assessment – of his ideas, and a stimulus to a greater direct involvement with them. In turn, my hope is that it will stimulate a greater involvement with the implications of prevention, not only as a set of ideas but also as an agenda of practical consequence in difficult times. It is, as I seek to show, relevant to a range of practical issues that confront societies at the start of the twenty-first century.

A word about the title is in order. As it was being written, my working title was 'The Genealogy of Provention', and indeed, that is what the book is. But there were problems along the way. For one thing, my dictionary and spellchecker do not understand 'provention'. Indeed, at one presentation I gave some years ago, a comment was offered to the effect that it was typical of Burton that he put himself out on a limb by tying his ideas to this 'provention'. Second, I was convinced eventually by the arguments of others that the title might deter rather than attract potential readers. The title this book now carries is thus correct: it is a story of John Burton's odyssey, from the world of power politics to the processes of conflict resolution in a much changed world. But it is, still, a genealogy of provention.

This book has been far too long in the making and I thank my publishers for their patience especially my editor Alison Howson, who has shown patience above and beyond the call of duty. I have thus incurred debts along the way. It is no excuse, but one reason is that, as I got closer to Burton's work I realised the enormity of what he was about and the implications of his work. Was I up to it? In due course, yes, I think (!) but it is up to readers to draw their own conclusions. This is just the first word and could hardly be the last. I myself want to move on in due course to look at the question of implementing 'provention' in practical realms. My conclusion, at least, is clear: there is much to be done.

Those to whom I owe especial thanks are Michael Banks, John Groom, Tony de Reuck and Chris Mitchell, from the days in Endsleigh Street and on many occasions since. Several audiences have listened to me talk about John Burton and I mention particularly those at the Australian National University, George Mason University, the London School of Economics, Rhodes University, the University of Bradford School of Peace Studies, and the University of Lancaster. I also thank the British Academy for the financial support that enabled me to visit Australia in 1994. This opened up a huge new perspective in relation to Burton in Australia in particular, and an engagement with the Australian view of the world more generally. Having been to Canberra, it is hard to imagine how I could really have got to grips with things from the perspective of the English Midlands. I thank also Jean Burlinge of the Open University for finding me a copy of the transcript of the Northedge–Burton tape, recorded in May 1975; as can be seen from the work that follows, I used it to much effect as a benchmark.

Over the years, the North Staffordshire Polytechnic – later Staffordshire University – provided support and a research environment where the pursuit of sound research work allied to teaching was always encouraged. Particular thanks to my former colleagues there – Professor Keith Hayward and Professor Trevor Taylor; it could hardly be said of either of them that they shared my involvement with Peace Research in general, or John Burton in particular, but I thank them for their good fellowship and friendship over very many years. Dr Sita Bali and Dr David Morrice were – and are – rather more kindred spirits when it came to more philosophical matters of 'theory' and paradigms and all the theoretical stuff, and they gave me their time when I needed to bounce ideas around. As did, more recently, Professor Andrew Linklater, at Keele University. To Philip Gabriel I extend special thanks.

It is conventional, at this point, to thank one's best friend, critic and source of support and encouragement during the completion of a work of this nature, and it is a convention with which I am delighted to be able to conform. I thank my wife, Gill. I, like her, often thought I might never make it to the finish. Now I have, and here it is, 'the John book'. This book is for her.

Some of the material presented here has appeared previously in a slightly different form: 'Articulating an Alternative: The Contribution of John Burton', *Review of International Studies*, vol. 21, no. 22 (April 1995); and 'John Burton and the Study of International Relations: An Assessment', *International Journal of Peace Studies*, vol. 6, no. 1 (Spring).

DAVID J. DUNN

Introduction

This book looks at the Burtonian idea of 'provention'. The word deserves attention: not least because 'provention' is not in the dictionary and is, as yet, beyond the capabilities of a computer's spellchecker. It is supremely ironic that Burton's preferred word, in developing an approach that seeks to illuminate the problems we face and how we prevent solutions from emerging, 'provention', seems to the spellchecker to be the nearest word to 'prevention'. For John Burton, the fact that we (or at least authorities acting for us, at all levels of society) seek to *prevent* things happening, in the interests of order and stability, is part of the problem. Provention is a preferred word because it suggests not a control or limit, but rather open-ended adaptation. It is akin in meaning to proactive as opposed to acting in response to a threat, problem or circumstance. It suggests taking the initiative (perhaps in response to a certain farsightedness, or what Burton might call a different definition of the situation). Moreover, provention is more than a word in that it signifies both a critical approach to existing assumptions about how societies work – at local, national, international and global levels of analysis – as well as a diagnostic/programmatic approach with regard to how the existing socio-political problems, manifest therein, might be addressed and properly resolved – as opposed to managed or contained.

It is the central aim of this book to trace the development of Burton's work through various, halting, stages with a view to explaining why such a new term was deemed necessary. At this stage, to repeat (and to suggest the direction that the following work seeks to address and understand) it may be contrasted with prevention. Whereas prevention suggests holding, order, containing and control, provention – as we shall see – shifts the emphasis to questions of change and adaptation.

Genealogy also needs attention. Provention is the label Burton put on much of his later work. He did not start out as a novice academic with a mission to demonstrate the validity of provention. He came to it late, through a mixture of chance, personal influences, circumstance and the like. Over time, he was able to say more, and then he was able to say not only what provention was but also what it promised. Thus genealogy suggests a searching for its roots, through an engagement with its pre-cursors and dead-ends. There never was a Burtonian project, mission or similar sense of purpose. Except to cope with, explain and suggest a way out of a sense of unease at the foundations, limitations and implications of the conventional wisdom. It is a measure of the man that, throughout his life, Burton has never felt comfortable with the notion of a/the conventional wisdom. Indeed, it is tempting to suggest that where he has encountered anything approximating to orthodoxy and the convential wisdom, he has challenged it. And with positive consequences.

The aim of this book is to survey the work of John Burton with a view to explaining the origins, development and significance of what he has called 'provention'. As a work it is principally about ideas and, more specifically, the development of a scheme of thought. If the notion of development suggests smooth progression, in Burton's case it was neither smooth nor continuous. If this is the overall aim, there are several objectives. These include an analysis of Burton's involvement with the practice, and then the academic study of, international relations; an explanation of his distancing himself from the orthodoxy of Inter-national Relations as an academic discipline, having necessarily engaged with it as a student and a teacher; his successive attempts to redefine the substantive issues, especially conflict behaviour; his development of conflict resolution; and the elaboration of what he describes as a philoso-phy of conflict resolution.

Why a book about Burton covering these issues, among others? First, a book about Burton's work is timely. He has in recent years retired to his native Australia, though 'retired' is a conventional term that is not entirely appropriate; he no longer has a formal teaching or research position, though he still continues to write, in his tenth decade. A survey is therefore a retrospective summary of achievement at this point in his life. Second, and perhaps more important, it is appropriate in terms of the point that Burton has reached in his own work. His four-volume 'Conflict Series', which appeared in 1990, can be characterised as a sort of point of crystallisation of his work, an achievement. What he has done since is a further articulation of some of the implications that follow from 'provention', but the more significant aspect of the Conflict Series is that it outlines an alternative frame of reference for the understanding of behaviour. In that respect, it represents a point at which Burton has long aimed as he sought to articulate an alternative to the power frame of reference, so long dominant in human affairs and in particular in international relationships. A survey thus records an achievement, 'provention', but one long in the making and sometimes, perhaps often, also difficult.

Such a work as this is timely in relation to other developments, too, specifically as these relate to the discipline of International Relations and in particular the agenda of security at the start of the new millennium. Towards the end of the twentieth century there appeared a series of concerns and comments that relate to degrees of confusion within International Relations. These pre-date the end of the Cold War and are more fundamental than the construction of a post-Cold War agenda. For Ken Booth, the problem is that, as he puts it, our work is our words, but our words do not work any more (Booth, 1990). More recently, Booth has argued that insights in the work of Burton, along with the work of Johan Galtung, Richard Falk and Kenneth Boulding, whom he terms peace research 'radicals', 'constitute a more original contribution to the present security debate than any of the articles that have been filling space in the workaday security journals at the closings of the Cold War'. At the same time he reminds us that the writings of these (and other) individuals were regarded as 'irrelevant (or worse) during the Cold War' (Booth, 1997, p. 86). Some years ago, Michael Banks sought to identify where International Relations as an academic discipline was to be located in terms of its development (Banks, 1985a, p. 215). He argued, with respect to International Relations (and the comment is perhaps even more valid now compared to the situation that obtained when it was first written), that 'there seems to be progressively less agreement about the core ideas that are supposed to hold the discipline together' (Banks, 1984, pp. xi–xii). He also offered the observation that Burton could assist us out of this impasse.

Apart from considerations of relevance and utility, there is another set of issues that surround Burton's relationship to International Relations. He has written not far short of twenty books, and countless papers and articles, yet he has been marginalised, and largely ignored by many, in terms of the community of International Relations scholars, certainly in the United Kingdom. Though he spent a good part of his teaching and research career in the United Kingdom he never achieved the status of professor, achieving that rank only later, in the United States, where his reputation stood, and stands, higher. Why, given his output, was he so marginalised by his colleagues in the United Kingdom, in a manner quite contrary to the way in which his fellow Australian, Hedley Bull, was not? Indeed, Bull was clutched to the collective bosom of the British International Relations community with as much enthusiasm as Burton was sidelined, standing, arguably, at the centre of what came to be known as 'The English School'. Burton is not without his supporters, however. He managed to gather around him a small but significant group of like-minded individuals who assisted in the critical articulation of much of his work, principally in London, later in Kent and then in the United States. These individuals included Michael Banks, John Groom, Christopher Mitchell, Michael Nicholson, Bram Oppenheim and Tony de Reuck, constituting the core of the Centre for the Analysis of Conflict and later the so-called 'London School', and came also to include Dennis Sandole, Margot Light and Mark Hoffmann.

For many of his colleagues, Burton's contribution has been enormously significant at both the personal and professional level. Herbert Kelman commented that meeting Burton literally changed his life (Kelman, 1984, p. xvii); and it is as well to point out that Kelman was not, at the time he met Burton, an impressionable undergraduate, but a mature academic in his own right, an eminent professor, a pioneer of peace research and a commentator on ethical as well as psychological issues. Banks also has repeatedly argued the case for the recognition of Burton's enormously significant contribution. Furthermore, he suggests that two of his books of the 1980s (*Global Conflict* (1982) and *Dear Survivors* (1984)) are tracts for their times (Banks, 1985a, p. 227), a sure indication of realism and relevance. Moreover, suggests Banks, although the work of Burton is 'too speculative, intellectually radical and inadequately substantiated: he is part guru, part gadfly, a source of inspiration and irritation.... It is likely that Burton's entire output will be seen, in future generations, as the beginnings of a fundamental shift in the way in which the entire discipline [of International Relations] treats its subject matter' (Banks, 1985a, p. 220).

Others have been equally enthusiastic, not simply in terms of their opposition to Burton (the late Fred Northedge, for example) but in their apparent dismissal of his entire approach. Susan Strange, a particularly important figure in the British International Relations establishment and arguably the pioneer of the approach known as International Political Economy, felt that Burton's approach to issues such as conflict was unrealistic, and has observed that

whilst my last son Adam was being born, John Burton appeared on the Gower Street scene [that is, at University College London] and like

[Harold] Laski was more interested in recruiting disciples than teaching students to think for themselves. Nor could I accept his unrealistic notions that all conflicts could be resolved with better analysis and rational discussion ... All the reports suggested that Burton wasn't an easy man to get along with if you didn't agree with everything he said. I thought it better to leave him to it. (Strange, 1989, p. 433)

Alan Ryan is not nearly as direct as Strange, but we are left in no doubt as to his view when he argues that Burton invented the term provention 'to preach the irrefutable truth that we ought to head off conflict before it breaks out, by getting rid of its underlying causes – but Professor Burton is necessarily short of advice about how in 1990 or 1991 we can prevent (let alone "provent") the damage done in 1917 and 1919 when the Allies carved up the defeated Ottoman Empire' (Ryan, 1991, p. 5). And, from Australia, Andrew Mack has been critical of the basic foundations (especially the concept of need) upon which Burton's framework rests, suggesting that 'his argument assumes that which is to be demonstrated' (Mack, 1985, p. 21) and 'if "need" cannot be adequately distinguished from wants, Burton's theory fails' (Mack, 1991, p. 95).

Nor are these views isolated or rare. John Groom, for example, in taking a wide perspective across the study of International Relations, observed that 'in Britain major contributors to the conceptualisation of world society were made by Mitrany and Burton, although neither was born in Britain and both were controversial figures there, unrecognised, indeed denigrated by the British academic establishment' (Olson and Groom, 1991, p. 139). It is clear, therefore, that in dealing with Burton we are dealing with an individual to whom many remain indifferent: he has his supporters and his detractors, and they appear to be vocal in defence of their views of him.

What makes these verdicts – suggesting that Burton is in some way prone to misunderstand, showing tendencies toward the 'unreal', contestable or contentious and in some way does not understand the 'real world of events' – paradoxical if not perverse, is that Burton was, for a considerable time and at a critical juncture in the conduct of his country's foreign policy, a practitioner in the 'real world' of power politics. He was, in point of fact, Secretary of the Australian Department of External Affairs before he was forty years old at a time, after the Second World War, when Australia was developing an independent foreign policy and its own stance as the Cold War evolved in Asia. Before that he was a close adviser to the foreign minister and attended the founding conference of the United Nations in San Francisco, amongst other events.

In short, we have a curious puzzle at the heart of a consideration of Burton's work. On the one hand is the view that he is essentially unrealistic, living and working in a world that, though interesting, is detached and incapable or otherwise of explaining what is going on in the realm of contemporary international relations. Conversely, we have the view that his contribution is comparable, in its way, to that of John Maynard Keynes, arguably the greatest of the modern economists. In short, we have a paradox to be addressed, among other things.

These verdicts on and views of Burton, as well as other issues, are to be addressed in what follows, the first general survey of Burton's work written by a single author. Work is under way by other scholars within the United Kingdom, focusing on aspects of Burton's work, but not an evaluation of the whole of it. Banks and others among Burton's colleagues contributed to a Festschrift in the late 1980s and the book served its purpose adequately then. Since then, of course, Burton has written more, and significantly more important, works. The work of Kenneth Boulding has been addressed by Cynthia Kerman (Kerman, 1974), and that of Johan Galtung by Peter Lawler (Lawler, 1994). One of the contentions underlying the present work is that Burton's achievement can stand, and is worthy of, comparison with both Boulding and Galtung. Indeed, a statement printed on the covers of each of the four volumes in the Conflict Series refer to Burton as the 'father of conflict resolution'. An exaggeration, perhaps, but only that because, arguably – and so argued here – Burton has made a contribution of no less importance than those of Boulding and Galtung. Collectively, they may legitimately be described as the makers of conflict resolution and peace research. In that respect, therefore, an assessment of his work is not only timely – for the reasons already outlined – it is overdue.

The aim at this stage is an assessment of Burton's achievement in articulating his framework known as 'provention'. As such, therefore, the present work fills a gap, but it also represents a gap through which others might be led to an appreciation, and further understanding and articulation, of the framework of provention. Much, it will be clear, remains to be done. Thus, there is no claim or pretence to a definitive treatment of Burton's scheme. On the contrary, it is to be hoped that this will be the first of many encounters with Burton and provention.

It is as well to address the question of the perspective from which the present work is written, and how it is arranged. It is written from within the discipline of International Relations, but not a 'mainstream' or orthodox perspective. Many have commented on the apparent crisis within the discipline of International Relations, evident throughout the

1990s. In part this is because of the demise of the state-centric perspective that dominated the discipline for so long, but is now inappropriate and inadequate to the task of explaining the modern world of state and other actors. We live in a world often described as interdependent, which is 'getting smaller', where time and distance render events immediate and often more difficult to influence or control. But there is something more fundamental than this. Arguably, the very construction of the discipline of International Relations is at issue; perhaps, even, its persistence as a discrete discipline. The old distinctions about the nature of international, as opposed to domestic, politics are collapsing; high and low politics are no longer significant or meaningful distinctions in a world where, for many, sport and culture are politics, as are trade and environment; and power is now diffused and coercion frequently dysfunctional, as attested on so many occasions. Cases abound where action is necessary or desirable, but where none is forthcoming because of the logic of the system itself. States will act only if they feel that it is in their own interest to do so, and if they perceive no benefit, they do not act, singly or collectively.

Problems perceived may therefore go untended, getting worse before they get better, if they get better at all. Rwanda, Somalia, Bosnia and East Timor stand as the most recent, but also the most telling, cases, where the very logic of the states system is at issue. In Rwanda, for example, there was a response of sorts, but the major issue appeared to be to get the refugee population out of an adjacent country and back into their own territory, consistent with the established notion of territoriality, citizenship and responsibility. But, as other cases also attest, it is clearly the case that governments are not the guardians of their citizens' welfare; rather, they inflict positive pain, harm and suffering on their own populations, with a freedom to do so consistent with territoriality and sovereignty. Witness Saddam Hussein's treatment of the Marsh Arabs or the Turkish treatment of Kurds. Essentially, the old framework is in need of replacement, rather than repair or renovation, and security, welfare, community, citizenship and legitimacy in need of reinvestment.

The community of International Relations scholars has responded variously to such changes, and a range of approaches, conceptual schemes and so-called 'islands of theory' have proliferated. To what effect, and with what consequences, are questionable. To the extent that John Burton has sought to redefine the issues or reconstruct them in novel and radical terms, then to that extent he has been marginalised or ignored, for there are many who see the essentials of international politics as unchanging, despite time and circumstance, represented in the persistence of power and interests. Burton has been found to be too unrealistic by many. Yet, for Banks, sympathetic but not uncritical of Burton's work, he offers a way out of the current impasse, because Burton's accumulated writings 'have gone farther than any other single body of work towards the creation of a genuine synthesis of the fragmented islands of theory that have so teased the discipline' (Banks, 1984, p. xii). Why, how and to what extent we shall discover in what follows. For the moment it is important to stress an affiliation with Banks' stance in relation to Burton, seeing great potential for addressing the central problems of a discipline in difficulties.

Yet it is important to recognise that this does not take us far enough. Many of those who encountered Burton or his later work saw him as working within a framework of conflict resolution, speaking a different language, employing a different ontology, and they were often unaware of his previous work in International Relations. What he has tried to do, often hesitantly, and often with difficulty, is to get *beyond* International Relations, as it were, with a view not to redefining its terms but rather to reconstituting the fundamentals of his own world view, rendering international relationships only a part of a complex pattern of relationships and not necessarily a uniquely different or difficult part. Hence his identification with conflict resolution. But even this does not take us far enough, as conflict resolution is just part of a larger whole.

More specifically, what is attempted here is a survey and explanation of how a sense of personal dissatisfaction at first gave rise to a critical stance in relation to the practice of international relations; then to a critique of the conventional assumptions about that behaviour, embodied in the discipline of International Relations; and from there to the construction of an alternative explanatory system. Moreover, as we shall see, that sense of dissatisfaction was latent and felt long before it could be articulated, either clearly or at length, and certainly to Burton's own satisfaction. In part, therefore, we shall be concerned with an attempt to articulate an alternative. But what kind of 'alternative'? Many social and political theorists can claim that what they are embarked upon is a task of systematic improvement of socio-political knowledge through a process of articulating alternatives, be they approaches, frameworks or whatever. In this, the issues surrounding Burton are surely not unique.

However, taking the story on a little further, the treatment of Burton's work that follows seeks to demonstrate how the personal unease and disquiet, or critical stance if you will, was just a prelude. But not simply that. Clearly, he tried to articulate an alternative approach to International Relations. But, in due course – forty years, in fact – he developed a framework for the analysis of the totality of human relationships, especially conflictual relationships, that would transform a sense of personal impatience and unease into what amounts to no less than a fundamentally novel approach to human relationships: indeed, a new political philosophy. This is a not inconsiderable achievement, representing, arguably, a distancing from – if not a full-scale assault upon – the fundamental tenets of much of Western political philosophy. We would be well advised to take such claims seriously, while also subjecting them to rigorous scrutiny.

Having said that this book is principally about ideas, it must also detail the life-stance and personal development, to some degree, of the man manifestly associated with them. But this is not a 'life', in the sense of a conventional (or unconventional, for that matter) biography. For one thing, the author has no claim to skills associated with the historian or biographer. (For another, a biography is already being written – especially in so far as it concerns Burton's work in Australia as a practitioner of politics, rather than as an academic – by Gregory Pemberton, in Australia.) And, further, the emphasis here is on ideas rather than personal details or events. It details the relationship between Burton's life and work to a limited extent, less concerned with the details of events than with the appearance of ideas in context. What follows constitutes less of an intellectual biography, co-locating person and ideas, and rather more of an analysis of the evolution of a scheme of thought. Some might, perhaps, see it as an exercise in the sociology of knowledge.

Such an approach also helps to define the preferred form of the book. One option that presents itself to an author dealing with people and ideas is to treat the issues thematically, establishing a framework of ideas. An emphasis on themes stresses order and system, relating ideas one to the other in a systematic fashion. It suggests, to some degree or other, the retrospective imposition of order on an emergent system of ideas. The benefits of such an approach are precisely that they see order in the search for ideas and system, covering the whole. Coherence is suggested. We are dealing here with ideas and images such as a seamless web, a slow evolution, a filling-out of an essential frame. (A model might be Cynthia Kerman's work on Kenneth Boulding, which represents an elegant mixture of his life and a coherent framework of ideas evolving; see Kerman, 1974.) In the terms of this approach, fuller frameworks are revealed, elements of consistency made explicit and interconnections evident, and growth recorded.

This is not the path chosen here, however. An early proposal to treat the work of Burton led to an observation that the chronological approach should be avoided: books like this, it was suggested, needed to deal with theme, rather than a book-by-book evaluation. Despite that advice, and much consideration of how to approach the ideas of Burton, the approach adopted here is broadly chronological, since a chronological perspective might tend to highlight points of discontinuity, or periods of confusion or stasis. In this perspective, there are key roles for the vagaries of accident, chance, discovery and rare, but valuable, conceptual leaps in particular circumstances that are seemingly incapable of clear explanation, certainly at the time they occur. The chronological/ evolutionary perspective stresses rather more the mood of unease and discomfort (and sometimes sheer angst and stress) that precede first discovery *and then* research, taking the issues further and assigning meaning and significance. It stresses the pragmatic rather more than the programmatic and driven. Driven by circumstance is not the same as driven to expand on what one already knows to be the case. Often it is unclear what people are searching for, though it is clear to them what they are reacting to or rebelling *against*, be it the limitations of conventional wisdom (where the limits of conventional wisdom are acknowledged) or a sense of unease that is felt, even when it is not clearly articulated.

This is the preferred route adopted here because, as we shall see, Burton frequently stresses the importance of chance, accident and moments of discovery; what is important is how one responds – to events, books, ideas, conferences – *at the given moment in time*. Frequently, we do not know how to proceed, though the need to proceed is deeply felt. These chance encounters, discoveries and accidents are instrumental and significant in terms of how we proceed. These are the moments that historians can only try to recreate or explain, their efforts only ever capable of being an approximation and partial re-creation. This has more than a passing interest to a consideration of Burton's own position.

In a light-hearted moment, Burton proffered the comment that he had been saying the same thing for over forty years. Therein lies a fundamental issue to be explored in what follows. In one sense he has been consistent. Yet he has, as it were, been saying the same thing hesitantly, incompletely, in different ways, with different concepts and with different frames of reference and at different stages of his career. Thus the title of the book is suggestive of an evolution – from power to provention. There never was a Burtonian project, but there is a Burtonian odyssey and a consequent achievement. As we shall see, as a significant participant in events now recorded in histories, written officially and otherwise, his own approach to knowledge and understanding has been much influenced by a view that what history records is not history as experienced by the participants. What the histories record as events are not necessarily events as experienced as far as Burton is concerned. Taking the point even further, this might help us in understanding why, by and large, Burton has stressed an approach to relationships based on an ahistoric, sociological frame of reference, rather than one based in history. The stance is rooted in the experience. But this is to get ahead of ourselves.

At this point it is important to stress that, at key points in his search for an appropriate, and adequate, framework, he has found inspiration in articles and books that have served as key instrumentalities. Though he may not have taken into his own framework the whole of what he encountered, he has, perhaps, on occasion, found a key concept, idea or framework that takes him further. Indeed, he might even have read into a piece more than the author intended. But the point is that he has found the piece useful, in part or in its entirety, and instrumental in taking his own work forward. Similarly with the influence of academic colleagues. An encounter and a discovery has facilitated further research.

But this is not all. Were this the story of an academic who sought a more complete framework for the discussion of ideas, albeit one who preferred a sociological or critical frame to a historical or conventional one, it would be really rather straightforward, commonplace even, for many scholars could claim with equal facility that they had sought ways of better explaining the social reality of which they are a part, in which chance, accident and the occasional intuitive leap play a part. So what, if anything, is it that sets apart John Burton as being worthy of study in terms other than these? What paradoxes or hidden truths are there to be revealed?

For one thing, Burton never intended to be an academic, a fact seldom considered as important or relevant in an evaluation of his work: it may be that people are unaware of his earlier life. He did not leave university with a sense of academic vocation and a burning desire to write and contribute to knowledge. Of course, he had studied, gained a first-class Honours degree and a doctorate. But even though he succeeded in academia, this was not his preferred route – at least not at first. His preference was for a more practical career, informed by a sense of duty and public service. This is important. He was a civil servant and diplomat (of extraordinarily high rank, for a young man of thirty-two years old); was thwarted in his search for a political career; turned to farming; and continued, in Australia, to comment to some degree on domestic and international politics. Though he was certainly not an insider, he was not entirely an outsider either. He had a reputation, of which some disapproved, but he still commentated, and forcefully, on events, sometimes seeking to influence them. He freely admits that he became an academic in circumstances that he could not and did not foresee. But when, in middle age, he did become an academic, his output was extraordinary. Within two years of his taking up a university teaching post in London, he had produced a book, and two others soon followed. By the time of his retirement, he had produced not far short of twenty books and numerous articles, together with countless discussion papers, and had been associated with institutional initiatives, both national and international.

Which ought, surely on any reasonable grounds, assure him of a place. The extraordinary dual career, the diplomat-turned-scholar, clearly relating theory and practice, would surely ensure at least a reputation of sorts. Others of his generation have followed a similar path. But Burton's reputation is mixed where it is acknowledged and, by another twist, many regard the work he has produced as being marginal to the study of International Relations at best, and irrelevant at worst.

The output is manifest, but what are we to make of it? What is significant about it? Part of the purpose underlying this book is to unravel some of the critical dichotomies that surround Burton. Almost the simplest of them is the diplomat-turned-scholar. But later we encounter the International Relations theorist who spurns conventional wisdom quite explicitly. In turn, people take up stances in relation to him: pro-Burton or anti-Burton. Few seem to be indifferent. He was never a professor in the United Kingdom, where much of his early work was done. Only later did he achieve professorial status, in the United States, where his works are very well regarded and where his reputation seems assured. This is far less true in Great Britain and Australia. Part of the reason may be found in personal animosity, but such an explanation is at best only partial. Burton, like everybody else, does not get along with everyone. The stances have to be explained by the ideas and the context. Not only does he move away from International Relations, first there is drift, then a positive shift and then there is a positive search for, and then elaboration of, an alternative frame of reference. In one sense (to be explored here, at some length) it could be said that Burton defines out of existence the autonomous subject of International Relations, with its own distinct set of assumptions, concerns and issues: what is known as the 'anarchy *problematique*', which is said to set International Relations aside from political science, history and other academic fields. For Burton, these claims to uniqueness are specious, and where they are not specious, they are hindrances to understanding, rather than enablers. For Burton, international politics is only one kind of politics, preoccupied with political power, but rooted in false assumptions about persons, power and states, assumptions that are more than misleading: they are positively damaging in their practical implications.

For Burton, there is no 'darker side of human nature', from which springs a lust and search for political power. Politics, for him, is about people. Thus, if politics is not about power, nor is international politics. The Realist foundation, rooted in traditional assumptions that, in practice, cannot be substantiated (there is always the case that proves that human nature is 'bad', that we struggle to contain this force within us, imperfectly; any pretence to the contrary can thus be dismissed as wishful thinking or idealism). Such a stance clearly sets Burton apart. But it makes him a realist, though not a Realist. It is inconceivable that Burton should tell us to find 'that which history teaches'. What we learn from history is what we want to learn, and when we learn it we learn it from the written records, the veracity of which (for Burton) must be suspect; they can at best approximate to mood and whim, but they cannot know the truth, even if they seem to approximate to an understanding of it. At this point, there is a clear thread that links the practical career of Burton the diplomat and the assumptions that have underpinned his academic career. One can 'know about' John Burton by looking at the records of Australian diplomatic history, the records of conferences, the official documents and the relevant biographies (of those for whom, and with whom, he worked; and of those he opposed or antagonised). But what do we know of Burton if this is all we 'know'?

There is thus a clear epistemological issue at stake in an assessment of Burton's work. His approach to knowledge and understanding, the mixture of ontological and epistemological concerns, are central to the evolution of his thought. His critique of conventional 'political philosophy' (well-known to us from the works of Plato, Aristotle, Hobbes, Locke, Marx and the rest of the classics) goes to the root of our understanding of not only men and women but also the structure and functions of politics, the nature of democracy and the nature of political institutions. He is not 'positivist' in the conventional sense of the term, but roots his assessment in an approach to an understanding of how people live: how they are, rather than what they should be; in what they need, not what they ought to need. In how they exist as people, communities, families, tribes, ethnic groups; not as artificial constructs that aid our analytical understanding, like 'economic man' – who has never existed beyond the confines of economic analysis; or the 'voter' casting preferences according to an assumed array of choices; or the strategic decision-maker, contemplating the thought processes of an array of opponents, assuming the nature of pain and damage, and constructing effectively punitive strategies. Burton eschews the notion of 'great leaders', making 'big decisions', preferring instead to focus on decision-makers as men and women, subject to their own relevant pressures and needs, and thus comparable to other men and women.

In this, his stance is holistic. He tries to see behaviour as a whole, interconnected and with its patterns replicated at all levels of social and political activity. He has not yet solved the problem of reconciling complexity with a necessary focus on the whole, but this is a secondary issue. His thought enables that debate to take place. What he does say is that making arbitrary judgements about what is important is misleading methodologically, whether this is an affirmation of the primary role of the state, the uniqueness of international politics, the essential difference as between leaders and led, the assumption that scarcity is the central problem in economics and the like. Behaviour has to be seen as a whole, and behaviour understood as it is, not as we suppose, expect, anticipate, want or judge it to be. In these terms, as we shall see, the notion of 'deviance' in society is all about compliance with established norms.

His treatment is scientific, but not in any crudely quantitative or behaviouralist fashion. The preferred approach is rooted in the life-stance. Recall an earlier emphasis on his sense of disquiet, fuelling a search for an alternative. Given this stance, his discovery (the conjunction is important) and incorporation of the American nineteenth-century phil-osopher, (and predecessor of Dewey and James in the development of the American Pragmatic tradition), Charles Sanders Peirce, is illuminating. Peirce, who called himself a 'pragmaticist', rather than the more familiar 'pragmatist', essentially constructed a philosophical stance of connect-edness between knower and known, a pattern of reflexivity if you will, a stream of hypothesis construction and testing against the evidence, with utility a key consideration, certainty allied to an operational doubt. (In this he perhaps pre-dates debate about the authority of science in the postmodern literature by some way, but is entirely relevant to it). Peirce did not enable Burton to think anew, rather how to give voice and a frame of reference to that previously internalised. (There is a dual similarity here with Karl Deutsch's introduction of the notion of feedback to Burton's system, in the sense that both were important enablers, and both stressed a similar relationship of thought: test and see.)

Drawing out some of these issues, it is clear that Burton rejects the particularist-authoritative style that is so typical of much of conventional

International Relations thinking. He rejects an emphasis on the state as *the* key level of analysis (and in doing so reminds us, in more than a passing mood, that the state was designed as an instrumentality, not as an end in itself) which is a foundation stone in the traditional frame of reference. He rejects an emphasis on governments as *the* centre of authority. He is more concerned with processes than structures, not least because the latter create their own elites, who then define the ends of politics in their own terms, and not least their own survival as an elite. As such, he has much to say about the problems of political systems in general, as well as conflictual behaviour in particular. He stresses change rather than order, legitimate social relationships rather than coercive relations. He stresses, in explanations of social behaviour, causes rather than symptoms, the fundamental rather than the superficial: needs rather than wants or desires; and needs rather than nationalisms.

Moreover, the more one reads the work, and then looks at contemporary events, the sense of a prescient mind evolving is inescapable. Burton has seemed to anticipate much that is contemporary, in both theory and practice. His relevance seems clear in the light of unfolding events.

This is not to suggest that his work, in particular and as a whole, is unproblematical. There are problems in the exposition, the references to the literature, and at times the positively assertive nature of the treatments. There is, at times, an impatience barely concealed, an impatience borne of frustration with the limitations of the literature and his own frame of reference.

Plan of the book

After a chapter that sets out the relevant context by surveying, relatively briefly, Burton's life and associations, the book is organised into four parts. Part one surveys Burton's work up to the point at which he became a full-time teacher and researcher in London in 1963. If, as he says, he has been saying the same things for forty years or more, then it is important that a work such as this, suggesting a successive articulation of thoughts and ideas, should also cover the earlier and less conspicuous work. Hence, attention is directed here to Burton's doctoral dissertation and some of his more conspicuous work done in Australia. Part two surveys the work done at a time when it could be said, with some authority, that Burton was located squarely within International Relations, engaging with its central concerns and addressing a shared agenda. This was a significant period of research and, perhaps more important, teaching, for Burton. Though it was significant, it was relatively short.

Part three charts the progressive disaffection for the discipline of International Relations, illustrating and explaining Burton's drift – and then significant break – away from the politics of states and power, with a special claim to a unique intellectual *problematique*. Part four deals with the nature, structure and significant elements of the framework of analysis, which he terms 'provention'. A concluding section assesses the significance of provention in terms of the contribution it represents in terms of its capability to explain the contemporary world. As such, Burton's claims for it to be treated as a new political philosophy are scrutinised and his achievement evaluated, with reference to International Relations and a set of wider concerns.

1
Life and Associations

As stated at the outset, this is not a biography of Burton. Nevertheless, on the very clear assumption that events and ideas interact with each other, it is important to establish a brief biographical frame of reference to Burton's developing ideas. This would be important for most surveys of the ideas developing in intellectuals as prolific as Burton, but in his case there is an added dimension, for he has been a practitioner as well as a scholar; his life and work have aroused controversy; and, perhaps most importantly for a man who has produced so much work and had an effect on conventional assumptions about conflict and society, Burton never intended to be an academic.

John Wear Burton Junior was born in Melbourne, Australia on 2 March 1915. His father is especially important and, even though this book concentrates on Burton's work rather than on the details of his life, the role of the father is important and deserves attention, for the traits of the father were in this case clearly to influence the son.

John Burton Senior was born in Yorkshire, England in 1875, the second son of Robert Burton, a joiner. The family left for New Zealand in 1883, because of the ill-health of Robert's wife. John left school at 12, working first as a fleece-picker and then later as an apprentice wheelright. At 17 he became a lay preacher, evidently influenced by a strong family tradition. By 1895 he had begun theological training in New Zealand and was ordained in 1901. In the following year he left for missionary work in the South Pacific, but not before marrying Florence Hadfield – on the day that he departed, 24 April. In due course the couple had five children: a son, John Jr., and four daughters. John Burton Senior returned to New Zealand in 1910, because of ill health, and wrote a book (many more were to follow), later described as 'his most influential and controversial' (Thornley, 1979), which drew attention to the poor working

17

conditions of the labourers in Fiji. Several years later he was invited to become the secretary of overseas missions in Victoria. At the end of the First World War he assisted with the demobilisation of Australian soldiers in London, where he became a pacifist. For twenty years (1925–45) he was General Secretary of the Methodist Missionary Society of Australasia, and from 1945 to 1948 President General of the Methodist Church in Australasia, 'his elevation having been deferred during the war because of his uncompromising pacifism' (Thornley, 1979).

During his long and active career, Burton Senr. evidently acquired a reputation as a radical, who disdained 'popular judgements ... adhering to principles of justice and utterance of Christian conscience'. Moreover, his writings and efforts were not without a significant effect on policy, particularly with respect to working conditions in the Pacific islands: 'Though criticised for his dominance, he was an outstanding leader during the depression and World War Two, with a natural organising ability and capacity for single minded pursuit of aims' (Thornley, 1979).

John Jr. was obviously influenced by his father. He showed a practical streak, characteristic of his father, and developed an interest in how things worked, trying to repair them if they needed attention. He did not, apparently, conform to the typical image of a bright son of a strong, driven father. Indeed, 'Burton told me that he was a bit of a dunce at school. He had suffered from dyslexia and was bottom of his class year after year' (Clack, 1991). He was also influenced by the religious air of the household. Indeed, it seemed natural that the son should follow the father in the direction of the Church. But what that meant, and what was involved, seemed to divide father from son, and that division proved to be consequential. For John Jr., 'religion' was about involvement in doing good and ameliorating social problems, rather than a mystical engagement with ideas and beliefs. In light of what his father – as a zealous and active missionary, critic and leader – had done as a minister of the Church, this was hardly a surprising view to adopt. But what John Jr. found difficulty with, could not, and ultimately did not, accept was the attendant theological apparatus, the quasi-philosophical speculations and the necessity for prayer. This, in his view, was not what 'religion' was about; speaking out and doing good – yes, but getting on one's knees and praying for guidance – no. He was not interested in the metaphysics or mysticism of the task, but rather the doing of it, and if the one necessitated the other (as might reasonably be argued), then he would have none of it. The Church, and religion, was not to be his career, earlier expectations notwithstanding.

Nevertheless, despite this difference, which might reasonably be called fundamental, there were similarities between them, which persisted over the years. It could be said of the son that he too could be dominating on occasion, and some saw his forthright expression of opinions as brusque, perhaps (unnecessarily) confrontational and 'flinty'. He was also single-minded and not afraid to speak his mind. It is tempting to suggest that both father and son shared a (typically, English) North Country cast of mind; as is often said in Yorkshire, 'I speak as I find.' Both, undoubtedly, did. And both were to find admirers for what they did, forthrightness and dominance notwithstanding.

The young John was educated at Newington College in Sydney, and Wesley College, Melbourne. He graduated in 1937 with a degree in psychology (first class) from the University of Sydney. Public service as a career seemed to be consistent with his early outlook (social improvement seemingly being associated with public service), and that is the direction Burton took. The first-class degree notwithstanding, the point of entry into the Commonwealth Public Service in Australia was as a postal clerk, the only point of entry at the time. What is interesting is that this mode of entry says a great deal about the continuing nature of the Australian civil service at the time. It was not many years before Burton's entry that the normal point of entry was as a 15-year-old school-leaver; graduates were exceptional. Soon Burton found himself at Australia House in London and he was quick to register for a research degree at the London School of Economics, just across the road from Australia House, taking advantage of a Public Service Scholarship. He soon switched from a Master's degree to a Ph.D. under Lionel Robbins, and was awarded a doctorate in 1942.

Burton arrived back in Australia just before the Japanese attack on Pearl Harbor. What happened next was both remarkable and consequential: remarkable because Burton went very far, very fast, achieving the status of Permanent Head of the Department of External Affairs by the time he was thirty-two; consequential in terms of how Burton did the job and what the experiences meant for his later academic work.

On arrival back in Australia, Burton worked first in the Department of Labour and National Service and then in External Affairs. In the former he was part of a staff concerned with post-war reconstruction, and of this group of people Bolton has commented that the ministers 'were supported by an outstanding group of public servants, mainly young graduates. They created a policy in an atmosphere of intellectual excitement seldom encountered in Canberra. Some of them were influenced by the ideas of Laski and Keynes' (Bolton, 1990, p. 29). It was while working in the latter, as a probationary Third Secretary, that Burton became Departmental Private Secretary to H. V. Evatt, the Minister for External Affairs in the government led by Ben Chifley of the Australian Labor Party. Of the appointment and, more significantly, its consequences, P. Hasluck, also a member of the Department of External Affairs at the time – and who was later to serve as Minister for External Affairs in the Menzies Government, has observed that 'Wilson [at the Department of Labour and National Service] did not mind losing Burton and Hodgson [at the Department of External Affairs] did not wish to keep him. Let the Minister have him. It was a fateful move. Burton instantly commended himself to Evatt' (Hasluck, 1980, p. 15). Burton is quoted as saying, of the appointment itself, 'I got a call on the telephone. "Come and see me and don't ask questions"' the minister had said (Clack, 1991). This was an extraordinary conjunction of opportunity and personality as far as Burton was concerned. In his mid-twenties, he had gone from postal clerk to graduate student to Third Secretary and on to his new position astonishingly quickly. Moreover, he got on well with a boss who effectively ran his own show – as far as foreign policy was concerned – which, consequently, gave Burton enormous scope: 'Evatt ran a substitute for the Department [of External Affairs] from his own ministerial office with Burton doing more of the fixing and arranging than any departmental officer did and having much more influence on shaping the minister's opinions than anyone in the department had' (Hasluck, 1980, p. 15). The point is compounded by P. G. Edwards' observation that 'Evatt seemed to develop an almost parent-filial relationship with Burton and to rely on him to the exclusion of Hodgson and other departmental officers' (Edwards, 1983, p. 145). Burton himself has observed that '[Evatt] respected anyone who had a view and stuck to it . . . [the relationship with Evatt was] very, very close. We understood each other. There was never a situation where he would give me much instruction. You know what to do, was the kind of instruction I got' (Clack, 1991).

Burton held the position of Departmental Private Secretary until his return to the Department of External Affairs in 1944. Apart from the experience, it is useful to record the verdicts on Burton's style and achievement. Edwards records that 'to many, Burton appeared to have inherited the father's missionary zeal in a secular form and to have become a crusader for his ideals in this world' (Edwards, 1983, p. 145). For Hasluck, Burton's 'influence on foreign policy during the time he was private secretary should not be underestimated. He had talent as a political operative and he had boldness. He also took a very flexible view of established rules. Thus he could get things done quickly, both by taking short cuts and disregarding the views of others. He was very valuable to Evatt in expediting action...My own view is that Burton was essentially a crusader. He had to advance a cause and was as ardent as any crusader because of his conviction that whatever cause he favoured was the only cause worth serving' (Hasluck, 1980, p. 35).

If all this sounds like the routine career development of an aspiring civil servant who met exceptional circumstances, it is important to stress the nature and context of the events. Arguably, Australia came of age in the period during and after the First World War; Gallipoli during and Versailles after stand as landmarks in the development of Australian autonomy within the orbit of imperial concerns. The Foreign Affairs brief was, for much of the inter-war period, in the hands of the Prime Minister, whose role was to relate Australian concerns to London, and vice versa, consistent with Australia's place in the Empire. Relatively speaking, it was far behind, for example, Canada, in its pursuit of independence and autonomy.

Australia at the time of Burton's ascent was still very much a dominion within the British Empire; all roads led back to London, and policy (certainly foreign and defence policy) emanated from there. (It is worth remarking that, even as late as the 1960s, many Australians saw that one of the things they ought to do, if they could, was to 'go home' – which is to say, visit Britain for the first time.) It was the business of the Australians to execute policy in these circumstances. The lines on the political map were drawn, *de facto*, from London, and probably with some influence from Washington. Indeed, evidently there were those who felt that Australia was too small to have a foreign policy. On the other hand, there were those who began to feel that the old order was ready for change, certainly in the circumstances of the war in Asia, where it began to become clear that the imperial networks were under strain, and local perceptions began to be made evident and were then asserted. Change was for some an opportunity and for others a threat, such that 'Britain's Dominions Office in London had become quite concerned at the rapid expansion of Australia's Department of External Affairs...even to the extent of raising a file on the subject in 1944' (see Pemberton 1991 for a further dicussion). Burton's position, evidently, was worthy of comment too (Pemberton, 1991).

It is worth stating the obvious here too; to leave it unstated is, perhaps, to miss the implications that follow from it. It matters that Burton was born an Australian and made policy as an Australian in a world where the country had a role to play, but a role defined and structured in relation to significant others. The politics of power are thus bound to look different when conceived from Canberra, Sydney and Melbourne as opposed to London and Washington, especially as far as reconstructing the post-war world was concerned. As we shall see, it was important for Burton that the role of Japan in world politics was perceived differently by him, an Australian in London, compared to the perceptions of others. Similarly, later in Australia, his views on the other countries and colonies in Asia. In these he was markedly unconventional. Furthermore, at this time Burton's views had not gone unnoticed, both within and outside Australia: 'British officials described Burton as "the power behind the Evatt throne" and "Evatt's ideas man". Australian Naval Intelligence was less kind, telling British and Dutch intelligence ... that Burton was a "strongman from Moscow"' (Pemberton, 1991).

Back at the Department of External Affairs (DEA) in 1944, Burton was part of a staff looking at the agenda of post-war reconstruction. He had attended the 1943 conference establishing the Food and Agriculture Organisation, and in 1944 attended the conference of the International Labour Organisation, as well as the founding conference of the United Nations at San Francisco and the Paris Peace Conference of 1946.

In March 1947, Evatt appointed him to the position of Permanent Secretary of the Department of External Affairs. In the light of the preceding account, we should not be surprised at Pemberton's observation that 'Burton was somewhat unorthodox as a Departmental Secretary'. He arrived at work early in the morning and answered telegrams himself before his staff arrived. But Pemberton also remarks that Burton showed a lighter side too, inviting his staff to his farm outside Canberra to play cricket – as well as to help with some of the farm work, 'an action which today would cause an uproar. But these were the days when some officers rode horses to work and brought their dogs in to sit under their desks' (Pemberton, 1991).

Burton's tenure at the DEA was marked by debate regarding Australian engagement with Asia. Traditional imperial and loyalist arguments were confronted by those of an emergent state seeking a foreign policy of its own, and the struggle was often intense. In the middle of 1947, the Dutch conflict in Indonesia worsened and Australia, at this time a non-permanent member of the United Nations Security Council, was active in a process to take the dispute to the Council. India concurred in this, but the British and United States governments did not, evidently believing that they could manage the conflict, with the British assuming that the *de facto* internationalisation of an imperial (Dutch) issue would have wider ramifications, beyond, but including, Asia and the Dutch. Burton took issue with this 'great power management' approach, determined that the issue was appropriate for the new United Nations organisation to handle. The British finally agreed, the issue went before the Security Council, the Australian resolution on the dispute was adopted and a cease-fire effected. Australia's action was such as to gain it much credit in Asia, and the Indonesian prime minister remarked that Australia's resolution at the UN had 'probably saved the republic' (Pemberton, 1991).

However, by the end of 1948 the Indonesian conflict had again taken a violent turn. In response to the European view that they should again oversee affairs, Indian Prime Minister Nehru called a conference of Afro-Asian nations to meet in Delhi in January 1949. Australia and New Zealand were invited to participate. To assuage doubts about the nature of Australian participation in the conference, the British were assured that Australia would have the status of 'observer' only. That the observer turned out to be Burton himself prompted the subsequent observation from Pemberton that sending Burton as an observer was rather like Bradman giving the ball to Keith Miller in an Ashes test and telling him not to bowl bouncers. More fundamentally, Pemberton, having surveyed the records, suggests that 'after Nehru, the 33-year-old Burton was the dominating figure [at the Delhi Conference] ... Many of the key speeches made, and resolutions initiated, were Burton's ... The New Delhi Conference was a triumph for Burton's foreign policy' (Pemberton, 1991).

By the end of 1949, and into 1950, the government in Australia had changed and so had Asia, in no small measure. After the assumption of power by the Communists in China in November 1949 and the proclamation of the Peoples Republic of China (PRC), under Mao Tse Tung, the issue was one of diplomatic recognition – or not. Here, the position of the United States was not inconsequential. Burton held firmly to the view that Australia should recognise the PRC government in Peking, on the grounds that such a move was both necessary and desirable from an Australian viewpoint. Less conventionally (he was still a public servant), he also published an article urging such a view 'under the ill-disguised initials "J.W.B." in which he vigorously championed recognition and warned that delay could only help isolate the Communist regime and "serve to crystallise the beliefs of Peking in Australia's hostility to it"' (Albinski, 1965, p. 27). If this were not enough to merit the label 'unconventional', Burton also sought preselection as a candidate for a new seat in Canberra, on behalf of the Australian Labor Party, thus incurring the wrath of the parliamentary Opposition (Albinski, 1965, p. 66). In fact, the recognition of the China issue saw a major rift between Evatt and Burton, because Evatt (and Prime Minister Chifley) took an opposite view from Burton politically, though he favoured recognition personally (Albinski, 1965, p. 42).

On 10 December 1949, Labor was voted out of office in a general election and the new Parliament met in March 1950. The election was a turning point for Burton, if indirectly. Had Labor won, he might have become Foreign Minister (Edwards, 1980, p. 184). With a new government in place, and events moving apace in relation to the new government in China and emergent instabilities in the Korean peninsular, Burton resigned as head of the Department of External Affairs just days before the outbreak of the Korean War, in June 1950, and went on extended leave of absence. According to Albinski the split was by mutual consent, resulting 'from the divergent political philosophies held by him and the government he was serving' (Albinski, 1965, p. 67). What is important, though a discussion of the issues is not appropriate here, is that Burton's engagement with China, his departure from government and the subsequent ramifications of these events was (and arguably still remains, for many) especially controversial. As indicated in Pemberton's comment above, there were those who saw Burton as a figure of suspicion, questioning his loyalty and integrity. He was subsequently appointed to the post of High Commissioner to Ceylon, 'never exactly a nerve center of Australian foreign policy' according to Albinski (1965, p. 106), a point almost certainly recognised then, and later, by Burton himself.

Burton did not stay long in Colombo, for an election had been called in Australia. Burton returned to Australia almost immediately to stand as a candidate in the election, having already been preselected as a Labor Party Candidate for a New South Wales constituency. He fought it, and lost

Thus ended a major episode in Burton's life. He was not yet thirty-five years old, but had been educated, served as a civil servant, assisted in policy-making, advised senior ministers, influenced them both directly and indirectly, made friends and enemies, resigned and resigned again, and then lost an election. He was married (in 1939, having met his wife when they were students in Sydney), with three daughters, and now had a living to make. It was not entirely starting from scratch on a new path, as Burton had bought a farm at Tuggeranong, outside Canberra, during the war, when he was a civil servant; it was to serve as a means of escape and provided a degree of independence, which he valued greatly, as well as a place where he could indulge his preferences for machines and physical labour, and bring up his growing family.

('"It was my salvation ... The farm gave me security and independence. When you worked with Evatt you needed an escape", he said. "I didn't want to become a yes-man"' (Clack, 1991)). Later he moved to a farm in the Weetangera district, now developed into the Holt and Higgins suburbs of Canberra, which provided him with a firmer foundation.

Yet now that he was no longer part of the policy-making fraternity, indeed being well outside it in formal terms, life solely as a farmer was not sufficient. What was Burton to do now? He had come a long way in a short time and it is hard to envisage him settling down as a gentleman farmer for the rest of his life. He did not, though having a farm (later, in the 1970s, in England and, later still, on his retirement to Australia, leaving the land in 1993) has been an important part of his life. And it is worth stating the other obvious consideration. This is not the place for amateur speculations about parent–child relationships, but it is surely the case that, given what his father had done and was still doing (in terms of output, status and influence), he had a hard act to follow, but the farm did not seem the place to do it – yet.

There followed a period, after resignation and electoral defeat – and before Burton embarked on an academic career in London – which looks, at first sight, to be rather fallow, the period between civil service and government and the academy. Certainly, anyone looking at the picture from well beyond Australia could be forgiven for thinking that Burton did little of great consequence, that these were essentially the 'wilderness years' at worst; an interregnum at best. The first sight is illusory. Of course, there was a living to make and, following this tack, Burton opened a bookshop in the Kingston area of Canberra. He also acquired a bus, filled it with books and took the shop 'on the road', selling books in remoter regions beyond Canberra. European immigrants working on the Snowy River project were good customers, for dictionaries especially.

But he did significantly more than this. He also wrote, travelled, lectured and took part in Australian party politics. He was not centre stage in any of these activities, but his reputation was such that he never was in the wilderness; at the very least, his reputation and temperament were to be barriers to doing so. His activities were often noted in the press, not always approvingly. He was, as ever, speaking out and thus became controversial. In May 1952, with four others, he went to China to establish the prospects for an exploratory peace conference to terminate the Korean War. On their return, the group reported their impressions of China. Needless to say, they did not accord with the conventional wisdom. They did not see a threatening Communist menace, Red Peril or the like. Rather, they saw a country that had fostered reforms, aspired to improve the lot of the mass of the people, and replace old and corrupt practices, and they publicised their findings in a report entitled *We Talked Peace with Asia*, published later in 1952 (see Albinski p. 124). To take one example, Burton applied the following test to China:

> If religious freedom, family life, and freedom of expression and freedom of association are tests, then I do not believe that China is a communist country. If the test was whether the revolution was directed against the owners of capital, again China is not communist because the revolution was directed against only those workers and capitalists whose motive was their own gain and who used corruption, exploitation including serfdom and gangsterism as means to their ends. (Burton, quoted in Albinski, 1965, p. 124)

Needless to say, this was a small but significant part of an emergent and interlocking structure of Cold War and colonial/imperial politics in the Asian region. Relations between Australia and Britain on the one hand, and Australia and the United States on the other, not least in relation to colonial independence, Communist issues and the often erroneous conflation of the two, were at the centre of the Australian and wider debates. And they were continuing debates to which Burton sought to contribute.

It was in these circumstances that he was to write (in a matter of just a few weeks) *The Alternative*, published privately in Australia in 1954.

In 1955, he received an invitation to attend, as a private citizen, the Bandung Conference of Asian and African Governments, which saw the establishment of what came to be called the 'non-aligned movement' in the context of the Cold War. (More than a decade later he was to edit a collection of essays on the theme of non-alignment (Burton, 1966)). In 1956, he wrote a pamphlet, *The Light Grows Brighter* (Burton, 1956) on the nature of democratic socialism in Australia (at that time the Australian Labor Party (ALP) was undergoing significant internal debates and conflicts about direction and stance), and in a preface to that pamphlet Evatt commented about Burton and the times:

> John Burton has already made contributions of value to the defence of basic freedoms in Australia. He resisted the onset of McCarthyism and helped beat it back. Like many others he underwent and surmounted the 'ordeal by slander' which is the very essence of McCarthyism. He took a leading part in the cultivation of the true friendship of Australia

with the new nations of Asia, including India, China, Indonesia and Ceylon. (Burton, 1956, p. 5, quoted by Albinski, 1965, p. 132)

Soon afterwards he wrote *Labor in Transition* (Burton, 1957), another contribution to the debate on the direction of the ALP, and in 1958 he delivered the Fifth Chifley Memorial Lecture (following, among others, Evatt, Lord Lindsay of Birker and Gough Whitlam) at the University of Melbourne, on the theme *The Nature and Significance of Labor* (Burton, 1958); significantly, the latter dealt with foreign policy and world politics. Nor would it be accurate to say that, even at this stage, he had given up on the prospect of a political career, as in 1960 he sought preselection as an election candidate again, this time with a view to standing for a Senate seat in the 1961 election; once again, he was unsuccessful.

In due course, an invitation from an American foundation (Rockefeller) arrived on his doormat, and he dismissed it. But when a repeat offer appeared, he took it seriously and in 1960 took up a Fellowship in the Research School of Pacific Studies at the Australian National University (ANU) in Canberra. There he wrote *Peace Theory*, published in New York in 1962. Gradually, he began to move in extended academic circles (involving, for example, international conferences, including Pugwash in London, Cambridge and Dubrovnik), meeting others, including Kenneth and Elise Boulding, and Karl Deutsch, and it was while in London in 1963 that he was offered a teaching post at University College, London (UCL), at just a few days' notice. He accepted. It was his first teaching position.

This is significant. He had not taught before. His training was in the ways of the civil service, where brevity is the aim and method. The style of *Peace Theory* is indicative here. There are few footnotes, the style is somewhat idiosyncratic, clipped rather than discursive. He is not, as it were, steeped in the tradition of the literature. This was to have at least two consequences. First, he was not bound by the discourse and assumptions of power politics and state-centric realism, the dominant approaches of the period. On the other hand, he had operated in the realm of politics where the realities of power at least had to be acknowledged – which is not to say that, in acknowledging them, Burton accepted them. The events already discussed lead us to the conclusion that the *modus operandi* was, for him, the problem and not the solution.

Second, as he encountered the literature of International Relations, he was able, as well as predisposed, to be something of a free thinker, not bound by the burden of tradition or the lessons of history as embodied in the established canon. He wrote lectures as he went along – almost always the task of the new academic. The exception here is that Burton was now not far short of fifty years old: a novice academic to be sure in one dimension, but with a career past that set him apart from the usual type of starting-out lecturer. He soon encountered Michael Banks, from the London School of Economics, and was joined at University College by John Groom, then a young teacher. Both were to be constant, though not uncritical, allies. From Banks he learnt much about the literature, drawing on Banks' strengths – reading widely, synthesising and digesting the issues and transmitting them with a sense of rigour and commitment. Groom's strengths were different in many respects from those of Banks, but none the less significant for being so, because Groom was an ally and assistant in the other, different branches of academe; he was the in-house ally, soulmate and assistant.

The first product of these first years at UCL was *International Relations: A General Theory*, first published in 1965, but with its origins at the ANU in Canberra. Most academics would count this as a significant product of their first few years, but Burton did not fit the mould of 'most academics'. He was active, as early as 1963, in the development of organisations. In London, he found like-minded individuals in Sir Charles Goodeve, Professor Jack Mongar and Professor Cedric Smith (both of these from UCL, and interested in the problems of conflict by way of personal inclination rather than, at this stage, professional involvement), who together assisted in the founding of the Conflict Research Society in Britain. A year later, in December 1964, with others, Burton was instrumental in founding the International Peace Research Association (IPRA) (which grew out of a Conference on Research on International Peace, with Burton as chairman of its continuing committee, with the IPRA modelled on the experience of Pugwash: the aim of the organisation was to improve the quality and quantity of scientific research on war and peace). Soon afterwards, the Centre for the Analysis of Conflict was established at UCL. This says something again about Burton the practitioner turned academic, almost as if he refused to acknowledge that some things were 'academic', which is to suggest distance and detachment. Burton had no qualms about establishing an organisation, setting the agenda and making the connection to the relevant people (whoever they might prove to be). After all, he had grown up in the shadow of his father; it would be reasonable to assume that he had remembered the tenets of the father's secular faith, even if he did not assume the burden of the religious faith: speak as you find, public service, challenges to face, injustices to right, and barriers to be confronted but never to be thought insurmountable.

The Centre for the Analysis of Conflict consisted of Burton and Groom, permanent members of the International Relations staff at University College, based in the Law Faculty in Endsleigh Street, with others brought together for the purpose and as money and circumstances allowed. In this respect they were in fact physically removed from the main body of the college, based in Gower Street and Gordon Square, as well as rather removed from the Law Faculty, being perceived, perhaps, as sorts of international lawyers, with whom they were affiliated. Also involved were Christopher Mitchell, recently graduated from UCL and a new tutor; Banks, who came up Southampton Row from the London School of Economics; Michael Nicholson; Tony de Reuck (who had played an important role as facilitator in his previous job at the London-based CIBA Foundation, through which Burton had made or re-made connections), and Frank Edmead, a former leader-writer on the *Guardian* newspaper. There was also a number of keen and enthusiastic graduate students who, together with the rest, created a sense of critical mass, moving and creating their own research agenda.

When Burton arrived to teach at UCL, the students studying International Relations were enrolled for the London University degree of B.Sc.(Econ) and examined jointly with the students from the London School of Economics (LSE). Soon, profoundly different intellectual emphases became evident, highlighting the different frames of references being taught at UCL and the LSE. The response to this was the development of a separate degree, still a B.Sc.(Econ), but both taught, and examined, by the International Relations staff at UCL. It bore a very different imprint from that taught at Houghton Street, with less emphasis on history and philosophy and more on the emergent issues associated with methodology, science, behaviouralism and systems thinking. These themes, as we shall see, were clear to see in the development of Burton's thinking. The confrontation with the conventional wisdom of power politics and the methodologies associated with this were at the root of the schism.

This also had another and perhaps even greater consequence. Burton, now with his own momentum, never quite fitted into the established International Relations profession in Britain. There, the tradition was associated with the works of Edward Hallett Carr, Charles Manning, Martin Wight and, among Burton's contemporaries, Alistair Buchan, Fred Northedge, Susan Strange and Hedley Bull. What unites them is an emphasis on the 'real world of power', whatever their different emphases. Whatever united them differentiated Burton from any and all of them. At one particular confrontation in the mid-1960s, Burton was challenged to proffer an explanation of 'the real world' from his point of view, if, as seemed to be to the case, he was so critical of existing approaches. In effect, the challenge was to the effect that, if he had some different views, then he should put them to the test. Korea, perhaps? Burton's response was to argue that what was known about the conflict in Korea was already 'known' from an established power perspective, so the challenge to explain anew something that was old was inappropriate. Typically, he suggested that he and his colleagues try to explain something that had not been explained effectively in the terms of the established framework of assumptions. What was needed was a new explanation of a conflict not already explained in conventional terms, and therefore necessarily a contemporary conflict. He chose the case of the confrontation between Britain and Malaysia on the one hand, and Indonesia on the other, then current and known as 'Confrontasi' or confrontation. At the time it assumed a significance that might not be appreciated more than thirty years later; which is to say that Burton selected a conflict that was significant, current and persistent. Soon he also started to come to terms with the ethnic Greek–Turkish conflict in Cyprus, where the fragile constitution established to facilitate independence from Britain in 1960 had collapsed in 1964, and where violent conflict was both intense and persistent.

The group of scholars at UCL were formally constituted as the Centre for the Analysis of Conflict (CAC), around the investigations of real existing conflicts. It was established *not* with the initial intention to develop an alternative approach to conflict such as that with which Burton was associated from the 1980s; this was a later development, emerging from Burton's engagement with the issues in theory and practice, as we shall see: at this stage, there is no immanent 'Burtonian project'. In fact, the CAC was established to test the applicability of the current assumptions of International Relations against emergent and current situations (the key term of the day was 'apply' – it is as well to remember that theory for policy was an emergent theme in the literature, especially that coming out of the United States as the war in Vietnam was entering a key phase; on the relevant literature, see, for example, Tanter and Ullmann, 1972). If there were problems with it, what were the alternatives, not based on a reading of history, but on the basis of a systematic analysis of the situation? Burton seemed determined to show that the problems resided in the operating assumptions of the day. New terms start to find their way into the Burtonian lexicon; 'wrong definitions of the situation', 'perceptual problems', 'steering' and the like.

All did not go smoothly, however. Though the engagement with practice was to produce its own literature (Burton published *Systems, States, Diplomacy and Rules* in 1968, and *Conflict and Communication* in 1969), by the early 1970s the teaching enterprise at UCL was in difficulties, but, perversely, a result of the success of the CAC rather than its failure. The members of the Centre had assisted with the teaching, but many were on essentially short-term contracts and/or being financed by grants that were not guaranteed to be renewable in the longer term. Yet the undergraduate programme was popular and growing, and Burton argued that resources for the longer-term financing of the operation should be found. The College authorities evidently took a different view, as the undergraduate teaching scheme was allowed to close down.

In some respects, the International Relations section was simply that, and a small one to boot. A section in a faculty to which it did not, arguably, really belong. It was detached from such social sciences as were in place in UCL, but they were in any case in something of a minority in an institution dominated by sciences and humanities. In terms of the permanent staff, they did not amount to a critical enough mass. In the interim, Dennis Sandole was brought in to assist with the teaching workload, other lecturers having already left.

John Groom had moved on to the University of Kent at Canterbury. Burton, now nearing official retirement, followed him to Kent and so, in effect, did the teaching nexus because, as the operation wound down at UCL, it grew at the new university in Kent. Burton and Groom were at the centre of things, with Chris Brown and, later, Keith Webb, who moved to Kent from the City University in London. By now, Chris Mitchell was based at the City University, and Michael Banks was back at the London School of Economics. It was in these circumstances that the Centre for the Analysis of Conflict took on a different, but still important, role. It was now, if not the mass around which a distinctive British conflict studies community could cohere, then an invisible college of scholars who met from time to time, exploring systematically an emergent agenda and changing its composition over time. Later the CAC was joined by Richard Little, Margot Light and Mark Hoffmann, among others. One of their roles, *de facto*, was the critical reception, and appreciation, of the Burtonian oeuvre.

But now Burton was to move again, the temporary stay at the University of Kent at an end. In 1983, he became International Studies Association visiting scholar at the University of South Carolina (where he encountered younger scholars, among whom might be noted Roger Coate and

Jerel Rosati, who added novelty and momentum, as well as effort, to the development of Burton's frame of reference, particularly the focus on needs, as we shall see). After this, he spent two years at the University of Maryland (working with, among others, Ed Azar) until, in 1985, he moved to the rapidly developing George Mason University at Fairfax, Virginia.

The university was growing rapidly in northern Virginia, transformed from a small local college into a new regional university, and Bryant Wedge had initiated moves to found a research and teaching centre devoted to conflict resolution, involving faculty across disciplines and professionals involved in dispute settlement and resolution at all levels of social and human interaction. Wedge became its first director, and an M.A. programme began in 1982. By 1988, as a Distinguished Visiting Professor of Conflict Resolution, Burton was on leave from George Mason, spending a year at the United States Institute of Peace as the Jennings Randolph Distinguished Fellow. Much of the work at George Mason was devoted to the consolidation of the Center for Conflict Analysis and Resolution, with both Masters and Doctoral programmes, drawing on dedicated faculty members in the Center and others from related disciplines. Significantly, Christopher Mitchell and Dennis Sandole, once at University College with Burton, were now at George Mason, along with Rich Rubinstein, Jim Laue and (in 1988 as visiting professor), Elise Boulding. Here again, just as at the Centre for the Analysis of Conflict in London more than twenty years before, there was a critical mass, creating and developing resources in the expansion of the conflict resolution field. What was particularly significant this time, however, was that the core faculty fitted into a relatively autonomous, directed and identifiable organisational nexus, with degree programmes, resources and an ongoing identity.

Burton continued to teach, research and travel to conferences and meetings throughout his time in the United States. But the culmination of the period at George Mason, arguably of the period that went before it, was the appearance of the four volumes that appeared in 1990, known collectively as 'the Conflict Series'. Burton wrote one himself, *Conflict: Resolution and Provention* (1990b); edited one, *Conflict: Human Needs Theory* (1990a); and co-edited two with a graduate assistant from George Mason, Frank Dukes, *Conflict: Readings in Management and Resolution* (1990a) and *Conflict: Practices in Management, Settlement and Resolution* (1990b).

On the back cover of *Conflict: Resolution and Provention*, Burton is referred to as 'the founder of the field of conflict resolution', and Harold

H. Saunders, a former United States Assistant Secretary of State, refers to the book as 'one of the early books of the twenty-first century'.

Burton has now retired to his native Australia, reluctantly given up farming and lives in a quiet suburb of Canberra in the Australian Capital Territory. He has not stopped working, but reads widely and writes when he feels the need to do so. He still has much to say, reworking old and new themes, articulating afresh the ideas within him.

2
The Prelude: International Relations from the Edge

As we have seen, John Burton became a university teacher of International Relations in 1963, when he joined the staff of University College in London not far short of his fiftieth birthday. At that point, taking on the task of interpreting and presenting International Relations to students and then writing himself, he joined an identifiable community of scholars in so far as he was obliged, in his new role, to engage with International Relations as an academic discipline, a set of intellectual concerns and a community of scholars. Yet he had written much before this, from several perspectives and in different roles, and much of what he wrote was about international relations, if sometimes only in passing or as part of a wider brief. What he wrote, and the significance of it, before he fully engaged with International Relations, is the subject of this chapter.

In the course of the period surveyed here he was, first, a graduate student in London and then a civil servant who assumed an extraordinarily significant role in terms of the conduct of Australian foreign policy at a critical period of that country's history. After his resignation from that role, there appears – at first sight – to be a period of stasis, perhaps a sense of 'nothing happening', with Burton rather lost from history; no longer a diplomat and civil servant, but not yet a scholar.

First glances, however, can be misleading, and this is so in this case. Closer analysis reveals that the decade covered by the 1950s was a period of significant transition, but a transition characterised by incremental and unplanned change rather than a programmatic and radical personal search for new direction and purpose. In due course, Burton was a mix of private diplomat, sometime political activist, lecturer and author. It is important to point out that when, for example, Burton wrote his doctoral dissertation, he had no thought of becoming an academic; he was destined for public service. When he wrote *The Alternative* (1954) he wrote urgently, within a matter of a few weeks, and in a polemical style in response to events unfolding and as a contribution to a contemporary debate. He sought to influence events rather than merely to offer a commentary on them. When he wrote *Peace Theory* (1962) he wrote it when an opportunity to do so presented itself. In retrospect, we can discern patterns of consistency and change in Burton's work. Yet it is important to establish that the path that Burton ultimately followed was not a path that was evident to him at the outset. Many of his career changes and achievements have been the result of chance meetings and unforeseen circumstances. Hence, the emphasis on genealogy is appropriate: we need to unearth how Burton got from where he was to what he became, and we need to search back.

Burton's doctoral dissertation was begun before the commencement of war in Europe in 1939, and was completed late in 1941, the degree of Ph.D. being awarded by the University of London in 1942. It was entitled *Restrictive and Constructive Intervention*. The dissertation supervisor was Lionel (later Lord) Robbins but, as Burton was at pains to point out in the dissertation preface (written at the end of October 1941), events had precluded any major involvement by Robbins in the writing of the work, apart from a reading of a preliminary outline. Burton seems to have been given a relatively free rein, allowing him the scope to be somewhat individualistic in style and tone, and rather novel and radical in his analysis.

At first sight, the dissertation rests in economics; there are discussions of trade and industry, transfer mechanisms, employment policies, sectoral and market adjustments and so on. In so far as the work involves itself with international dimensions, and it clearly does, locating the roots of international disputes in the dynamics of domestic policy, aspects of it might legitimately be construed to lead a reader to the view that it constitutes an early effort at what was later to become known as 'International Political Economy'. It is, in fact, a disquisition on the causes of international strife. More specifically, it seeks to demonstrate that the root causes of international strife (especially in the period between 1919 and 1939) are to be found in the conditions of states and their domestic economies. A constant theme running through the whole work is the issue of change, and the associated issue of responding to change and stances of resistance to it.

For a number of reasons, as we shall see, Burton's doctoral dissertation is a remarkable document and one that is perhaps overlooked by even those familiar with the rest of his work. This is not surprising: it is not easily accessible and was not turned into a publishable book. Events took a different turn. Yet what is most striking is the approach and the line of argument that Burton, still only in his mid-twenties and with a first degree in psychology, adopts. It stands out in stark contrast to so much of what was being written at the time about the causes of war in general, and of the First and Second World Wars in particular. It is as well to recall that the work which set, and largely reflected, the tone of the times, was the work of Edward Hallett Carr, *The Twenty Years' Crisis* (1939), which was to influence the study of International Relations for a generation and more, (and of which Burton was very clearly aware, and to which he refers, but it was an approach he did not share). There, we should recognise, Carr established that scholars in International Relations adopted one of two broad approaches: Realism or Utopianism. For the Realists, what was being studied was the essence of international politics, the struggle for power. To see it as anything else, therefore, was to be classified as an Idealist or, as Carr would have it, Utopian, a term of derogation that would last for many years. In these terms, Burton was not a Realist and, though he refers often in the dissertation to the notion of a 'harmony of interests' (which has often been said to be the hallmark of the Idealists), nor was he an Idealist either. He was concerned with an explanation of the causes of conflict, and he saw it in the conditions, internal and external, of states. In the course of the dissertation he refers to Germany and Japan, but he does not seek explanations of conflict in terms of crude clashes of national interest, balances of power, the authoritarian personality, human nature, devil theories of war, totalitarian systems and the like. In point of fact, these are conspicuous by their omission. What, then, is Burton's frame of reference? In so far as he seats his analysis in the behaviour of states, he is consistent with much of the then conventional wisdom, adopting what he later came to call the 'power frame' of reference. However, for the most part he sets out a rather individualistic perspective, with two key terms around which the argument turns – restrictive and constructive intervention.

Burton argues that there existed in the nineteenth century something approximating to a self-regulating system based on the market mechanism, which permitted gradual and continuous change in relation to changing circumstances. Britain and the world economy in the nineteenth century were capable of effecting continuous and gradual change, consistent with the existence of a free market. There was a reasonably efficient shift of resources, and little or no resistance, since there was no sudden displacement of industry. Factors of production were relatively mobile in this system, arguably something that resembled what he terms an ideal state of production, where an ideal state of production 'is one free from maladjustments, that is a structure which gives maximum output including leisure, but not one implying equality of distribution of real income' (Burton, 1942, p. 83). Much remains to be explained, of course, but this is not a major concern at this point in the exposition. Yet what is important for the argument here is that the key assumption underpinning the notion of this ideal system (by which, of course, he does not mean perfect) is an assumption that the powerful adjust, change takes place and the equilibrium of the system of relations is restored. In short, this ideal system admits of change and the appearance of novelty, to which adjustment is made by all. Continuous change is consistent with the operation of the market.

However, Burton argues that this dynamic was interrupted after 1918, with the introduction of what were essentially influences that disturbed the regulated market system. Here the period is marked by discontinuous change, attributable to extra-market factors, such as the development of armaments industries in states that seek such industries to assist in the search for security and national defence, defending the industries as required, and the growth of government-sponsored protectionism. Discontinuous change is marked by sharp changes, little time for adjustments to be made and maladjustments that distort. At a time when there are no expansionist trends in the international trading system, discontinuities are especially difficult and, says Burton, when these appeared in the period 1919–39, this aggravated pre-war trends and resulted in an end to the market mechanism and government intervention. By then there were problems associated with the transfer process (Burton, 1942, p. 95). Interestingly, when illustrating the dynamics of the transfer process, Burton makes much of the interests of producers in Australia, and especially wheat as a commodity.

What happens in these difficult circumstances is that special interests start to coincide and then coalesce in their resistance to change, indeed even seeking alliances between employers and employees to resist unwanted change. Special interests dominate the political debate at the expense of the wider interests of the whole of society. Hence, an emphasis on what he calls restrictive intervention on the part of authorities. Conversely, where there is a process of appropriate adaptation to circumstances this is termed constructive intervention.

Essentially, what Burton is developing here is in one sense consistent with what the dominant Realist thinker of his time, Hans Morgenthau, was to argue; namely that politics in general, and international politics in particular, was part of a struggle for interest defined in terms of power. This, after all, was what needed to be explained against a backdrop of the rise of Fascism in Germany and Italy; the Chinese war in Manchuria; the civil war in Spain; the inter-war depression and so on. These were in fact the very events that served to validate the assumptions underpinning Morgenthau's analysis (and subsequently many other Realist thinkers); in the light of these events, how could anyone come to a radically different conclusion as to the real question and the nature of their explanation? Yet the reasoning and the relevant frame of reference for Burton was far removed from that adopted by the German Jewish émigré Morgenthau. Burton did not rely on an asserted human nature, nor did he argue that what was taking place was inevitable and intractable. Indeed, in the light of his critique of restrictive intervention he presented the means to effect a policy of constructive intervention. He did not rely on unstated assumptions about harmony of interests to any great degree, relying instead on what amounted to a programmatic approach to the problem of restrictive attitudes and policies.

In short, given that Burton had graduated in psychology, studied in the field of economics and come from a socially committed family background, he developed his analysis despite an engagement with the literature of political science and international relations, not because of it. (Like his fellow pioneer in peace research, Kenneth Boulding, Burton did not study – and become a prisoner of – assumptions rooted in the historical approach to international politics.) To that extent he was not captured by the essential concerns of politics and international relations as coming to terms with, or necessarily discussing this, that or the other. He did not engage with Hobbes, Locke, Machiavelli and the like. For all that he was at the London School of Economics at the time of Laski's supposedly greatest influence, the dissertation is not written in his shadow. Where there is engagement with the literature of political science, it is very much with the salient issues of the day, rather than with the perennial themes and issues. He looks to Evan Durbin, very much a rising star of the time in terms of the development of the nature of democratic socialism, as a relevant influence on occasion.

That the dissertation was written from an Australian perspective and from outside political science is itself significant, not least because it sets the stance of Burton as standing outside the mainstream assumptions of politics and diplomacy in some significant sense. Which is not to say that he lived and wrote in a world of his own; he did not.

This is not an appropriate place to précis the entire corpus of issues that Burton covered in 1942. Nevertheless, there are salient features of the analysis which it is appropriate to identify in the light of what follows, sometimes much later.

First, Burton recognised the interplay between the domestic and international political systems, explicitly in terms of the shifting of the burden of change (set in motion in one realm) on to others in the international system. This may sound a rather obvious point to make, but it is not quite the same as saying that international politics is different from domestic politics, and that, as it came later to be said, foreign policy begins at the water's edge. Nor is this merely a question of distinction; it is also a crucial question regarding origins and directionality, causality if you will, in the matter of strife, as he was to argue explicitly that 'To hope for the "withering away of the state" in conditions of growing economic nationalism and industrial organisation by governments... is to be utterly unreal and to ignore the crucial issues. The basic causes of disharmony arise within domestic economies' (Burton, 1942, p. 287). Furthermore, 'our contention is...that government intervention which hinders the adjustment of production to change is a major cause of structural maladjustments and that because it causes maladjustments in the world's productive structure it brings about unemployment and political strife' (Burton, 1942, p. 22).

Second, there are further questions of perspective, more particularly the problems associated with limited perspectives – and their practical consequences. Frequently, he argues that there needs to be a radical shift of perspective in order that the interests of all be placed ahead of the interests of sectors or groups. Furthermore, he is critical of established frames of reference, arguing that

> economists have resorted to the development of separate theories – one to cover unemployment, another concerning international trade, another to explain the causes and effects of imperfect competition... This has suited economic theory very well...From the point of view of policy, however, it is becoming startlingly apparent that another method, a method that treats society as a whole, must be adopted. (Burton, 1942, p. 17)

In other words, there is a need for a radical change of perspective where holism is at the centre of the analysis, allied to a break out from disciplinary constraints and partial theories, in order that issues and problems be seen for what they are – incapable of being understood partially, and widespread, rather than limited, in their consequences. 'Once it was reasonable to make a fairly clear-cut distinction between economic theory and political science; now any such separation must be misleading' (Burton, 1942, p. 19). (Recall that Burton was making this point many decades ago, when, for many, the very nature of political science itself was a matter for discussion.) Furthermore, he is not insensitive to the question of methodology, as he argues that 'economic and political scientists have already gone a long way in the development of economic and political theory; but further progress may depend on the solution of problems of method and exposition' (Burton, 1942, p. 17).

In the matter of problem-solving, which came to feature large in his later work, he was quite explicit:

> the central problem of constructive intervention is to formulate an unemployment policy by which adjustments are effected in a manner socially and politically acceptable and at the same time in a manner which brings about an international harmony of interests... This objective cannot be achieved in practice either by purely national or purely international intervention. There must be a fusion of the two. (Burton, 1942, p. 285)

It is important, given the events of the time, to see what Burton did not say, as in this respect the dissertation was rather extraordinary, if not idiosyncratic. Given the events unfolding when the dissertation was being written, he did not explain the war in Europe and in Asia in terms of totalitarianism, authoritarian personalities, mass movements and crowd behaviour, nor in terms of arms races *per se* or the aggressive side of human nature. He was surely aware of these, given their salience in the literature (scholarly and more ephemeral) of the time, but chose instead a framework of analysis that showed an interplay not only of the domestic and the international, the sectional and the general, but also the crucial interaction of structures and processes – focusing on the way threats to structures prompted resistance to change, rather than adaptation to it, and the attempt to shift the burden of change on to others, often with disastrous consequences. In short, those with the power sought to resist change and make others do the changing – a process they sought to resist, by force if necessary. A theme running through the whole is the central notion of perception, more specifically that perceptions of parties in what Burton called 'conditions of strife' are valid and real to the parties themselves, and need to be understood as such; thus, questions of 'right' and 'wrong' may be more problematic than helpful in understanding conflicts. The relevant response is to shift the relevant frame of reference within which events are perceived to have consequence – and for whom.

He wrote about a world of power and interest, yet in a radical frame of reference, and very soon after the dissertation was completed, he was back in Australia practising in a world of power internationally and party politics domestically. His assumptions were to some degree unconventional, but they were still rooted in his understanding of, and a search for the explanation of, power politics. But this did not make him a power politician, nor did it make him a political realist *à la* Carr and Morgenthau. Yet his analysis was of the real world that he saw, and thus realistic. He explained it in terms different from those employed by others.

In terms of an engagement with an analysis of socio-political structures and processes, the dissertation written in London probably seemed to be both a beginning and an end, for Burton now returned to Australia as a civil servant with a clear set of tasks to address. Returning to an Australia at war, Burton's career path was upward and rapidly so. It is not part of our main purpose here to chart Burton's progress through the events of the Second World War and Canberra. For our purposes here it is germane to the argument that Burton ascended very rapidly through the civil service hierarchy to become a key adviser to key decision-makers. He was at or close to the centre. As such, he had scope for great influence and he exercised the options available to him. His role was consequential rather than minor. His medium of communication was the minute and/or the conversation, not the academic paper or textbook. He moved through what C. P. Snow came to call the 'corridors of power', but it is important to recognise that in Canberra at this time the corridors were not overly long or labyrinthine. The role of Canberra and Australia in the still largely imperial scheme of things was important but still minor in some degree, to the extent that the role of Australia was that of a state whose foreign policy agenda was pretty much administered from London rather than radically devised and articulated from Canberra. In other words, the role of Australia and Burton should not be overestimated, but nor should it be made light of.

Burton, the war over, was a frequent participant in the major post-war conferences devoted to reconstruction and reform, principally the conference at San Francisco that led to the foundation of the United Nations in 1945, but also the Paris Conference of 1946, the British Commonwealth Foreign Ministers Conference of 1946, Imperial Conferences of 1946 and 1948, and the Delhi Conference on Indonesia in

1949. For a relatively young man he was well-placed, experienced and skilful. Soon he was appointed to the post of Secretary of the Department of External Affairs. Yet if the Second World War presented the young Burton with a full agenda, the dynamic transition into the Cold War was even more difficult, not least because he did not share the dominant mind-set. In conventional terms, the Soviet Union and China were clear and present dangers to security as defined from the Western perspective. The problem for Burton was that he did not share this perspective. What Burton wanted was a re-perception of the issues that saw, as a better guide to more successful policy-making, the perspective of the Chinese: What was it that they wanted? Why had the revolution been thought necessary? What were the interests and perceptions of the Chinese leadership now in power in Peking? In the course of the next few years, matters of great (and lasting) controversy were at the centre of Australian politics but, in a book devoted more to ideas rather than to events, this is not the place to survey them. What is certain is that Burton was at the centre of these events, until he removed himself from them. In the new circumstances, he resigned from the civil service. Soon he was appointed High Commissioner to Ceylon and set out for Colombo. Having barely arrived in Ceylon, he returned home to stand as a Labor candidate in the recently-called general election, but was not elected.

What was Burton once he had resigned from the Australian civil service? Indeed, what was he to do? A career in public service was what he had set his mind on many years before, indeed as a boy. Now he found himself at odds with many (most?) of those he sought to serve. He had sought election as a candidate for the Australian Labor Party and he had lost. He visited China in 1952, and in the light of this and his criticism of Labor Party politics, his endorsement for the next election was withdrawn. He had bought a farm and this was now to be his living, if not his career. Yet he did not drift from the scene, nor was he silent.

In the 1950s, the Australian Labor Party went through a period of great change, perhaps even turbulence. Two issues were central to the party's development – one domestic and the other international. Domestically, the issue was about what constituency Labor was to serve in the changing post-war Australia. In due course, the Labor Party in Australia split in two, with the Australian Labor Party on the one hand and the Democratic Labor Party on the other. The international issue concerned the new politics of the bipolar world, split as it was between the West and Communism, and more specifically what kind of policies needed to be adopted in relation not simply to Communism in general but Communism in Asia in particular; Australia may have still retained very close ties with London, but Washington mattered too, and so did China. So also did the emergent anti-colonial movements in Asia.

The domestic issues gave rise to *Labor in Transition* (1957), *The Nature and Significance of Labor* (1958) and *The light grows brighter* (1956). All these were inputs to the domestic political debate in Australia. To make the point directly, all this debate was not simply a matter of internal party politics. If it was simply a matter of squabble or debate, the issue would be of only passing interest. The debate was about more than this: it was about the kind of world that was evolving around Australia, how this was to be interpreted, and what the consequences were to be for Australia itself. In the post-war decade, what was Australia, and what was it to become? From the perspective of the twenty-first century, it is perhaps too easy to miss the nature and significance of these debates about the form and direction of policies, both domestic and, perhaps more importantly in the circumstances as they then presented them-selves, internationally. The cosmopolitan state that is Australia today, engaged with Asia, is not what it once was. The transition has been a difficult one, and Burton – in his apparent wilderness decade – was a player in the politics of the transition. He was not just a former civil servant, nor was he merely a farmer, nor a critic of domestic politics. He was 'Burton'.

To make an obvious point, but one that might be overlooked; the fact that Burton was writing on matters of moment – indeed, that he was invited to give a lecture in memory of a former leader of the Labor Party and Prime Minister, Ben Chifley, belies the superficial interpretation of the 1950s as some kind of lost decade or wilderness years for him. He was not centre stage, but nor was he entirely in the wings. He was most certainly not lost from view, nor was he quiescent or acquiescing: he was vocal, critical and controversial. It is thus as well to note that many who came to know Burton as an International Relations scholar or, later, as an innovator in conflict resolution practices, probably unaware of this Australian background, would be wise to recognise that all this experience was consequential, if not directly and immediately, then incrementally and in the longer term. These events also serve to illustrate the personal and political credentials of one long thought to be an 'Idealist'.

Thus the domestic political debate saw Burton writing pamphlets and giving speeches in the middle years of the 1950s, but it was the question of attitudes to Communism and Asia that gave rise to his first published book, *The Alternative*, which appeared in 1954. Burton wrote the book in a matter of just a few weeks, and it was published by a friend in Melbourne. Even then, it was not exactly an 'academic' treatment of the issues. It certainly had a radical stamp about it, as Burton argued not only that Communism was established, it was also spreading, but that this spread of Communism was not necessarily a mark of aggression:

> The view is here advanced that Communism is firmly established, that it is spreading more rapidly than the system of free-enterprise, because it is better suited to the more pressing needs of under-developed countries, that this spread is not itself aggressive nor the fruits of aggression but rather an indigenous development and that Communism will not gain support within the boundaries of developed democracies because it can make no contribution to their welfare and hence would not be successful. (Burton, 1954, pp. 25–6)

As the argument proceeds there are clear influences from the dissertation written fifteen years before in London. There are references to investments, the internal demands for change (with a special emphasis on the United States), the question of full employment as a political issue (and the way it came on to the agenda of the 1943 Hot Springs conference on Food and Agriculture) 'where the Australian delegation [of which Burton was a member] argued that unless the main consuming areas such as America and Britain maintained a steady level of consumption, the agricultural producing countries of the world must suffer. This meant that the level of employment in America in particular had to be maintained' (Burton, 1954, p. 35). And then there is a clear echo of restrictive intervention again, since Burton argues that in changed circumstances it would be desirable for the United States to adjust to the changed availability of resources, 'but these adjustments are strongly resisted and the reasons are not hard to find' so that 'what is being resisted is the trend toward the control of private enterprise so as to force it to operate in such a way that it provides for the requirements of consumers and not for the greatest return to producers' (Burton, 1954, pp. 36–7). There are international implications because

> as there is a determination to maintain the present system in the United States, and therefore throughout its trading world it is not surprising that any increased influence of Communism or Socialism, or any form of planned economy, is regarded as a security threat. For these reasons the United States is prepared to see the end of a colonial

system or of feudalism only when it is clear that it will be replaced by a system acceptable to America. Any expression of nationalism that does not take this form is regarded as Communist inspired and an object of suspicion. (Burton, 1954, pp. 37–8)

This is a very clear indication of a question that Burton, a decade later, was to address explicitly in terms of what he called 'wrong definitions of the situation' which led, in turn, to wrong policies and self-defeating strategies. Indeed, though Burton subtitled the book 'a dynamic approach to our relations with Asia' he might have subtitled it, were he at that time to have had the means to do so, 'change, misperception and failed strategies of resistance'.

The alternative approach Burton proposed was a mixture of the domestic and the international, aimed at land reform (that is, change), the ending of colonialism, to be replaced by self-government, with the existing power-holders (be they indigenous leaders or colonial powers) facing the option of resisting Communism and risking making it seem more attractive to the indigenous populations, or reforming appropriately to make a reformed local society more attractive than a Communist one. Burton identified a constructively interventionist role for the United Nations in this process, consistent with the expanded competence of the UN in the new post-war world.

In positing that Communism would not be a threat to domestic societies that provided security, welfare and democratic participation, Burton hints here at what he came to argue much more explicitly later, for the clear implication of his analysis is that where societies fulfilled needs (in the dissertation he often talked not of need but rather the then-prevalent terms of 'want' and 'freedom from want') they were prone to feel more secure and therefore less valuable to outside inter-vention or destabilisation. By the same token, where societies exist that are divided by wealth and power, where the needs of the few are satisfied at the expense of the needs of the many, then the many will deem that society one of which they do not and cannot feel a proper part and will, in consequence, look elsewhere for an alternative programme of action and/or reform. In these terms, the persistence of Western policies exacerbated the problem and resisted change when change was needed to satisfy widely felt needs.

The latter part of *The Alternative* focuses on Australian involvement with Asia, and though it is not appropriate here to summarise the whole, selected comments indicate the thrust of the argument, couched in terms which, by now, we can recognise. For example, 'Fear of unemployment resulting from cheap imports made by Asian "sweated labour", and the fear of cheap labour in Australia prompted by the importation of Asian labour for the cane fields of Queensland, have prejudiced Australian trade unions and the Labor Party against Asian peoples' (Burton, 1954, p. 79). Moreover, 'Australian fear of Asia is based on the general belief that there is throughout Asia a pressure of population on resources. But this belief arises out of a lack of knowledge of present conditions in Asia.' Reform, development, access to markets and resources would unleash the positive potential of Asia, argued Burton, thus 'the stability and security of the area would be assured' (Burton, 1954, p. 80).

Not exactly the conventional wisdom associated with dealing with the various manifestations of colonial insurgency, the spread of Communism, the Red Menace, the nature of containment (of which, not surprisingly, Burton was a vocal critic) and the like, which were all part of the dominant mind-set in 1954, a mind-set that informed socio-political and cultural discourse, root and branch, at this time, arguably the coldest years of the Cold War. The need was for change, while the policy response was stasis and containment. What Burton was engaging with here were the political consequences of wrong assumptions, a question he was to address much more articulately at a later time. *The Alternative* was very much an individual response to the political circumstances of the time. It was born out of a need to comment on the faults of the conventional wisdom that informed policy at that time. In so far as Burton relied on others for authority, information or insight, those upon whom he called were the radical American journalist, I. F. Stone, the British Socialist politician, Aneurin Bevan, and the Marxist economist, Paul Baran.

The attention that came to Burton by virtue of his writing *The Alternative* led him towards an engagement with the academy, a fellowship permitting him to take up a position as a Visiting Fellow in the School of Pacific Studies at the Australian National University in Canberra. It was there that he wrote *Peace Theory*, published in New York in 1962, and even a cursory glance at the footnotes and references reveals a clear engagement with – indeed, a foot in, the academy – for he begins to engage more deeply with the scholarly treatment of the issues, ultimately locating his argument within a broader pattern of academic concerns. The footnotes and references clearly demonstrate an engagement with the literature, though often this is taken as a point of departure. He acknowledges the thanks owed to his colleagues and critics (notably Arthur Lee Burns), and acknowledges the input from his encounter with the Pugwash movement (founded by Cyrus Eaton to form a scientific–academic bridge between East and West during the worst of the Cold War political confrontations and taking its name from Pugwash, Nova Scotia, where the group first met), particularly its 1960 meeting in Moscow.

Peace Theory is an engaging title, if a little misleading. The book is not rigorously 'theoretical' in any positivistic fashion, nor is it concerned with the nature of peaceful societies, widely defined, or speculations as to what a peaceful society might resemble. What it is, is a study of international relations in a changing world, where the sources of change are many and varied, but where the responses to change are likely to be limited in practice because they are little understood 'in theory'. The study is concerned with the nature of peace and, as the reverse of the coin, so to speak, the causes and conditions of conflict. It is, if you will, diagnostic in tone, with hints of a cure interspersed with the elements of the analysis. A persistent theme is the process of change, which he assumes to be a constant in modern political life. The causes of conflict also change (and he lists several, including what he calls 'classical conflict' – involving issues of territory, contested rights of exploitation and colonial rivalries, revolt against suppression, revolt against poverty, ideological conflicts, and armaments competition) but he argues that the classical lexicon of international relations – and policies that follow from the prevailing wisdom – is increasingly inadequate in dealing with these dynamic conflicts. The sources of conflict are systemic and lasting, not ephemeral or trivial, more particularly systemic change and adjustment, yet traditional policies are not enough, for they are anachronistic and, though perhaps right for their times, are not useful in addressing new and emergent forms of conflict. If times change radically, there is a demand for thought to change too.

Burton argues that

the general approach to the study [of peaceful relations] has been traditionally in terms of international institutions, international politics, power rivalries, international strategy and enforcement procedures...Deterrents, balance of power, international enforcement and other devices which are conspicuous in traditional studies of international relations, we have found incompatible with a condition of peace. They cannot, therefore, be regarded properly as part of the study of peaceful international relations. (Burton, 1962, p. 195)

Indeed, 'the studies which purport to be studies relating to peace are in fact studies of political warfare, of military strategy, of international organisations, of power balances and of other enforcement devices. There has been no endeavour, so far as one can ascertain, to develop a study which would be concerned with peaceful relationships' (Burton, 1962, pp. 196–7). In other words, conventional wisdom is an impediment and not a means, to the constitution of a peaceful society. Traditional assumptions and practices may be consistent with the maintenance of order in a system of inter-state relations, but order is not to be equated here with the condition of peace. Where there is a dynamic process at work – such as Burton identifies in contemporary conditions of revolt against colonial rule and the status quo – then devices designed to contain, resist, manage or 'hold the line' are simply inappropriate and counterproductive. They do not solve the problem. At the same time, Burton is keen to establish that there is an intermediate step between the changes in world politics and the responses of state authorities towards them: this focuses in on the process of perception, since 'it is the *perception by other nations* of the nature of change which determines their responses' (Burton, 1962, p. 55). And therein lies a danger, since, to take just one pertinent example,

> changes preceding World War Two were undesirable from the point of view of the Western powers; but they were in a large measure a reaction by Germany and Japan to the refusal of the West to make the necessary adjustments once an economic injustice had been demonstrated. Such situations form the great majority of 'unwarranted' changes in history. Popular thinking on this issue is confused by misleading analogies. (Burton, 1962, p. 23)

What, then, does he propose by way of an alternative approach to the subject of peace? 'Rethinking is now required in the general problem of conflict' (Burton, 1962, p. 45). That is a major aim of this book, and a key distinction appears early on: the problem is not conflict *per se*, but rather circumstances where 'the study of peaceful international relations ... seeks ... to ensure that conflict is resolved and not merely repressed; for the repression of conflict merely suppresses grievances, and unsatisfied grievances create a condition not of peace but of potential hostility' (Burton, 1962, p. 4). We shall come to see more of this distinction in due course. In discussing system dynamics, he pays attention to the nature and significance of change, making a distinction between primary and secondary change. The first involves major changes to the environment related to human activity (such as geographical changes), while the second involve 'acts by governments which are deliberately intended to alter economic, social, political, strategic or other interstate relationships we shall call "secondary". Deliberate acts to prevent alterations are, in a dynamic world, reasonably included in this category' (Burton, 1962, p. 55). He leaves us in no doubt as to the primary issue underlying the whole:

> a condition of peaceful international relations ... is the study of a relationship in which change continuously takes place, but by means which do not necessarily destroy a condition of peace. The condition of peace is therefore itself a function of change and adjustment to it. Consequently, the starting point of peace theory is an examination of change, rather than an examination of a hypothetical and static position of peaceful relations. (Burton, 1962, p. 48)

In summary, the problem to be addressed is the problem that inheres in systemic mal-performance, not speculation about some abstract 'peace'.

These are particularly pregnant passages. They are certainly more subtle when compared to the style of *The Alternative*, for here he is keen to make clear distinctions, to finesse the argument in some degree. His style is rather more disciplined, if not always crystal clear, and is located within the contemporary literature of significance. Moreover, having highlighted the problems that reside in the conventional approaches to war and conflict, the rest of the book is clearly constructive. In other words, as well as being a critic, he also acts as an innovator: not only does he say what is wrong, he also suggests a more fruitful approach. Furthermore, he also finds a clear role and purpose for the academic: it is not passive, nor speculative, nor detached:

> Before disputing parties can come together and usefully ask each other what the strife is about and what agreements are to be made, an analysis of conflict has to be made on an academic plane with all the objectivity of science. The initial responsibility devolves upon the scientist in the field of peace theory, and no useful progress on the political level can be expected until theories are formulated, made public and widely accepted. (Burton, 1962, p. 188)

He is radical in terms of methodology, no prisoner of established approaches to the study of international relations and searching for more than a rather selective-eclectic methodological stance: 'Many behaviorist studies, sociological studies of the modern state which throw light on national responses, adjustment processes in various types of economic and political organisation, and other matters affecting the ability of nations to register passive responses are all relevant to a study of peaceful international relations' (Burton, 1962, p. 199). The interesting thing here is a recognition by Burton that the inter-state dynamic is not unique, not constituting a special kind of political system that can be understood in, and on, its own terms. This had long been an established view: international relations, it was argued, were relationships unlike any other, for they were constituted in a particular realm – devoid of central authority, characterised by self-help, where there was only a modest international society (at best), and where this society could descend rapidly into anarchy. By positing that we could expand the research frame of reference, Burton acknowledges that this claim to specialness or uniqueness is spurious, since we can learn much from 'various other economic and political organisations' and in particular processes of adjustment that take us into a study of behaviour (his use of the term 'behaviourist' was typical of the time, but soon this would be replaced by a more generalised term 'behaviouralism', which much influenced the study of International Relations in the 1960s). But he does more than this. He goes beyond a focus on states to a wider analysis that encompasses the macro (involving the interactions of states), and the micro-analysis of individual and group processes: his emphasis on perception is important in this respect.

His very clearly expressed sense of what was required in light of the issues addressed in *Peace Theory* were stated unambiguously: 'A complete rethinking of international relations is required. War, once accepted as inevitable or as a necessary evil, has to be eliminated. Traditional thought processes have to be challenged' (Burton, 1962, p. 47). *Peace Theory* was thus a symptom of the perceived poverty of conventional thought, and at the same time a pioneer effort in the search to replace that conventional wisdom. Locating it within the corpus of Burton's work, the book has all of the hallmarks of a work of transition. There are still clear links to what he was saying at the London School of Economics, but he was also well aware of the changes to international structures going on around him, especially in Asia. There are many signs and hints of the issues that were to be engaged and addressed more fully in the future. The opportunity to do so soon presented itself. Burton, in London, was now not only a student of International Relations, he was also a teacher. But as well as engaging with the literature as part of the teaching task, a professional involvement with it – and the continuing debates about it that were to be such a part of the crucial decade of the 1960s in International Relations – afforded Burton the opportunity to embark upon the task of rethinking it.

3
Engaging International Relations

Burton thus arrived in London to teach International Relations. Up to this point, Burton had been able to give voice to his personal views as he saw fit. He had quit the Department of External Affairs, had criticised domestic and international policies and, as a Research Fellow in Canberra, he could carry on being critical, with an eye to the demands of being rather more 'scholarly', now engaging with the academy in some degree, and to the extent that he did, he needed to accept the idea of academic procedures, if not rules, and engage with the collective concerns of his colleagues, widely defined. *Peace Theory*, as we have seen, saw that process beginning.

London presented different demands. Now he was not at the edge of the debate (in two senses, as a Research Fellow and in Australia) but rather close to the locus of power and influence in International Relations, characterised as it had been since its inception by dominant Anglo-American concerns and institutional identities. Given that his new academic department was headed by Georg Schwarzenberger, an avowed power politics thinker, it is interesting to speculate how Burton and he got along, given what we already know about Burton's critique of the power politics approach. Yet there is a more important issue, of which, perhaps, the Burton–Schwarzenberger relationship is just one illustration: in so far as Burton was now engaging with 'International Relations' as a full-time academic, what was it he was engaging with? This was not at all clear and the very subject itself was beset by much introspection allied to debate and no little controversy. An assessment of the nature of International Relations as it was in the 1960s is therefore necessary at this point: only in the light of the discipline then evolving can we make sense of Burton's work after *Peace Theory*. Nor is this merely a case of setting a context by way of completeness. Part of the problem was that many in the field disagreed fundamentally with regard to what International Relations actually was, what it was ceasing to be, what it could become, and how.

Consider the following comment: 'The field of international relations is currently experiencing a period of great research activity which some see as growth and others as dismemberment, which some see as intellectually invigorating and others as intellectual pretension, some as socially relevant and others as an escape into social irresponsibility. It has not always been thus' (Platig, 1966, p. 4). Some in Britain saw this as an unnecessary and undesirable import of fashionable ideas from the United States, from where many (though not all) of the major new trends emanated, characterised by neologisms and 'scientism'. Many of those working within the limits of the conventional wisdom saw it as a shift away from the real and fundamental issues at the centre of the discipline. Burton was fairly clear in his assessment of the significance of it all, suggesting that the changes under way in International Relations marked 'what will for a long time be regarded as the most important decade of thought in international studies' (Burton, 1968, p. ix).

International Relations emerged as an identifiably independent discipline in 1919. This is not to suggest that there was no significant body of thought extant with regard to the conduct of international relations generally, or more particularly war and peace, for there was. Much of the Western political tradition, indeed, had been concerned with the nature of human nature and the appropriate conduct of practical political and social intercourse, given that nature was thought to be flawed and not entirely benign. St. Augustine, Hobbes and in particular Machiavelli still loom large in the old tradition, centuries after their deaths. Set against this, however, was a significant body of thought that had tended to stress the associative, if not entirely peaceful, tendencies evident among, or potentially within, human beings, and in various circumstances, notably voiced by Kant, Proudhon, Owen and Saint-Simon. In the light of centuries of human thought and conduct, war and peace were sure to be accorded status as major issues of intellectual and practical concern (see Manuel and Manuel (1979) on the development of Utopian thought).

There were also organisational initiatives before the First World War. The World Peace Foundation and the Carnegie Endowment for International Peace had been established in the United States before 1914, with the aim of eradicating war – and when that was accomplished, the American steelmaker and philanthropist, Andrew Carnegie, decreed that the funds left in the Endowment be diverted to solving other social problems. Such was the mood of optimism. After the First World War, the first university departments appeared – at the University of Wales in Aberystwyth, in Oxford and at the London School of Economics and Political Science. Outside the universities, the Royal Institute of International Affairs was established in London. University departments were also founded in the United States, and the Council on Foreign Relations was founded, in New York, in 1921 (on which, see Schulzinger, 1984).

The dates are important, as the institutionalisation of International Relations was part of a mood of reformism and improvement that attended the conclusion of the First World War and attempts to prevent a similar occurrence. The regulation of international politics could not be assumed to be always stable and self-regulating in light of the war. More knowledge and institutions were required. At a practical level, it was embodied in the project to establish a League of Nations, aimed at establishing and preserving an international order where war was to be minimised. Indeed, part of the Covenant of the League embodied a provision for states in dispute and wishing to go to war to give three months' notice of their intention to do so; it was assumed that, in the three-month period, reason would prevail. At an academic level, the impetus was to learn more and establish a new framework of understanding. Of course, the practical and the academic were closely related. As Morgenthau long ago observed, the letter sent to Aberystwyth offering the new chair in International Politics described its purposes as 'the study of those related problems of law and politics, of ethics and economics, which are raised by the project of the League of Nations, and for the encouragement of a truer understanding of civilisations other than our own' (Morgenthau, 1971, p. 300).

Essentially, therefore, International Relations has been a discipline with a problem at its centre; it is not a subject studied as an interesting issue and for its own sake. The problem is how to order a system of states where there is no central authority, and where the power in the system resides with the members who do not acknowledge any obligation to others unless they decide that doing so coincides with their own interests. In short, how is a state-centric and self-help system to be better ordered, given that when it is disordered it is likely to be beset by increasingly destructive wars?

The question was not entirely new. It had been confronted in 1815 after the Napoleonic Wars, and, more importantly, before that in 1648 at the end of the Thirty Years' War. It was to be confronted again in 1945. But 300 years previously, the Treaty of Westphalia (there were in fact many meetings and several treaties, but the depiction of the singular is conventional) established the roots of the modern international system of states. It did so as a search for order emerging out of disorder, namely the butchery and instability that were associated with the Thirty Years' War. From 1618 to 1648, most of Europe was in chaos as disputes proliferated with respect to who ruled, over whom, where, why and for how long. The settlement of 1648 was based on a fiction, but a necessary fiction, in that all the participants were to be treated as equal, differences notwithstanding. Second, they were to be treated as sovereign, with a right to rule in the territory they represented. From this flowed a concomitant rule, the rule of non-intervention. Subsequently, despite its being transgressed on occasion, the rule of non-intervention has shown a remarkable persistence as the basis of international relations between and among states. Similarly with the notion of sovereign equality and the right to use force and resort to war, which persist with equal force and validity in a system still recognisably with Westphalian foundations even into the early twenty-first century.

What changed over the decades after 1648 was the context within which the Westphalian system was located. Societies changed, ideologies changed and technology applied to war affected the conduct of war and the operation of ordering devices such as the balance of power and alliances. When modern society was brought together with modern war in 1914, the shock was overwhelming: millions were killed in a war that lasted for over four years, and which many had expected to last a few weeks at most. The so-called 'century of peace' (of course, it was no such thing, except on one particular reading of the word 'peace'), was brought crushingly to an end. The war changed attitudes to war, society, culture and politics (see, for example, Fussell, 1975).

The post-1918 mood was directed at reforming the behaviour of the states system by developing understanding and effective international organisation at a global level, through the action of the League, beyond a narrow view of politics and encompassing, to some degree, social conditions. The mood was one of optimism (though not entirely undiluted, for motives of revenge and retribution were allied to reform in the making of the post-war peace). Subsequently, this approach to reforming international relations came to be labelled Idealism, but it did not last long after 1918–19. For critics of the Idealists, 'real-world' considerations began to encroach upon the reformist path. The battle over the participation of the United States in the League, German reparations, treaty-making with the defeated powers, instability in Europe, then the collapse of Germany, followed by Wall Street, then Weimar, all led to a sense of Idealism being replaced. Power and interest were replacing co-operation and reformism: this, it was argued, was the enduring reality, as ever. This was the view of those who were to be known as the Realists, and it was their approach to the study of International Relations which was to dominate for the following three decades.

It is appropriate at this point to flesh out these labels, Idealism and Realism, especially since they have been used frequently in the foregoing discussion. The terms are long-established in many fields of intellectual enquiry, as, for example, the use of 'Idealism' in philosophy and 'Realism' in art, and they have come to denote particular approaches to International Relations. Moreover, they have been the source of some confusion, especially where Realism is often referred to as a 'dominant paradigm'. We should therefore clarify the terms paradigm, approach and model at this stage also.

A *paradigm* is a widely shared view of, or set of assumptions about, how the world is constituted, with an emphasis on 'widely shared'. From 1918/19 to about 1960 there was, in International Relations (IR), a widely shared view that the world was comprised of states, that we were studying a state-centric system. This is what was taught in universities, researched in graduate schools, and embodied in monographs and textbooks. It was a paradigm shared by both Realists and Idealists: they both worked with the image of a world of states. Where they differed was on the possibilities that inhered in the system. They shared a *paradigm*, but adopted different *approaches* in consequence.

For the Idealists, the system was capable of more: it could improve performance through co-operation, lessening competition and minimising the prospects of war while also extending co-operation into expanding areas of human behaviour. Some asserted that there was an underlying harmony of interests, despite the differences that set societies apart. The Realists, on the other hand, saw co-operation as being likely only where interests coincided, and this was likely to be less rather than more, as states were driven ultimately by their own interests, rather than those of any other states, or collective interests. Power and influence were the driving forces, competition the norm. This was not necessarily an approach to politics that denied the power of morality, but it did elevate interests and power. Significant terms used in the Realist depiction of international relations in practice and in theory were the balance of power, alliances, geopolitics and the like. In adopting the view they did, the IR Realists drew on a long-established tradition in Western political philosophy; namely the power of might and interest, going back to Machiavelli and Thucydides, and, significantly, embodied in the pervasive and persistent Roman notion of 'if you want peace prepare for war'.

An *approach* is therefore narrower than a paradigm, and the term is often used interchangeably with 'perspective'. Consider the following, rather more prosaic, example. Two people perceive a bottle. They agree that it is a bottle, that it is green and that it is designed, made and used for storing something, usually a liquid, but that it could be used to hold certain solids – such as salt or sand. But they agree that it is what it looks like. Their view is shared, indeed widely shared by many when confronted by a bottle. But they may disagree as to whether it is half-full or half-empty, depending on their perspective or approach. A pessimist says that it is half-empty, an optimist that it is half-full. Their perspective or approach depends on their own value system, but this does not stop them agreeing that the bottle is a bottle, and that it is a certain colour and so on. Similarly, with paradigms and approaches.

A *model* is an abstraction, or pattern, used by an analyst or researcher, in order to permit him/her to study a thing or subject more simply, reducing that being studied to manageable proportions. An example might be a model of an economy as one comprised of stocks and flows, or producers and consumers. Using this model they can test assumptions, accumulate findings, establish that some things are repeated and others are not, and thus accumulate knowledge about how things work. They are then on the way to developing explanations and constructing theories or sets of general explanations.

Realism dominated the study of International Relations for as long as it did, since it both captured and reflected a mood and was, arguably, right for its times, described by Hannah Arendt (a close friend of Hans Morgenthau, it should be noted) as 'dark times'. These were the decades of, successively, Stalinism, Fascism, depression, total war, division and Cold War in Europe, and the development and proliferation of nuclear weapons. There were many European émigrés to the United States who adopted a so-called 'Realistic' view of politics; John Herz, Robert Strausz-Hupe, Stefan Possony, Nicholas Spykman and Arnold Wolfers among them. After 1945, they were to be joined by others – not all Realists – including Karl Deutsch and Stanley Hoffmann. Major texts of the time were written by Schumann, Hartmann and Niebuhr. (For a survey of political realism in American thought, see Coffey, 1977.)

The British historian, Edward Hallett Carr, is also important, and his 1939 work *The Thirty Years' Crisis* proved to be particularly influential, especially in so far as he had much to say that was critical of what he called 'Utopianism' in International Relations, suggesting that 'if therefore purpose precedes and conditions human thought, it is not surprising to find that, when the human mind begins to exercise itself in some fresh field, an initial stage occurs in which the element of wish or purpose is overwhelmingly strong, and the inclination to analyse facts and means weak or non-existent' (Carr, 1939, p. 5). Carr was to describe all of this in terms that were to construct the debates about the study of International Relations for decades to come. Burton was well aware of all of this at an early stage, when first in London.

If anything, Hans Morgenthau proved to be even more influential: his text, *Politics Among Nations*, first appearing in 1948, going through several editions and dominating the study of International Relations in the United States. If one text summed up the subject in a readily assimilable form, this was it. E. R. Platig, for example, placed *Politics Among Nations* at the top of a list of ten 'significant' and ten 'typical' books reviewed by thirteen scholarly journals, the significant books being adjudged those which 'have made a substantial contribution to the international relations research community in the postwar period' (Platig, 1966, p. 207). Not only did it dominate the research community, it was also significant in terms of what was taught. The concerns that connected the Realists as a more-or-less coherent group were, as we have seen, the politics of power and interest, as perceived from a European-Atlanticist perspective. Many, to reiterate, were European émigrés, mostly to North America; Georg Schwarzenberger left Germany for the United Kingdom in 1933, and his major interpretation of International Relations was entitled, not surprisingly, *Power Politics* when it first appeared in 1941 (see Schwarzenberger, 1964).

A rather more subtle approach to the state-centric system is illustrated in the work of the British scholar, Martin Wight. Bull and Holbraad (1979, p. 19) suggest that he did not embrace the Realist position and was ambivalent in relation to it. Nevertheless, there is not a huge distance between the Realists and Wight, and he was to have great significance with regard to how the subject was studied in the United Kingdom. Wight's work was a foundation for what later came to be called the 'English School' in International Relations (and associated with some members of the IR Department at the London School of Economics). He wrote two particularly influential works, *Systems of States* and *Power Politics*, both republished at the end of the 1970s, some years after his death (Wight, 1979a, 1979b). Arguably, he set the tone and agenda of what was later to be called the 'English School' in International Relations, concerned as it was with the notion of a society of states, combining elements of statist thinking, Grotian elements of international society, and hopes for reform of that society of states. According to his editors, 'the whole emphasis of Martin Wight's work is on the elements of continuity in international relations, rather than on the elements of change and that references to contemporary events are only illustrations, not essential to the central theme' (Bull and Holbraad, 1979, p. 9). Moreover, the *Power Politics* of 1979, just as an earlier edition had done,

> present[ed] world politics as comprising chiefly the relations among powers, or states in their external aspect, whereas most studies today assert that states share the stage with 'other actors' such as classes, political parties or business corporations and that transnational or trans-state relations among these various groups are no less central to the subject than international or interstate relations [but, for Wight] 'modern man in general has shown greater loyalty to the state than to church or class or any other international bond'. (Bull and Holbraad, 1979, p. 13)

Furthermore, despite the finer points of whether or not Wight was or was not a Realist, what is inescapable is that the world he described and sought to understand was a world of states where power was an operative – *the* operative? – force.

Traditionally, after the First World War, International Relations had 'three main interests . . . history, international law and political reform' (Morgenthau, 1971, p. 300). Later it was to encompass what Quincy Wright was to call a series of 'root disciplines', upon which it drew in order to enlighten its own concerns. These involved international law, diplomatic history, military science, international organisation, international trade, colonial government and the conduct of foreign relations, among others (Wright, 1955). Whatever else International Relations was, *and is*, a constant theme has been that it has been eclectic, drawing on other disciplines in order to enlighten its special concerns. It would be as well to remember this as a characteristic of the discipline; one person's lack of focus may be another's eclectic approach, after all.

John Herz developed a modified view which he called 'liberal realism' (see Herz, 1976), but he is as notable for what he had to say about the way the subject was studied. He prefaced his hugely significant work, *International Politics in the Atomic Age* (Herz, 1959), with the observation that the book was decidedly old-fashioned in terms of the methods he had employed to write it. He had written it himself, without teams of researchers; he had not used 'an IBM facility', nor had he interviewed anybody or gone in for data analysis. As a matter of fact, he said, 'the book does not contain a single chart, map, graph, diagram, table or statistical figure' (Herz, 1959, p. v). He had thought and then written. There is much of significance in terms of what these remarks from Herz represented, for the fact that he could term his work 'old-fashioned' is to suggest that much was changing, even as the 1960s approached. A decade later, graphs, charts, tables and the like were very much the norm, consistent with an entirely new mood about how to study International Relations. What is important is that there was a developing sense that International Relations was changing in terms of relevant and appropriate methodologies. When comparisons were made with economics, for example, it was clear that economics was capable of making statements that appeared to be scientific, and that economists could make law-like statements and offer concrete advice to policy-makers.

Economics, long the preserve of 'Political Economy' in the nineteenth century, had made progress in so far as it was able to develop theoretical constructs – rigorous models of how economies, firms and sectors worked; it was capable of offering policy-relevant advice (many economists had been recruited into government service in the course of the Second World War – especially, but not only, in the United States: see, for example, Galbraith (1981)), and in the United States there was a Council of Economic Advisors to assist the President. It was able to deal in models and theories, making predictions and offering policy advice. It was thought to be a hard science and thus taken seriously for being so.

The study of political science in the United States was more advanced than International Relations. Much influenced by the innovations associated with Charles Merriam at the University of Chicago in the 1920s, there was an emphasis on the study of political behaviour, as opposed to the study of institutions and a focus on individuals and groups as levels of analysis (it was in this environment in Chicago that Quincy Wright was to commence his monumental *Study of War* in 1927: he completed it in 1942). Graduate students who worked with Merriam and Harold Lasswell (whose work, *World Politics and Personal Insecurity* was described as 'a work of great precocity' (Fox, 1968, p. 12)) included David Easton and V. O. Key, Jr. and among the first inroads into a scientific study of politics were to be found the studies of voting behaviour, sampling and prediction of outcomes. Note the emphases on behaviour and prediction.

There was, too, a well developed tradition in the United States of 'social science', the American Social Science Association being founded in 1865, by those seeking to understand and improve society (see Haskill, 1977) – though, arguably, it came rather late to International

Relations – and a deep-rooted philosophical tradition of Pragmatism, to be found in the works of William James and John Dewey, relating knowledge to practical social impact and function. The eminent American scholar, W. T. R. Fox, reflecting that tradition, was to observe that 'American professors of International Relations, no matter how little policy-orientated their intellectual interests may be, generally believe that deeper and more widespread knowledge of International Relations will somehow result in better public policies, and therefore in a better world for Americans to live in' (Fox, 1968, p. 16).

There is therefore some credence to claims that International Relations received a major stimulus to growth after 1945, when the United States assumed the role of a great power, prompting a demand for knowledge of the world with which it sought to engage. But it was a boost and not a spark of creation. Yet to emphasise the boost after 1945 should not lead us to ignore the important social and philosophical influences that so moulded International Relations in the United States. Nevertheless, it is incontrovertible that for much of the period since 1919, and especially after 1945, the United States has been a dominant force in the study of International Relations. The number of courses, research institutions, research grants, 'think-tanks' and the like is impressive. Indeed, W. J. M. Mackenzie, surveying the field of politics and social science in 1968, was moved to remark that the United States had 'in political science, as in so many fields...in effect bought predominance' (Mackenzie, 1968). The American higher education sector is large and the book market significant, and there has been significant spillover into the rest of the English-speaking world. But size is only one indicator. National style and philosophical roots, allied to an evolving American role in the world, are important determinants of American predominance in a field that has long been Atlanticist in character, though this may now be changing. For many students of International Relations in the 1950s and 1960s especially, doing postgraduate work in the discipline meant doing it in the United States, such was the gravitational effect of American dominance. Some Britons (John Vincent, for example) went to Australia.

So, could International Relations develop in a manner similar to political science and economics, capable of rigour rather than comment, predicting rather than explaining what had happened in the past, being taken seriously as scientific study rather than a mere admixture of intuition and speculation? Such feelings about status cannot be discounted in assessing the significance of the move towards a different, 'scientific' International Relations agenda. Indeed, the roots of that mood are to be found in writings dating from years before. Writing in 1949, Fox remarked that many who entered the study of International Relations in the 1930s had found little esteem in doing so, and that this sense of lack of esteem, allied to a search for legitimacy, and related to events in the wider world, led to a period of soul-searching. Fox, for example, noted the work of no less than twenty-four professors of International Relations in the United States who had been appointed before 1930, and observed that 'their research is to a high degree characterised by a high technical competence and lack of chauvinism. Much of their research which has proved to be of great importance to the field could be, and was, completed without any special International Relations technique having to be developed' (Fox, 1968, p. 7). Moreover, he continued, in the absence of a sharply defined focus, the International Relations scholar who rejected current history had few other options.

Not all engaged with the changes that were evident, gathering momentum even. In later editions of *Politics Among Nations*, for example, Morgenthau acknowledged that a debate about method and science was going on, but he refused to engage with it. So, too, did Wight: 'the behaviourist school – with its calculated exclusion of moral or ethical questions, its lack of attention to historical enquiry and its underlying utilitarianism of purpose – was one whose claims he was not able to take seriously' (Bull and Holbraad, 1979). Many 'behaviouralists', as they would have preferred to be known, would not subscribe to this view of themselves, one suspects. Despite these essentially conservative statements of non-engagement, dissident views on the role of science, and alternative futures for International Relations thinking, the pace of change was swift and accelerating.

Methodological influences were to come from other disciplines too. Set against what had gone before it, the impact of two works by Karl Deutsch was extraordinary. His *Nationalism and Social Communication* (Deutsch, 1957) reinvested the study of nationalism with new form and dimensions – based on studies of communication and behavioural relationships rather than assertions of shared heritage, history and values – and his study on the *Nerves of Government* (Deutsch, 1963) had a profound effect on the emergent study of foreign policy analysis, indeed perhaps even served as a kind of lexicon and conceptual core for much of what was to come later. At this distance, it is difficult to recreate the mood engendered by the appearance of *Nerves of Government*. It is easier to observe that it transformed the language and concepts employed subsequently in the analysis of decision-making generally, and foreign policy decision-making in particular. Screening, filters, feedback and the like were essentially novel before Deutsch, and the norm afterwards.

This was all symptomatic, not only of the debate about *what* was to be studied. It was also a question of *how*, as in the 1960s the IR discipline was subject to influences that flowed across the several social sciences with respect to questions of methodology. IR sought to become more scientific, in the sense of aiming to construct meaningful generalisations, credible explanations of behaviour having some empirical content and going beyond commentary, to offer statements of predictive value and hence potentially useful in enhancing the quality of policy-related advice and subsequent performance by governments. In this, many proponents desirous of making IR more scientific sought insight and pattern in the achievements of a positivistic science employed in the natural sciences such as physics, chemistry and biology. Evidence was important, but so too was method. In this, proponents of science sought to transcend the limitations of the deductive methods often employed by the Realists. Criticisms related to imprecision in the use of terms (as, for example, in the use of the term 'balance of power' as policy, description and goal), selection in the use of historical evidence (often with reference to the 'lessons of history') and a method rooted in assertion rather than demonstration (such as that related to the primacy of power or the existence of human nature, the latter being timeless and universal – but based on what evidence?).

This mood is encapsulated appropriately in a short comment, with appropriate footnote, from James Rosenau, written when the methodological transition was well underway. Commenting on the limits of the conventional wisdom in the emergent field of foreign policy analysis, he observed that 'since foreign policy analysts do not set out to test explicit hypotheses, they can never be wrong. Their analysis might be inappropriate, superficial or out of date, but they cannot be wrong... The analyst with a scientific consciousness, on the other hand, cannot ignore his errors.' The footnote cites Zbigniew Brzezinski as follows: '"If Krushchev could not predict his downfall, how would you expect me to do it?"' (Rosenau, 1969b, pp. 26–7).

Computers mattered, as we shall see, and so did the images associated with them – images of information processing, systems, organisation theory and the like. Herbert Simon's *Administrative Behavior* (Simon, 1957) was influential in terms of how decisions were made and, before it, the seminal monograph of R. Snyder, H.W. Bruck and B. Sapin again focused on behaviour in the context of *Foreign Policy Decision Making* (1962). What these and similar initiatives served to do was to open up a research agenda associated with the prevalent image of the state. From this time onwards it was not to be, indeed could not be, represented as a hard-edged, unified actor separated from external influences by a relatively impervious shell. The state-as-billiard-ball image was under pressure when it became clear that leaders often followed public opinion; that the concept of 'a decision' being made by a few leaders was open to question in the light of new practices involving an articulate public opinion; that rationality was not always the norm in decision-making; and that 'political factors' often influenced how an ostensibly unified bureaucracy worked in practice. Images, perceptual processes, and the activities of gathering, filtering and processing information were important and often problematic. Bureaucratic politics mattered too. Fundamentally, in light of all this, the notion of the unified state, allied to some notion of the national interest existing as some sort of objective criterion that should inform policy choices, was seriously challenged. But defining national interest was itself a political issue, and a complex one at that. There was to be more to 'the state' than a convenient starting point from which to embark on a study of international order.

Science and rigour were central issues that figured in two seminal collections. Stanley Hoffmann edited a collection of essays on the theme of *Contemporary Theory in International Relations* (Hoffmann, 1960) and assessed three sets of issues: the nature of International Relations as a discipline; a range of contemporary approaches to theory; and suggestions for the study of International Relations. They were symptomatic of a search for a new identity and scope. Why else, more than forty years after the appearance of the discipline, should its roots, boundaries and concerns be re-examined? At about the same time, a special issue of the journal *World Politics* (later issued as a book by Knorr and Verba, 1961), explored the nature of theory and the international system. That theory and the international system were the subject of debate, given the traditions of International Relations, was significant in itself. Of the book, F. V. Meyer said that the authors sought 'at the highest level, a theory of the world polity and, at a lower level, a theory of the role of the component state within this polity. They are dissatisfied with the more established approach in international relations, with its narrower interest in the relationship between states and its ego-centric one-country or two-country models' (Knorr and Verba, 1961: comment on rear cover from review in *The Economic Journal*).

J. N. Rosenau's *International Politics and Foreign Policy*, a collection of fifty-five essays published in 1961, stands as a benchmark and an indication of the nature of the dynamic methodological foundations of

International Relations in the 1960s. The frontiers of research activity in International Relations, he commented, had been alive with activity during the late 1950s and early 1960s. The purpose of the volume was to collect material together, make it available and accessible, and close the gap between research and teaching, thus bringing the theoretical concerns of those he termed the 'frontiersmen' on the cutting edge of research nearer to the teachers whose concerns tended more to relate real-world and topical concerns in contemporary teaching (Rosenau, 1961, pp. 1–3). By the time a revised edition of the work appeared in 1969 (Rosenau, 1969b) only five of the original essays, selected in part on the basis of their significance and lasting quality, had survived. Such was the nature of the changes that had affected International Relations in the course of a decade.

If these were landmarks of the literature that bore testimony to the change in mood, the ferment gave rise to what came to be known as the two 'Great Debates'. The first involved another Australian scholar, Hedley Bull, who, based in Britain, argued the case for what came to be known as a 'classical approach':

> the approach to theorising that derives from philosophy, history and law and that is characterised above all by explicit reliance on the exercise of judgement and by the assumptions that if we confine ourselves to strict standards of verification and proof, there is very little of significance that can be said about international relations, that general propositions about this subject must therefore derive from a scientifically imperfect process of perception or intuition, and that these general propositions cannot be accorded anything more than the tentative and inconclusive status appropriate to their doubtful origin. (Bull, in Knorr and Rosenau, 1969, p. 20)

Morton Kaplan, based in the United States, argued the case for a scientific, as opposed to a traditional, approach, commenting that 'the traditionalists are often quite intelligent and witty people. Why then do they make such gross mistakes? Surely there must be something seriously wrong with an approach that devotes so much effort to such ill-informed criticism' (Kaplan, in Knorr and Rosenau, 1969, p. 61). The debate was perhaps predictable, interesting in itself but, in the longer view, now seems especially symptomatic of the emergence of methodological rigour and pluralism.

The second debate took place just a few years later and can be contrasted with the Bull–Kaplan debate in so far as the later debate was not about wisdom *contra* science, but rather the merits of science, as debated by two 'scientists', certainly not traditionalists, who were much informed by the need to go beyond the limits of the traditional frames of reference. On the one hand, Bruce Russett (1967) argued that the advent of computers had made possible new methods in International Relations. Progress had been 'enormous over the past decade', he argued, but probably because work had started from a low base. More pointedly, computers had made new things possible and 'without such facilities, the inductive taxonomy that forms the heart of this analysis [*International Regions and the International System*] would have been quite impossible'. O. R. Young (1969) argued that this work by Russett illuminated some of the emergent problems in theorising in the new environment of computers, and so on. For Young, Russett had produced 'an elaborate presentation of data whose purpose is unclear and whose utility is undermined by the absence of a conceptual foundation'. Moreover, 'the new toy of social science, the computer, presents an invitation to become preoccupied with questions of puristic induction' and 'it is time for us all to stop being fascinated by numbers for their own sake and get on with the job of explaining important political phenomena' (Young, 1969).

Young is not wholly critical in his consideration of Russett, arguing that Russett has illuminated certain aspects of regions in the international system, and indicated that prediction may be possible. Again taking the longer view, Young's significant contribution was to remind his colleagues that explanation of political phenomena was the guiding issue, not a preoccupation with methodology *per se*. Which is not to suggest that what Russett and others were doing was without merit, but rather that Young represented some sort of corrective influence, warning against over-reliance on the computer. Particularly notable products of the quantitative-behavioural mood are to be found in Singer and Small (1972), Singer (1968) and Rummel's several volumes that emerged from the large-scale Dimensions of Nations Project based at the University of Hawaii. Not least of the virtues of this type of work was that it provided some kind of empirical content and foundation (or not, as the case may be) to long-established beliefs about how the international system was supposed to function (whether or not alliances contributed to stability was one of the questions Singer confronted early on, for example). And the provision of empirical evidence was to demonstrate that assumptions that the international system was 'peaceful' were formed and entrenched at times when violent conflict and wars were the norm in the international system; of course, there was no general war involving the 'great powers', but many people were killed in scores of wars, a large number of them undeclared and not conforming to the established rules of inter-state relations. In short, peace was a peace for some, and war was the norm for many – so much was demonstrably accurate in the light of the evidence.

This concern for aspects of behaviour – of states, individuals and other entities – has been described as a different approach in itself, often termed 'Behaviouralism'. In fact, this was a mood, and perhaps even a fashion. Yet it was not only a fashion, as it was in fact instrumental in effecting changes within International Relations. It was part of a shift away from the traditional concerns with states as unitary and undifferentiated entities, locating states on a continuum of relevant actors which were part of an emergent global political dynamic, be they states, organisations (formal or informal), alliances or individuals. States were not shifted immediately from the centre of the agenda of International Relations, however. Indeed, J. Vasquez made the point persuasively that many of the Behaviouralists continued in a tradition associated with power politics (see Vasquez (1983) for an influential view regarding the power of power politics). Nevertheless, this does not invalidate the major point at issue here; namely, that there was a shift to look at the roots of state behaviour in terms of human interactions within the state, and a shift to look at other actors beyond the state. The formal-mechanistic view that there existed 'the state' and that 'it' in some way 'made decisions', or that 'the Americans went into Vietnam' became problematic statements in themselves rather than statements of an accurate, conventional and uncontroversial nature. The nature of the 'governmental decision-making apparatus' was to be revealed by reference to the evidence, rather than merely asserted. Much of what was going on in the various social sciences (and International Relations was now widely assumed to be one of them) was subsumed under the label of 'Behaviouralism'. What this in fact meant, in terms of the form and future of the social sciences, was the subject of some debate (see, as a typical stock-taking assessment of the time, Charlesworth (1967)). By 1969, David Easton, in his presidential address to the American Political Science Association, proclaimed the arrival of the new revolution in political science in a time of social and political crisis. This was to be termed the 'post-behavioural revolution' and, according to Easton, the watchwords were now to be relevance and action (Easton, 1971). The impact on International Relations was fundamental. From now on, state-centricity would not suffice in the way that it had done at the start of the decade; nor would a narrow and relatively detached stance. The troubled times, as the 1960s were left behind, demanded more.

This was the realm that Burton entered, but he was no *naif*. As we have seen already, he was not to let the grass grow under his feet in London: he made contacts, attended conferences and seminars (including that held in 1963 devoted to the nature of aggression, where Burton presented a paper, alongside Konrad Lorenz, Anthony Storr, Stanislav Andreski and James Fisher, among others, and where discussants included Sir Julian Huxley and Desmond Morris (Carthy and Ebling, 1964)), and sought successfully to establish organisations and institutional structures. He was, clearly, no ordinary novice teacher of International Relations.

International Relations: A General Theory (Burton, 1965) was the first major product of Burton's UCL and London experience. Not surprisingly, the first part of the book represents his contribution to the developing debate within International Relations, and this section commences in a typically direct fashion where Burton is at pains to make several distinctions critical to his own work and critical of much that had taken place within the discipline: 'International Relations as a science is concerned with observation and analysis, and with theorising in order to explain and predict. As such it does not seek solutions to problems of peace and security' (Burton, 1965, p. 5). Here Burton offers a definition of International Relations 'as a science' – he does not ask whether it can be, and if so of what sort: it is a scientific enterprise – and his view of the enterprise is clearly informed by the practices established in the natural sciences. The task is one of observation, the identification of patterns and their explanation. The next step is clearly identified and distinguished from the first. The first task is explanation and, on the basis of explanation, prediction. This is entirely consistent with established practices in 'naturalism', where science is comprised of a series of conditional statements of the 'if . . . then' variety, familiar across time and culture: 'if we add x to y in the correct quantities, z will be the result'. This is a well-established practice within naturalism, seen in schools, universities and research laboratories. But there is a next step that is not related to the first. What is to be done with such knowledge as is developed is a policy question, and scientists, when asked about what ought to be done on the basis of the knowledge they discover, argue to the effect that 'it is not a decision for me to make, it is for society'. Entirely consistent with the practices of naturalism, he suggests that certain policies are likely to create certain consequences 'but their selection is a matter of policy' (Burton, 1965, p. 5).

In International Relations, 'the distinction between analysis and policy is not always made: many theoretical treatments of international relations conclude with a chapter in which some policy or remedy is advocated' (Burton, 1965, p. 5), thus blurring the distinction between policy and analysis, indeed even informing the analysis. Therefore, 'International Relations as a science which can contribute to problem-solving has been slow to develop and to achieve results, largely because of such unscientific excursions into policy, and the advocacy of single solutions' and 'International Relations has been further impeded by a confusion with analysis of policy problems... [and where] the "theories" or "solutions" advanced in respect of these problems are quite separate from general International Relations theory, which is concerned with the revealing and explanation of relations between states in any given set of circumstances' (Burton, 1965, p. 5). Therein lies the task suggested by the book's title, which doubtless many saw as presumptuous and audacious: to separate analysis from policy, observe patterns of global interaction and explain them, in a world of change rather than stasis. There was a key shift in the level of analysis evident here too: the analysis was to involve states, but it was not entirely state-centric, since there was a perceived need to analyse the structures and processes at the centre of the state and unite this with an explanation of general patterns of international relationships. The aim, in other words, was to establish a general explanation of relationships as these operated at the international level, but with a view to explanation *per se*, rather than a confused conflation of aim and method, analysis and policy goals. This was the goal, cast in terms of 'general theory'.

It is in a world of change that analysts re-examine their assumptions and theories, and it is in this context that Burton draws a distinction between two kinds of peace. In seeking a stable order between states where there was the ever-present prospect of war, order here was construed as a kind of peace. Peace as 'non-war' has been a characteristic of much of the conventional literature, where war is avoided by power balances, armaments and strategy. But a second meaning of peace is the conception of peace as a process (interestingly, Burton has moved to a more sophisticated conception of peace here, as compared to that employed in *Peace Theory*, where peace was repeatedly referred to as a condition) which does not rest upon enforcement or armaments: in other words, where peace is based more on a dynamic legitimacy rather than policies of control. The themes of control, as resistance to change, as opposed to a recognition of, and engagement with, change manifest themselves again as central elements in the Burtonian analysis. Turning to events to demonstrate the changed nature of the environment – where force is likely to be less relevant in bringing about preferred states – he looks at economic development, decolonisation and the conditions of 'powerless states'. In terms of the relationships now obtaining in international relations, he argues, the limitation of thinking in terms of power relationships are now revealed. In other words, even conceding that thinking in terms of power politics might have been right for a certain period of history, the new environment is such as to reveal the intrinsic limits of the conventional set of assumptions. Part three of the book is devoted to a lengthy analysis of the changed world environment.

Change, and the search for meaningful explanation in the light of it, also allows innovations in methodology and model-building, says Burton, and it is especially notable that he draws on the work of Karl Deutsch, and specifically on *Nerves of Government* (Deutsch, 1963). Here, Deutsch sought to explain the activities of states in terms of decision-making, information selection and effective screening (and re-establishing the nature of the link between the established idea of 'government' and the new approach to 'cybernetics', the science of information and control). Innovation in one area of thought can spill over into others, so that 'the introduction of cybernetics as a basic model instead of, or in addition to, a power-balancing model, is evidence of the shift of interest to processes underlying relations between states, and of an interest in consideration of a self-supporting condition of peace; it was a shift provoked by circumstances and made possible by the availability of new concepts' (Burton, 1965, p. 9). Of course, International Relations had long been thought of as an eclectic discipline, importing ideas in order to assist in a consideration of its own particular problems, but Burton was now drawing on the new ideas from elsewhere in order not simply to illuminate the existing agenda of intellectual problems in the discipline: he was seeking to redefine and re-perceive, suggesting that 'International Relations is now far more interested, than was the case even in the late fifties, in the processes by which these options are presented and chosen. A power model describes the resultant of decision-making processes. The significance of the new model is that it explains how decisions are made' (Burton, 1965, p. 22). This may not sound radical from our contemporary perspective, looking back more than thirty years, but it is important to recall that for many years preceding the changes of the 1960s, it was assumed that the state was some kind of self-contained entity, with the boundary of the state being conceived of as some kind of hard exterior shell, with interactions taking place where these exterior shells came together. For many – and for many years – this 'billiard-ball model' constituted a very clear idea as to what International Relations was about.

If this represented one challenge to orthodoxy, it was not the only one, as Burton also addressed the very idea at the centre of the power politics approach, namely the nature of human nature and, by extension, the idea of the security dilemma that sits at the centre of so much discourse about war, peace and insecurity. For long it was argued that human beings were innately aggressive. From this it was inferred that if this was the natural condition of humans, this was also the natural condition within which states existed. Of this continuum in thought Burton is especially critical, suggesting that 'when the biologists and psychologists assert that there are aggressive tendencies amongst individuals within nations, and imply that for this reason nation-states tend to act aggressively, then they are encouraging every state to have an expectation of aggression, even though there is no discernible enemy. The defence policy of the state will tend to produce just the results it seeks to avoid' (Burton, 1965, p. 37). Having made the general observation by way of introduction, he then proceeds to look at examples of circumstances where actions have been deemed aggressive, and the political consequences of doing so. Turning to Asia, Burton suggests that activities in Laos, Vietnam, Taiwan and Korea through which Western policies provided support for unpopular regimes 'has had the appearance to the Chinese of a deliberate encirclement and aggressive intents have been deduced from frequent, though unofficial and irresponsible, statements coming out of the United States. Chinese responses in each of these areas have in turn appeared to be aggressive and have seemed to justify Western policies' (Burton, 1965, p. 40).

So here we have Burton assessing the state of International Relations, questioning its traditional approach to matters of analysis and policy, criticising the orthodoxy in terms of its basic assumptions and its consequent errors of policy. What is it that he proposes by way of an alternative frame of reference? Some elements of his alternative have been identified already, but it is interesting to note especially two later sections of the book. One of them quite clearly engages with an issue of which Burton had some special experience, given his previous activities. Non-alignment was a political stance associated with roles for Third World states in the context of the Cold War stand-off between East and West. Burton came to see this as an alternative role for states acting outside the limits of power balances and spheres of influence, where they could assume an important role: 'insofar as the nonaligned states form a bloc or give expression to a community of interest, this is entirely on the basis of communication. The organising pressures are not related to power' (Burton, 1965, p. 233). The significance of this comment lies in the emphasis that Burton gives to the bases of behaviour located outside the nexus of power; the non-aligned states that emerged out of the altered circumstances that he was at great pains to point out changed the role and nature of power after 1945. (Nuclear weapons were also an important limiting factor.) Traditional conceptions of power politics were now emerging as limited in terms of their capacity to explain in changed circumstances. More to the point, those who acted within the logic of power politics, to see the search for interstate security as being a struggle over a scarce commodity, often made a bad situation worse, according to the logic of the self-fulfilling prophecy. A point germane to these issues, being hinted at rather here than addressed explicitly, was the question associated with perception and what he would come to call 'wrong definitions of the situation' and consequent wrong policies.

Pulling together these consideration of the limited roles of military power, the process of change, the new roles for states and an emphasis on information processing/decision-making as a focus of analysis (utilising the fresh inputs from Deutsch) saw Burton arguing the case for a transition 'from power to steering' (Burton, 1965, p. 141). The role of new inputs was immediately clear, since 'fresh concepts and terminology help overcome what could reasonably be described as habits of thought, if not traditional prejudice. New terms – the jargon of a discipline – are not generally welcome ... [but] they should not lightly be rejected in favour of customary language, for it is by a slight switch of emphasis, or the slightly altered perspective of new terms, that thought has developed' (Burton, 1965, p. 141). The shift from power to steering makes possible a more sophisticated approach to the functioning of international systems, the interactions of states and the bases of interstate behaviour, allowing us to move on from the limited explanatory capability embodied in ideas of balances of power (and Burton is at pains to point out that these, and simliar, terms were imported into socio-political analysis from the fields of physics and engineering; these too were once fresh inputs to a limited conceptual apparatus), 'billiard-ball' images of the state and self-evident national interests: 'It is the process of national data collection, sifting, screening, and course determination prior to action which is of most interest in international relations' (Burton, 1965, p. 146).

This is a significant reorientation of the nature of the problem at the heart of International Relations. Long thought to be embodied in the so-called 'anarchy *problematique*', with states existing in a fragile order and on the edge of chaos, the insecurities that inhered in the system were deemed to be the starting point of the analysis; the key was the achievement and maintenance of order in these conditions of uncertainty, with states looking after their own interests in the absence of any central authority representing an ultimate guarantor of states' security. How, it is asked, can a system of this nature – intrinsically fragile, dangerous and insecure – be made to work, given the nature of states and the inevitable clashes of interests that would be entailed in a competitive search for security, a scarce commodity in such a dangerous environment? In shifting to the perception, information-processing and decision-making procedures in states, Burton shifts the source of the problem from the central systemic *problematique* associated with order and stability, to the very sources of state behaviour, as determined by their (mis)perceptions of the actions of other states in general, or a certain particular state. In other words, the sources of international conflict and instability could and should be sought not by an analysis of the *problematique* of anarchy, but in the internal conditions that operated in the member states of the system. Simply stated, sometimes they see things wrongly: they see aggression in others where none is intended, they perceive threats where there are none, and they are the prisoners of their own belief systems as embodied in history, culture, value systems and decision-making procedures. Improved decision-making procedures, correct perceptions of others and changed circumstances and the like – overall, an improved efficiency in foreign policy decision-making and implementation – could lead to more successful steering of the ship of state, avoiding problems, limiting conflicts with others and enhancing the prospects for a peaceful system of international relations. There is a clear element of radicalism in this approach, but it is also a more sophisticated restatement of an old theme that had long preoccupied Burton: he had, for a long time, argued that the roots of international strife were to be found in the internal conditions of states, especially their perceptions of change and their (in)appropriate responses to it.

Given what he had to say about notions of peace earlier in the book, and his new emphasis on the roots of state actions, it is interesting to note what he has to say about the new initiatives in Peace Research, in which activity he had no little part to play. Having identified the fledgling organisations, he asserts that 'the active members of some of these organisations in the West belong to natural science and to disciplines other than International Relations. Their general view is that the established discipline has failed to adapt to the nuclear era and in particular has been tied to a national-interest approach to relations between states' (Burton, 1965, p. 87). Pugwash, of which Burton had some experience, was another manifestation of the disaffection with orthodoxy. Why, after all, would there be a felt need to found new organisations if the extant ones were doing the job properly? The difference as between International Relations, on the one hand, and Peace Research, on the other, was that the conventional approaches assumed that conflict was inevitable, unless constrained by deterrence – in which case conflict would take a different form rather than disappear (thus explaining the idea of the 'Cold War', presumably) – whereas peace researchers were not prisoners of the assumption regarding the inevitability of conflict, but sought instead to explain its origins, its dynamics and its consequences. Peace Research was thus a movement of protest, and what it protested against was the frequently-asserted view that war and conflict were an inevitable part of the human condition from which there could be no escape: the best we could hope for was not to solve the problem of war and conflict but to manage it as best we could, given our human frailty, proneness to error and our 'nature': 'Peace Studies are differentiated by the fact that they make no assumptions regarding the nature of men or states' (Burton, 1965, p. 93). And the existence of Peace Research was itself instrumental, its very existence as a protest movement changing the environment within which International Relations existed, since it was 'goading International Relations to develop improved techniques and more realistic models' (Burton, 1965, p. 94). Especially worthy of note here is the emphasis on the need for more sophistication in methodology ('improved techniques') and greater care in the construction of models that related to the world as it is, not as it is asserted or presumed to be, hence the need for 'realistic models'. The full-frontal challenge to the power-political Realists to become more realistic is especially notable here. International Relations, in short, was deemed to be part of the problem, and not a means to problem-solving in a world of change; this established the need for conceptual innovation, and scientific analysis seemed to be an appropriate method. An important task in the development of theory for Burton was to make clear the distinction between analysis and policy, not least because he was clear that these had become conflated in the established discourse, that this was wedded to a statist perspective to such an extent that the terms of that discourse were value-laden rather than scientific or 'objective'. The task, for Burton, then and later, was to develop some kind of free-standing analysis of the international system, firmly rooted in the terms of 'general theory'.

Apart from a consideration of detail, what did *International Relations: A General Theory* in fact represent, as a statement from Burton only relatively recently arrived in International Relations? It was very much of its time, showing the persistence of the old – especially states and power – and inputs of a novel nature. It was a transitional work for Burton, though a transition to what final destination was not yet at all evident, though there were signs of what was to follow. It was also reasonably typical of a general type of literature of the time when power politics and state-centricity were insufficient (though a necessary part of the analysis for many), but where there was a struggle to get to grips with emergent questions of method, ontology and conceptual innovation. It too represented a means of goading International Relations to develop improved techniques and more realistic models. For Burton it was something of a reconstruction of the field, more inclined to questions of ontology (what International Relations was actually 'about') rather than a refinement of state-centric analysis. And it also showed that Burton, feeling viscerally opposed to the conventional orthodoxy (as he had been for a very long time indeed, we should recall), was open to thoughts from beyond the traditional boundaries of the field. At the same time, as compared to *Peace Theory, International Relations: A General Theory* demonstrated a much greater engagement with the discipline of International Relations: not a profound accept-ance of, but an engagement with, it. And out of this seemed to come a greater, and more articulated, statement of the need for innovation in, indeed escape from, the dominant frame of reference. He had restated again the nature of the problem: and he was moving towards a greater articulation of some of the solutions.

Soon, Burton was challenged to come up with some novelties of his own. If, he was challenged, the conventional wisdom was limited, partial or inadequate, what did he propose in its stead? Why not come up with an alternative explanation of conflict? This challenge was to prove remarkably consequential. More significant than the challenge was Burton's responses to it, for in effect they accelerated and made more vocal his criticism of the International Relations discipline, culminating in his passage through it, as it were. A discussion of that exit necessarily follows from a discussion of Burton's immediate reactions and medium-term consequences.

The immediate response to the challenge was not to explain a conflict anew, but rather to explain an unfolding conflict in new terms. We should remind ourselves that he did not start out on this road going into uncharted territory because, as he had himself said,

> Before disputing parties can come together and usefully ask each other what the strife is about and what agreements are to be made, an analysis of conflict has to be made on an academic plane with all the objectivity of science. The initial responsibility devolves upon the scientist in the field of peace theory, and no useful progress on the political level can be expected until theories are formulated, made public and widely accepted. (Burton, 1962, p. 188)

The means or instrument of this in London was the nexus of scholars and colleagues that formed the Centre for the Analysis of Conflict (CAC) at UCL in 1966. If Burton sounded full of conviction in 1962 that this should be done, when it came to practical consideration involving actual participants in conflict, he and his colleagues stepped forward very cautiously indeed. They knew that there was a role for the academic in the analysis of conflict, but precisely what this role was now had to be established.

At the same time as the innovations in the CAC were taking place, 'normal work' had to proceed; which meant that Burton and his colleagues still had to attend to the tasks of teaching, keeping up with the literature in the rapidly changing discipline, and writing by way of response to it. It was not, for Burton at least, a case of 'either/or', since he wrote a great deal at this time, with the effect that his further articulation of the issues already engaged with in his written work and the lessons coming out of the CAC both enlightened and fed upon each other. This process gave rise to two major and related studies: *Systems, States, Diplomacy and Rules* (Burton, 1968) and *Conflict and Communication* (Burton, 1969), and they are best regarded as two sides of the same coin: throughout, they are regarded as companion studies, reflecting the work of the CAC, which was not confined solely to the novelties associated with the new approach to conflict, but where most of the time of the CAC was 'taken up with developments in theory, examining techniques employed in other social sciences, making comparative studies and typologies of conflict and advancing theoretical writings. The conduct of the actual case studies, and the processing of data generated, rest upon this theoretical work' (Burton, 1968, p. xi).

Taken together, they mark a step change in Burton's work, since he was now less concerned with the problems inhering in the conventional approach and rather more concerned with the alternatives to it. He sought a fresh approach from a radically new perspective. Whereas the emphasis at the CAC's level of practice looked at the dynamics of human conflict at the micro-level, *Systems, States, Diplomacy and Rules* was a type of macro-level analysis, with an emergent emphasis on what Burton called 'world society', and wherein he argued, informed by a clear distinction between theory and policy, and mindful of the examples in other areas where impact on policy was a significant question, that

> it is being argued in this study that there is a body of theory concerning world society that could serve as a basis for the scientific practice of diplomacy, and therefore for the formulation of commonly observed rules of international behaviour. Like all scientific theories it needs more development and testing to make it adequate for more purposes; but it is at a stage when it can serve as a valuable guide to practice. As is the case in medicine and economics, it would become increasingly more advanced and useful as a consequence of its application. (Burton, 1968, p. 149)

The very idea of a scientific practice of diplomacy clearly stands at odds with the established – and by no means 'traditional', even now – ideas of diplomacy as the subtlest of arts, but clearly points the way forward, to different foundations of knowledge, method and, not least, practice.

The importation of ideas and techniques is abundantly clear from even a cursory survey of these two works. There is a clear utilisation of the work done in General Systems Theory, which had its origins in the 1920s but came to the attention of a wider audience and began to have an effect on thinking about political systems in the 1950s, with the work of David Easton representing early major breakthroughs (Easton, 1953, 1965). There was some affinity here with the work done in the area of cybernetics, but the aims of the systems thinkers were grander in scale. The goal was to establish no less than a unified theory of social behaviour, with emphases on how systems develop, maintain order, set goals, change and adapt.

This provides the means for a new approach to the understanding of what is thought to be well-known. Thus, for Burton, 'states are better regarded as the resultant of the interacting behaviour of systems' (Burton, 1968, p. 10): in other words, he is suggesting that the nature and forms of the state can be explained in terms of the concentration of interactions of people in a place over a given time span, to such an extent that these interactions take on a permanent form and identity. What is being suggested here is that the state – as one form of human behaviour and interaction – can be explained in terms of the observable behaviour of human beings, what they actually do when they behave socially and politically. This is a radically different approach when set against established approaches explaining the state in terms of it having a monopoly on the legitimate use of violence, its legal status or its unique territorial basis. The state and the behaviour associated with other systems of interaction – within and beyond the state – could now be discussed in terms radically different compared to what was possible before, and in a way that was not tied to the supposed lessons of history, the verdict of the classical literature or the established authority embodied in the texts of power politics and state-centricity. Moreover, there was a clear conception that the state was a dynamic entity, consti- tuted by its people, with values, desires and aspirations, some of which went unheeded or unsatisfied, and with socio-political consequences.

Similarly, Burton borrowed from the relatively new approach to human behaviour that stressed the nature of social exchange in the development of communities and societies. More specifically, he got from Blau (1964) a framework for the explanation of power differentiations in communities, which did not rest on explanations of nature, greed or the lust for power. Blau argued that groups form and cohere around the practice of mutually beneficial exchange, which permits members of the group to get more than they could acting alone or in smaller groups. Over time, reciprocal exchanges become unbalanced, since some people have more of the things that others want. In due course, reciprocation gives way to unequal structures of differentiation and power. There is nothing evil or malicious in this, since it emerges out of the way that people behave in given sets of circumstances. One effect of this, among many, is to allow us to develop alternative explanations of power relationships in societies, quite distinct from those embodied in the traditions of Machiavelli and Morgenthau.

The import of ideas from beyond the boundaries of International Relations is significant in so far as it seeks a positivist-behavioural foundation for the analysis – rooted in what people do and who they are; not what they ought to do by reference to the prescriptive norms of ideology (of practice and scholarship), but the way the world is actually constituted. Here was the search for a more 'realistic' model of the political world. This is why the impact of the behavioural revolution in socio-political analysis was so significant for Burton: it provided him with potentially useful tools with which he could go beyond the limitations of conventional analysis and construct an alternative set of explanations, aimed at developing free-standing theory, different and distinct from the requirements of statist policy-making, or preconceived goals (such as order and stability, which were deemed to be loaded in favour of existing power interests).

The focus on systems is not an end in itself, since 'concepts of systems and states, of their needs and values, of legitimisation and intervention, and an analysis of the processes of decision-making, provide the means of examining the nature of communal and inter-state conflict, the conditions in which it is functional and dysfunctional, and how it escalates and spreads' (Burton, 1968, p. 80). Several points are worthy of further discussions here. Note the emphasis on states and systems: an emphasis on states is necessary but not sufficient to explain conflict. At this stage, Burton still found a role for states in the analysis, perhaps because he still had not found a radical enough way to define them, such that they did not dominate or predetermine the agenda of analysis. Note the recognition of the importance of needs and values, rather than the traditional emphasis on the interests of states. And the clear recognition of the processes of legitimisation, as opposed to sole emphasis on legal status and authority. And note too the emphasis on the dynamics of the conflict process, as well as the recognition that conflict might be functional in certain circumstances rather than destructive by definition. And, finally, note that what is to be explained is not solely inter-state conflict but also communal conflicts.

There is clear evidence here of a shift towards searching for a general set of principles that could explain the processes of conflict in particular, but also more than this. In *Conflict and Communication* Burton is quite explicit about the task, and the passage is especially revealing: 'there is ... a broader academic interest in conflict. There is an interest in the operation of the system concerned, how it works, why it broke down, how it can be altered to improve its efficiency, and how other systems of a similar construction operate. The study of conflict is not merely because it attracts attention. It is largely because by examining it the normal operation of the system can be understood' (Burton, 1969, p. xii). The focus on conflict is thus the focus on a problem, a systemic breakdown if you will, an analysis of which is but a means to the greater end of constructing systems that are legitimate, stable (in a dynamic way), adaptive and successful, reflecting the values of system members and fulfilling perceived needs. This is a rather more sophisticated statement of the issues compared to *Peace Theory*, though this too was informed by the same goal.

As evidence of the method of uniting issues in a general framework, consider the following comment on the nature of diplomacy:

> the student of international politics who holds that a scientific diplomacy may be possible is asking the fundamental question: would perfect knowledge induce peaceful community relationships, or is the character of interactions of states such that there must inevitably be conflicts of interest leading to violence? In short, are the issues of peace and war primarily a function of decision-making or power relations? (Burton, 1968, p. 148)

The focus on systems of interaction, steered by decision-makers, mindful of values and needs, accepting adaptation as a goal of dynamic systems, relating system to environment, the focus on behaviour, and the possibility of generalisable statements about how systems (all systems) work, are all clearly evidence of Burton's constructive shift away not only from the power frame, but also from the idea that International Relations constitutes some uniquely defined realm of politics. The state was to be perceived as a type of system, but not unique, and capable of being compared to others, with the results learned from other system analyses enlightening how states and international systems function. It is especially notable that the book concluded (Burton, 1968, pp. 225–44) with a restatement of a set of propositions – in fact, hypotheses – emanating from the discursive analysis, which suggested that the next stage of theoretical development was empirical testing, where mature theory consisted of a set of logically related and testable hypotheses and where appropriate testing would lead to constructive feedback and refinement of the original model. By way of example, we may cite proposition 3: 'legitimisation of authority rests upon performance in the satisfaction of values, and not upon the political processes of attaining office'; and proposition 9: 'when any administrative system fails to satisfy expectations, there will tend to be conflict between communities within the state'.

Incrementally, Burton was leaving International Relations behind, though not yet able to escape it completely and convincingly, evidently even more convinced that its claims to special status, by way of its unique *problematique*, special actors and a unique kind of governance were specious. The focus on general systems of behaviour was not only a means to greater unity in the social sciences, it also highlighted the claims to status made by disciplines, and helped to expose them. For, as Oran Young argued, the systems thinkers 'protested against the rigid compartmentalisation of disciplines and the consequent reduction of cross-flows between various fields of research leading to duplication of effort' and, moreover, the innovators in the field were concerned 'that the tendency of many disciplines to concern themselves with specific phenomena and detailed studies to the exclusion of abstract and general theoretical considerations was leading to an inability to integrate meaningfully the knowledge acquired in other disciplines' (Young, 1968, p. 14). This was a view entirely consistent with Burton's outlook, as made manifest in *Systems, States, Diplomacy and Rules*, and it was to be echoed by another conspicuous innovator in social theory and peace research, Kenneth Boulding, who argued: 'I became convinced at least twenty-five years ago that all the social sciences were studying the same thing, which is the social system, even though they were studying it from different points of view and with different vocabularies' by way of an introduction to a major work of systems thinking some years later. Just as statements (as recently as 1957) to the effect that political science was the science of the state (see Young, 1968, p. 2 for examples from the literature), seemed very passé, so did the new work put the traditional claims in International Relations into a new – and essentially limited – perspective. (A major section of Mackenzie's (1968) extraordinary survey of political science looks at the nature of politics without the state, a clear measure of the dynamism evident at the time.) We shall return to this conjunction of the established and the (Burtonian) new in the next chapter, but attention must now be devoted to Burton's second piece of work of this period.

Conflict and Communication dwelt less on the nature of states and systems, and rather more on questions of conflict resolution at the level of the individuals involved in it. In this respect it tended to complement the macro-analysis which was the systems work with the micro-level of conflict analysis, and this complementarity is always evident. It also saw Burton set out towards a different destination, and witnessed, in the long term, not only a redefinition of the world of social systems – to which we shall turn in due course – but also the establishment of a framework for the understanding of conflict, analysis allied to skills, which would be important in its own way and not only allow conflict to be understood differently, but also to facilitate its resolution. This too would be a major improvement on the record of arbitration, dispute settlement and diplomatic bargaining. At the risk of repetition or overstatement, it is important to set the developing system of Burton's thought in the context of the problems he then faced, as well as the opposition, allied to the still-incomplete conceptual toolbox he was himself filling. He knew what he wanted to get away from, and at this point had only a limited idea of where he was going.

But there was not always scepticism or uncertainty. Of the benefits of an approach rooted in science he was in no doubt: 'the greater the insights into a problem the easier is understanding, even though the greater is the number of variables and the more elaborate are the techniques. There is thus a simplicity in science, despite its apparent procedural complexities, which is absent in the elusive concepts of metaphysics and unsubstantiated generalisation' (Burton, 1969, p. 229). This is especially revealing and worthy of special comment. We appreciate by now that Burton set great store by the scientific method as it prevailed in social science in the 1960s. But he makes clear his lack of sympathy with metaphysics (for which read 'political philosophy'?), with its endless and relativistic debates about the nature, meaning and significance of concepts such as government, right, justice, war and peace. This, he assumes, is unproductive in terms of history (Have we made any progress in these terms of the discourse? Why are we still struggling with the implications of systems of thought thousands of years old when we have pressing problems in need of solution?) and shows no promise or potential as a way of solving our problems. It is unhelpful, indeed a hindrance to our proper understanding. He is not thinking in the abstract either when he mentions unsubstantiated generalisations, as this was the hallmark of much of the Realist framework that had so dominated the discipline. Here too there were problems, in so far as issues were asserted to be so (rather than demonstrated), such as the nature of human nature, humans' 'lust for power', the view that security is a limited commodity and that states must get as much of it as they can, that more for one means less for another and so on, at length. Indeed, it was article of the Morgenthau faith that 'international politics, like all politics is a struggle for power'. But is it true that all politics is a struggle for power? Is coercion a necessary foundation for social order and stability? Does this not admit of altruism, selflessness and charity – or are these just alternative means of gaining social acclaim and value, and thus more 'power'? And is this view of politics valid across time and cultures? Why not entertain the notion that people are sociable by nature, and that social practices are important elements of the analysis? All these types of assertions and generalisations were taken as givens, and the analysis started from there. Yet clearly the analysis was predicated on very insecure foundations, even though these were deemed to be sound enough by their proponents.

Burton is also very clear as to the nature of innovation. By way of conclusion, he argues 'the bringing of parties to an on-going communal or interstate dispute into a situation of controlled communication is an obvious way of examining their relations, of stimulating theories, of arriving at hypotheses and of testing them. One might wonder why it has not been done before' (Burton, 1969, p. 228). Quite so. The influence of entrenched resistance, habits of thought, assumptions about the impossibility of escaping from dominant structures of belief, about how the world is and how it always will be should not be under-estimated. But it was these very things that the controlled communication method was designed to take on, specifically that there was some kind of endless and unchangeable set of assumptions about which nothing could be done. These were asserted to be part of the 'reality', taking the form of assumptions that 'I do not like them; they are not like us; they are different; they are inferior; they will attack us if we are not vigilant'; and so on. It is worthwhile recognising the extraordinary mental and intellectual acrobatics performed, by individuals and groups, to main-tain some kind of consistency in the face of the evidence (is this one of the functions of nationalism?). How often have we encountered some-one convinced that he/she does not like 'them'? When told that his/her friend is one of 'them', he/she asserts that his/her friend is untypical, he/she likes him but holds to his/her established beliefs?

For Burton, the controlled communication exercise is informed by the notion that

> the conflict behaviour of communities and states comprises alterable components such as perception of external conditions, selection of goals from many possible values, choice of different means of attaining goals and assessment of values and means in relation to assessment of conflict. The method hypothesises that conflicts of interest are subjective, and that experience and know-ledge alter these components, thus producing altered relationships. (Burton, 1969, p. ix)

The original aim of the endeavour was to explain conflict, within and between states. That had been a long-standing aim of Burton, and this was the gauntlet thrown down to him: explain conflict anew. This was the 'limited research purpose' that underpinned the workshops, but it went beyond this, because out of it came a series of observations that could be cast in the form of testable hypotheses and tell us more about generalised processes of conflict:

> the experience suggested that an important technique might have been involved, as it were by accident, for the avoidance of conflict, and for the resolution of conflict even during violence, because the parties themselves seemed to gain from the exercise in some ways not possible from more traditional procedures of conciliation, arbitration and negotiation. Thus, the method came to have a second objective – the resolution of conflict. (Burton, 1969, p. xi)

Conflict resolution is

> a process that comes from the decision-making of the parties. It involves a reappraisal of values and alternatives and costs, and the appropriate international institution is one that facilitates this process. It is also critical of traditional diplomatic practices … the practice of diplomacy has been little influenced by research. (Burton, 1969, p. xv)

The importance of this discovery needs to be acknowledged. From our perspective it is clear that it marked a clear shift in Burton's frame of reference and his consequent agenda. Yet he was still aware of the need to address not only the nature of science and the search for good theory, but also to address and solve the problems associated with war and conflict. The goal was still the problem of peace, and how to attain it: 'The purpose of controlled communication is to provide a clinical framework and a means by which an applied science of International Relations can develop' (Burton, 1969, p. xiii). Theory and improvements in knowledge were the means of improving the performance of the system, to allow it to solve problems rather than merely to struggle through as best we can, given the nature of the insurmountable problems we face. The technical innovations were clearly aimed at examining the idea that the problems were not insurmountable: the problem was that we assumed that they *were*.

Perception was clearly a major element of the analytical framework, but there was also an emphasis on the nature of the parties to a conflict, the processes of representation of these parties, and the construction of the workshop environment prior to the establishment of effective communication between the parties. On the basis of the evidence, 'parties are helped not by the third party as such but by the ordinary academic tools of analysis, to stand back from the conflict, and to understand its origins and manifestations. Once each party is in a position to perceive the problem from the behavioural point of view of the other, communication is effectively controlled, and tends to become constructive' (Burton, 1969, p. 72). The underlying assumption is that 'analysis will reveal, after perceptions are corrected, that neither side may be required to compromise, and that solutions will be found by which all gain' (Burton, 1969, p. 70), which represents nothing less than a clear assault on the very central notion established in International Relations certainly – and most probably in other frames of reference that approach conflict in society – that conflict is about the struggle for 'resources' (tangible or otherwise) which are by definition (unsubstantiated assertion) in scarce supply, and where a gain for one is a loss for another.

But what of the old chestnut, the 'absence of political will'? 'It is no defence of the traditional method or of failure of mediation, merely to argue that there was an absence of political willingness on the part of governments to employ these methods. This project has suggested the hypothesis that willingness and method are related' (Burton, 1969, p. 118). This is an example of the style of the whole. It is not definitive, nor yet is it an enterprise lacking in confidence. It is clearly a pioneering effort and out of it comes not new articles of faith, but sensible hypotheses – from a limited number of cases – that could be tested in order to establish their validity and the extent to which they could become useful propositions, worthy of transfer to other conflicts and capable of resolving them.

Taken together, therefore, what is it that *Systems, States, Diplomacy and Rules* and *Conflict and Communication* represent? The first is a further articulation of what is wrong with conventional assumptions about International Relations in general, and the problem of conflict in particular. The second is an unintended – perhaps even an accidental – consequence of a response to an academic challenge. From here on, there was to be a dualist element in Burton's thought. On the one hand, he was desperate to escape the limitations that inhere in a focus on states (and traditional aspects of interest, diplomacy, war and violence) and was edging away from established ideas, without (yet) any clear set of what the final framework he sought would look like. Systems was a key idea that he picked up, and apart from the focus on systems *per se*, the focus on systems allied to behaviour was shifting him towards something more general, more generalisable, less cogniscent of discipline boundaries and concerns, stressing what it is that individuals do – but not only as individuals. Burton sought to explain behaviour beyond states, as well as of and within them. He had not, yet, found a clear means of escape from these limitations. Conflict resolution saw a focus on behavioural processes at a rather more specific level, where the limitation of established procedures were revealed again. What united these two strands was a need to focus on what it was that people as human beings needed and wanted in the micro and the macro settings that constituted their relevant behavioural worlds, in the local and the wider worlds. This last was to be Burton's next focus of attention.

4
Leaving International Relations for…?

Burton's next book was *World Society* (Burton, 1972). It was written as an introductory text, drawing together much of his preceding work. It is the book most usually cited by contemporary scholars in International Relations, illustrating a developing concern for the explanation of a world constituted by actors other than states, where states have a role to play, but where there are a wealth of other transactions and relationships to be engaged with, and where these are not merely setting the context within which states interact: they represent something substantive in their own right and are a challenge to established assumptions about state-centricity. What is even more remarkable is that Burton wrote the book as one appropriate for younger readers, not least because he argued that school-leavers were increasingly interested in the dynamics of world society and were likely to be less resistant to new approaches to interpreting the world.

In point of fact, the book is ambitious while at the same time also rather difficult and demanding, not because it is written in a difficult style (which it sometimes is) but because it represents a further example of Burton's grasping and groping to 'get beyond', as it were, the limits of the conventional, and it is this difficult phase which merits attention here. In this chapter, three works are surveyed, with a view to assessing this difficult and transitionary phase of Burton's thought. Not least of our concerns is to illuminate Burton's struggle to get to grips with a methodological holism, which was hinted at in the previous chapter, and which received further attention, not only in *World Society* but also in a particularly illuminating debate with Fred Northedge (dating from 1974) and a similarly illuminating discussion involving Burton and several of his colleagues in London.

The book contains discussions of ideas and themes now clear in the development of Burton's work: the limitations of conventional approaches, the nature of self-defeating strategies, and the key role played by perception and decision-making. More instructive are the emergent novelties. International Relations is now conceived of as the study of world society (Burton, 1972, p. ix), but it is conceived of in a manner that is recognisably more difficult than previously, and dramatically different in terms of method as compared to preceding approaches: 'the studies of man, that is the social and political sciences, are becoming as difficult to understand as have been the natural sciences... because scientific studies move from observation and description to analysis and theories. In behavioural studies, as in physics, there is first observation and then theories about the behaviour of the systems being observed...which the social and political sciences have now reached [and where] scientists concerned use a language that is unfamiliar to others' (Burton, 1972, p. ix). Burton argues that, a decade earlier, International Relations was essentially descriptive diplomatic history, concerned with governments, diplomats and statesmen. In the intervening decade it had been transformed, infused with the elements of scientific thinking, and consequently become esoteric to some degree. Burton argues that there is a need to relate changes in world society, and that the essentials of the new world society can now be explained. Hence the synoptic work that is *World Society*, designed not simply for a specialist audience, but for one seeking to engage with this new and changing world of science and technology that is, by definition, more complex. This is the key issue to be addressed: 'It seems to be a mistake to use inadequate and unrealistic approaches to a subject just to make it more simple. Young people want reality and relevance... [and] they are not content to learn just what was taught to a generation that appears to have had no effective answers to the serious world problems of underprivilege, under-development, revolt, communal conflict and war' (Burton, 1972, p. x).

The charge here is fairly clear: the established frames of reference are partial, descriptive, anachronistic and irrelevant – and incapable of solving the problems on the agenda of modern world society. As part of the process of re-invigoration, reconstruction and a search for relevance, Burton highlights new conceptual tools: principally, a focus on transactions (what he calls the cobweb model), values and the resolution of conflict.

The focus on the cobweb model essentially calls for a reconstruction of our world view, with the space we inhabit redefined, less in terms of its spatial and geo-political dimensions and with more reference to the relationships and transactions that constitute the globe as a set of relevant and meaningful behavioural relationships. In other words, the world is how we engage with it, not how it looks as a spatial depiction:

> Which is the more representative view of the world – the world of continents, islands and states or the world of transactions? This is not a superficial question. If we adopt the nation state [model] we will use the language of relations between states and their relevant power and have one set of solutions to world problems. If we adopt the transactions [model] we will use a different language and a consequently different set of solutions. (Burton, 1972, p. 43)

He continues, 'the source of conflict between states is in internal politics, in failures by states to adjust to altering conditions, in the struggle of states to preserve their institutions and in the conflicts between states and systems that cut across state boundaries. Conflict cannot be prevented by external coercion or by great power threats' (Burton, 1972, pp. 44–5). So much is, perhaps, predictable, in the light of what we know of Burton's work to this point, but he goes further here:

> Development and stability must rest on internal conditions or political organisation, that is, a high degree of participation so that authorities are strongly legitimised... a form of world government cannot rest on collective security and must be based on the transactions inherent in functional organisations... Viable political units can be very small provided there is a high level of transactions with the wider environment. Communications and not power are the main organising influence in world society. (Burton, 1972, p. 45)

This is radical indeed. The new elements of the analysis are communication, participation, legitimised authority, human beings co-operating to address and achieve co-operation in defined (functional) areas, and 'viable political units'. This does not resemble state-centricity as constituted in the usual analyses of world politics. Burton takes this a step further, when recognising the relationships that exist between the parts and the whole: 'the systems approach, which the cobweb model depicts, has some methodological advantages... It is a means of seeing wholes... It is a means of detailed analysis without losing sight of total interactions' (Burton, 1972, p. 45). This focus on the whole, constituted in what people do when they interact with each other, allows innovations that are not possible within the essentialist approach which is state-centricity. It does not assert that states are the most important focus. Nor does it omit the behaviour of ordinary individuals as they interact (increasingly) globally. And methodologically it inclines to the positivist, rather than the normative/prescriptive: the focus is on what people do – and sometimes they challenge the authorities that exist in states because these authorities are deemed to be irrelevant, poorly-performing, lacking in legitimacy, presiding over poverty rather than progress, and partial rather than representative. This goes beyond the inter-state *problematique* for one very simple reason: it addresses the problems as they exist and manifest themselves, rendering traditional approaches redundant.

Burton never loses sight here of the idea of models and new conceptual problems being relevant, capturing the reality of world society, as it is behaviourally constituted. Apart from communications, he recognises the important role of values:

> it could be that people of all races and creeds have some common values and similar objectives, and furthermore, it could be that these could be achieved by cooperation. It could be that these common values are hidden from view and that people cannot cooperate in attaining them because they are overwhelmed by the values and objectives of institutions, including states...We need to remind ourselves from time to time that our study is the study of man. (Burton, 1972, p. 124)

In this respect, Burton gets to the heart of the matter, redefining the vexed question as to the appropriate levels of analysis – the key is human beings in a world society, constituted by transactions and communications. While he recognises that the question of values has received considerable attention from political philosophers over the centuries, he suggests that this has been focused rather more on institutional values (the requirements of good government, stability and the like) rather than on social-psychological values, pertaining to the status of being human. But he goes beyond even this conventional view, suggesting that 'Our interest is in those [values] that are fundamental in human behaviour and for this reason presumably universal.' These he calls 'social-biological, because they are closely related to, if not direct expressions of, biological drives and motivations. They must form part of an analysis of any aspect of world society' (Burton, 1972, p. 128). We shall have occasion to return to Burton's engagement with the idea of socio-biological values in due course, but at this stage it is significant to point out why it was that Burton focused on the idea of such values. In seeking a total explanation of world society, he sought a positivist analysis of actually existing conditions and processes. Similarly, in focusing on the human constituents of world society, he was seeking a means of explaining why and how it is that they act as they do, or would prefer to do. In this respect he wanted to get beyond the issues of values associated with states and other institutions, not least because they could be thought of as creators of values (associated with institutions rather than human preferences), indeed themselves constituting limits on the expression of values. The focus on the idea of a biological component in all of this is of most significance, and for this reason: he sought a means of explanation that was devoid of any kind of ideological/institutional cause or component. This was the problem with so many of the established analyses; they were, in some sense, loaded and influenced by preferred values rather than the values associated with being human, as it were. He wanted a frame of reference that could be located in the real, the problems and the appropriate explanation of them. Just as Blau had enabled him to explain power relations in terms of exchange, and Deutsch had provided the means to employ cybernetic images of decision-making, so the focus on these particular needs, he assumed, could allow him to get further along to his preferred mode of explanation. What we can say, with some certainty, is that Burton was making a transit out of the academic discipline he had entered not long before. Where he was bound for was uncertain; he engaged potentially useful concepts and ideas as and when need or opportunity allowed, but he was well short of a coherent and articulated framework. At this stage it seemed that there were still unresolved problems.

The extent of the differences, both substantive and methodological, between Burton and International Relations are nowhere more clearly expressed than in the confrontation constructed for the purposes of debate between Burton and Frederick Northedge in 1974. It is of passing interest by way of an indication of the nature of the variety of literature involved in the study of International Relations more than twenty-five years ago. But, for our purposes here, it shows a clear gap between what we might call the conventional approach (embodied in a commitment to an analysis suggesting the clear, indeed self-evident, engagement with inter-state behaviour) and Burton's then-current framework of analysis which, whatever else it was, was radical for its time and, for our purposes here, evident of a period of transition, in terms of both substance and epistemology.

The two were brought together as authors of two set texts for the Open University course 'Interstate or World Society'. Each had written a book that had become a set text for the course. For Northedge, it was *The International Political System* and for Burton, *World Society*.

What is especially notable is that Burton and Northedge were opposed in matters of both substance and methodology. Northedge was four-square in the statist, international politics camp. For him, the key questions confronting scholars of international relations related to the activities of states. Quite explicitly, he was clear that he was not interested in the activities of men and women as individuals, but only in so far as they were leaders of states. When leaders act as leaders, they are subject to the kinds of pressures that are incapable of being experienced by others: there was something of a question of 'degree' here. Similarly, the activities of those outside the formal mechanism of decision-making were to be regarded as essentially peripheral: they might have something to do with policy-making, but their role was not significant. For Northedge, the 'big things' that occur in the world happen because states make them happen. This was a key assertion, defining the significance and focus of attention. International Politics was therefore a focus on the particular and special kind of politics that related to states, while International Relations was thought to be something rather wider, involving other types of relations.

Burton took an entirely different position. International politics, he suggested, has nothing to do with the real world: it is a game. To that extent, a focus on states was at best only partial, and was in fact misleading. Moreover, consistent with a focus on systems of behaviour, he argued that the inter-state system was one of many relationships that characterise world society, and that it might not be the most important one in terms of how world society in fact operated. Burton focused on the explanation of relationships in general. He was concerned with the behaviour of men and women, in terms both general and specific, and argued that findings learned in one realm of behaviour could be especially useful in understanding other realms. So much was consistent with a further engagement with a general systems approach, where similar patterns could be identified and explained in terms of homologies and system dynamics.

Rather than assert that the big things happen because of what states do, Burton argued that we needed to be more philosophical and see the issues from a holistic perspective, however difficult and challenging that might be. Northedge opted for what he called a 'focus of interest' which would make the study of international politics both interesting and intellectually satisfying. Burton shunned Northedge's idea of a focus of interest in favour of a position that looked at the nature of the whole, however difficult this might be. Burton still had no solution to the difficulties of looking at the whole, but he was aware that there was a fundamental task of epistemology here: Northedge was assertive in making the essentialist case, and Burton was predictably sceptical. Northedge, he suggested, was being descriptive rather than providing explanations.

Burton argued the contrary case in terms such as to make a significant debate with Northedge quite impossible. Whereas Northedge described a world of states, national interests and important decisions that came out of the machinery of government, Burton was preoccupied with a quite different set of concerns. Indeed, Burton was arguing the case on the basis of an emergent – and radically different – ontology allied to a sympathetic approach to questions of epistemology, each of which needed to be made explicit rather than left implicit or unaddressed. He was not, yet, where he wanted, and needed, to be with respect to these concerns, but he was well aware of the requirements that underpinned the foundations of any new set of explanations. He had some of the components: the issues were about participation, legitimacy, transactions, communications, adjustment to change, values and so on. There was virtually no reference at all to any notion of an engagement with an inter-state system, and one, above all else, that had a unique – and uniquely difficult – *problematique*.

Apart from any intrinsic interest or merits in the confrontation with Northedge, it was indicative of two things: the clear distance between Burton and the mainstream of International Relations – we could guess as much at this stage in any case. But there was still this difficult phase for Burton, a phase which received a better articulation when he engaged in discussions with some of his more sympathetic London colleagues – John Groom, Chris Mitchell and Tony de Reuck. What characterised them, said Burton, was two things: first, their focus on world society rather than international relations, and, second, their focus on the relatively unconventional,

> in a wide literature and an extensive field of behaviour, including the nature of authority, especially the spillover of domestic politics into the wider environment, in peaceful change, in mechanisms that insure that change serves a felt need and is not just for its own sake, in deviance at all levels and many other related behavioral matters that mostly do not receive specific treatment in international relations

texts ... I suppose that what we tend not to discuss also identifies us: we do not spend much time discussing public administration, history or law. (Burton *et al.*, 1974, p. 1)

In so far as they had made any intellectual progress, it was thought to be incremental, as a result of their empirical work and 'our deductive thinking' (Burton *et al.*, 1974, p. 1). The major question before them was simply stated but enormous in its implication – and particularly the cumulative effects of a radical new theoretical breakthrough: 'what is the reality we try to describe and understand ... the system of states or is it the wider world society?' (Burton *et al.*, 1974, p. 3).

In developing the discussion, Burton employs the metaphor of a floor arrangement, where the study of the ground floor is concerned with inter-state relations, and the 'basement level is concerned with world society as a whole, making no arbitrary boundaries between that which is national and that which is international and consequently no arbitrary boundaries among the general body of knowledge about man and his environment – psychological, sociological, economic or political' (Burton *et al.*, 1974, p. 5). There are also important questions of methodology since – following on from the theme addressed in the discussions with Northedge – at the ground level the method is descriptive, inductive and rests heavily on personal hypotheses, and where scholarship in this area might be thought by some to belong in the Arts. By contrast, at the basement level the emphasis is on deductive reasoning and systems analysis, which 'are the means by which a boundless field of interest can be examined' and where deductive reasoning 'rests on generalisations based on observable behaviour and empirical evidence at different levels of interaction and systems analysis is the means by which propositions regarding behavior at one level can be applied to behavior at others' (Burton *et al.*, 1974, p. 5).

There is, with the analysis now more advanced, a clear recognition of the magnitude of the problems being tackled, intellectually and politically/emotionally, since 'we have only recently – after two thousand years or more of experience and thought – come to appreciate that the goal of society is not to maintain itself and its institutional forms but to develop its members' (Burton *et al.*, 1974, p. 21). What follows from this is in fact rather significant: it throws into sharp relief the value placed upon the 'classical literature' or the canonical texts that underpin socio-political discourse. In other words, their value and utility might be severely circumscribed as we shift to new circumstances and social arrangements. Age here would not necessarily be a virtue, nor would novelty be a hindrance. A healthy stance might be to assume that much of the classical literature – from the Greeks onwards – might be misleading, appropriate to their times but not to ours. (What might be more appropriate are the innovations in socio-political thought as exemplified in, say, Burton, Johan Galtung and Kenneth Boulding, to name just three pioneers of Peace Research... but this is to get ahead of ourselves.)

There is also a recognition of the need to engage with the perceptions and perspectives of others, usually defined in conventional terms of right and wrong, but where now 'we may deplore the violence of the IRA or of the Japanese in the last war: but both... were the victims of a violence imposed on them by the structures in which and to which they had to respond' (Burton *et al.*, 1974, p. 21). The significance of these perceptual shifts should not be underestimated and it is worthwhile reiterating the point that the perspective being employed here is less judgemental and more one of comprehending the values, stance and perspectives of those usually described as the causes of problems, the instigators of violence, and those 'in the wrong'. In this same vein, society is not an end in itself, but rather a means to the social improvement and human betterment of those who constitute it. What follows from this is that there is a shift in directionality, authority and purpose: society and associated institutions are to be organised to change as the demands, needs and values of persons change, compared to the more usual pattern, where individuals are made to conform, as a matter of course conforming to 'the norm' – and where those who do not are marginalised, incarcerated or labelled as deviant. There is a radical shift in priorities here and a radical re-engagement with what the 'real problems' are assumed to be. It is to the further engagement with – and articulation of – that radical shift that we now turn.

5
The Ontological Break

We now engage with a period of thought which demands particular explanation. For a prolific author such as Burton, the fact that he published no significant major work between 1972 and 1979 (when *Deviance,Terrorism and War* appeared), is notable and needs some attention. This is not a trivial point. It has been a constant theme of much of the preceding account that Burton had shown great antipathy – both personal and professional (and as both diplomat and scholar) – to the established explanations of international relationships, and more particularly the approach concerned with the dynamics of power relationships. What he found extremely difficult to do was to acquire the means to replace the power frame of reference with an alternative. As he became more skilful as an academic, his frame of reference became more sophisticated, but it was still partial and incomplete. It is not unkind to say that he was groping, if not entirely in the dark, then in a half-light: some things were illuminated, clearly important and relevant but others needed discovery and incorporation. In the same vein, *World Society* (1972) is symptomatic of that process. It was not an end in itself, but rather a means of redefining the problem, beyond the system of states, but at a basement level, involving an all-embracing focus on human behaviour and a necessarily holistic perspective. This was fraught with difficulty and confusion, some of which we have encountered earlier in this account.

What he sought desperately was a new framework. Others had helped him along the way. What now happened was hugely significant, and it is referred to here as Burton's 'ontological break': over the course of several years he again borrowed ideas and concepts, melded them together and was, at the end of the process, capable of imposing some coherence on the matters at issue and how to approach them. He also gained experience outside communal or inter-ethnic confrontations that was the stuff of the CAC approach, and put that experience into a wider perspective. In short, he redefined the reality, he engaged a radical new ontology. But what happened next was far removed from international relations and from world society. What he had at the end of this process was a novel view as to what all of this human interaction – especially conflict and socio-political dynamics – was all 'about'. It was a radical reconstruction that resulted in a new system of ideas, ultimately an engagement with a different conception of 'science' and a radically new central organising concept, and an approach not confined to any conventional academic discipline.

As well as moving onwards intellectually, Burton was also on the move physically in that he left University College in London and went to the University of Kent at Canterbury. It was there that he encountered the sociologist, Steven Box, and it was Box who was to give Burton a new perspective on deviance. But before we turn to that element of the discussion we need to say something more about Burton's encounter with sociobiology.

Sociobiology was especially fashionable in academic circles in the 1970s. A key figure in all this was E. O. Wilson, whose *Sociobiology: The New Synthesis* (Wilson, 1973) set the mood. It was clearly a new input into the then-contemporary debate, but it was of a type similar to General Systems Theory (GST) in the 1950s and 1960s: for many, as GST had done before, it represented a means of imposing coherence on potentially disparate approaches to social knowing. It had its own precursors in the decade of the 1960s, when the roots of aggression in humans were explained in terms of the similarities between human beings and the higher apes. The most visible literature of the period was represented by Konrad Lorenz's *On Aggression* (1966). Wilson carried on in this vein, stressing the biological bases of behaviour in rather more general terms than a limited focus on aggression.

For a time, Burton found this topic rather attractive, and a chapter he wrote in a relatively little-known book is particularly instructive (Burton, 1975). In a treatment of 'Universal Values', Burton had this to say about the influence of biology:

> what precisely are the socio-biological values postulated is an empirical question...elements are discovered after they are hypothesised... Whatever they are, they must form part of an analysis of any aspect of world society. They are fundamental particles of human behaviour [and] are connected with survival, personality development, and

self-maintenance within any social environment. They are not unique to men [and] are like more basic reflex behaviour. (Burton, 1975, p. 73)

Thus they are less likely to be influenced by social forces such as ideology and culture. This is the thing that attracted Burton, for he was keen, above all, to develop concepts free of an ideological taint. The relationship between sociobiological values and conflict is made clear and shows a sense of limited advance, beyond an emphasis on perception problems, since they 'are universal and provide a basis on which parties in conflict can identify with each other and begin to understand the nature of mirror-images. Parties in a conflict struggle to attain the same values – security and certainty. But these are not scarce products. Their availability is increased by fundamental cooperation in securing them' (Burton, 1975, p. 81).

For someone so keenly aware of the importance of methodological questions, Burton is also remarkably frank about the difficulties encountered by academics in pursuit of methodological sophistication. We indulge in issues of methodology, necessarily, but 'it is only by working on the subject matter that the methodological problems will be resolved... Getting on with the job is more important' (Burton, 1975, p. 81). This was to be a lasting influence in Burton's work and would find greater articulation once he had encountered the American philosopher, Charles Sanders Peirce. Sociobiology was not a lasting influence but rather an area that Burton encountered and then left for something more fruitful. By the late 1970s sociobiology had become controversial, perhaps too simplistic, too reductionist and overly deterministic, and it largely passed from the scene in terms of being a major influencing factor.

Soon Burton was to find something better, with more lasting effects. Box (1971) focused on deviance, and Paul Sites (1974) led Burton to stress needs. Deviance is a well-established notion in the analysis of both social systems and human behaviour: it suggests behaviour beyond acceptable norms, but also suggests the breaking of established rules. In common parlance, it is a term often used to classify certain sorts of behaviour that are thought to be freakish, abnormal, outlandish, 'wild' or perverse. Burton melded together aspects of deviance, norms, authority and system change to emphasise the dynamics of societies and structures. More pertinently, he seemed to shift the directionality of the argument, to stress rather less those being classified as 'deviant' and rather more to illuminate the nature of the system or society that was classifying behaviour as 'deviant' – deviant in relation to what exactly? This was a major shift away from the equilibrium postulated in classical Parsonian-type functional sociology.

The influence of *Control: The Bases of Social Order* (Sites, 1974) cannot be underestimated, since it provided Burton with the key conceptual leap. From this point onwards, more could be said, and earlier attempts to encompass 'the problem' could mostly, if not entirely, be left behind. Once the key concept of need was at the centre of the conceptual map, other things were also made possible. Most important, more could be said about how to proceed to solve the conceptual problem, rather than repeat again that a conceptual problem existed. This Burton had long known. Now he had got a key idea of how to make significant progress.

The point of departure in Sites is the conception of society embedded in classical functionalist sociology (and, more specifically, adaptation in the face of needs). Here, the emphasis is on the development of an essentially stable, coherent society. Parsonian 'functionalism does presume that societies are self-equilibrating systems ... Societies by definition will tend to a condition of stability. Deviance therefore evokes mechanisms of social control whose effect is to counter and contain it' (Callinicos, 1999, p. 241). For Sites, 'even though Darwinist thought contained both adaptive and conflict orientations, the functionalist has tended to emphasise the adaptive element and to ignore the conflict. Thus, adaptation to the system is emphasised at the expense of conflict within it' (Sites, 1974, p. 2). Furthermore,

> recent evidence shows that the relationship of the higher animal to its environment is not a one-way process. That is, the animal goes beyond an instinctually forced adaptation to the environment and attempts in some way to control it ... The functionalist ignores this control potential in man ... [and] sees the individual as internalising that which he must internalise in order to adapt to his physical and social environment as it is given to him. He is given little or no autonomy. (Sites, 1974, pp. 2–3)

Sites attempts 'to show that the individual seeks to control the environment (physical and social) in order to obtain gratification of needs and to maintain himself' (Sites, 1974, p. 3).

There is thus a shift required to emphasise not only conflict but also system dynamics. But there is also an element in Sites which is demonstrably an improvement of the Darwinist-sociobiological focus:

There is of course a potential problem involved in talking about needs, for there is always the danger of falling back into the mistake made by earlier instinct theorists, who attempted to account for every specific human activity by positing the existence of a corresponding specific instinct. The functionalist makes the same mistake when he insists that a specific human activity occurs because of a specific kind of socialisation, without recognising the importance of the individual as an intervening variable except as a perfectly socialised carrier of culture. Both instinctual and specific socialisation approaches are unacceptable because they ignore certain dynamics of the socialisation process and the individual's capacity for and use of control. (Sites, 1974, p. 7)

In other words, he looks not at the biological or the cultural determinants of behaviour but at their interaction. In stressing the importance of needs in the analysis, Sites is not a prisoner of the need for methodological precision: rather, he is utilitarian, suggesting a likely fruitful method of analysis, while also accepting that we can back-track if necessary:

In using the need concept we must ever be conscious that we are operating at an abstract conceptual level and that in the last analysis the actual basis of the need is tied up with certain psycho-physiological processes which are in interaction with the environment and which are not at this point in our scientific development directly observable. The fact that these processes are not directly observable, however, should not prevent us from working with the need concept if it allows us better to understand and to explain human activity. (The atom was conceptualised long before it was 'observed'.) That is, if we observe certain kinds of activity (or lack of activity) in human behaviour which we need to account for, and can do so with the use of certain concepts which do not do violence to other things we know and which are consistent with other data which cause us to think in the same direction, there is no reason why we should not do so. We can always admit we are wrong. To be more specific, if we find that men have certain anxieties and perhaps engage in bizarre activity under conditions of insecurity, we might fruitfully posit the need for security and see where it leads us. (Sites, 1974, pp. 7–8)

If this utilitarian approach to the development of social theory was enlightening, then so was the relationship between needs, society and the human being, as Sites argued:

It is the very existence of needs in man that makes society possible. That is, if the individual did not have needs, others would have little possibility of controlling his behaviour. It is the individual's needs, then, which make it necessary for him to attempt control of his environment and at the same time permit the possibility of his being controlled by others, thereby making society possible. We insist then that the individual is not a piece of inert protoplasm which is infinitely adaptable to the social environment; instead he becomes self-consciously alive with certain needs which cry out for gratification. Since the latter, and not the former, is the case, we hold that the individual's relationship to the interaction process is first and fundamentally one of using it. The individual uses culture and the interaction process in any way possible, within feasible limits, to gratify his basic needs. (Sites, 1974, pp. 10–11)

We have quoted Sites at length here since he was such an important influence on Burton's scheme of thought, and the line of reasoning employed by Sites (as indicated in the preceding passages) as to how to advance the analysis was especially important. It was this line of reasoning that led Burton, in due course, to engage with the work of Charles Sanders Peirce. Yet it was the emphasis on needs that was the key: this was to be Burton's conceptual breakthrough. On the basis of needs he could develop a coherent frame of reference that took him to his preferred destination. The concept of human needs provided the coherence that systems, perception and sociobiology had promised, but which proved to be insufficient.

And what were these needs? They could not, with Sites, be precisely observed, but their existence could be hypothesised:

we have demonstrated the emergence of eight needs in the individual: a need for response, a need for security, a need for recognition, a need for stimulation, a need for distributive justice, a need for meaning, a need to be seen as rational (and for rationality itself), and a need to control. The relationship among these various needs is extremely complex. The last four needs emerge because the first four, which emerge out of the necessary dynamics of the socialisation process, are not and cannot be immediately and consistently satisfied. (Sites, 1974, p. 43)

We shall soon encounter Burton's frame of reference utilising Sites, but in acknowledging the significance of Sites, it is necessary to acknowledge that his was not the only influence on Burton. At this time, Burton's wife, Leone (herself an educationist), was much concerned with the nature of problem-solving. Burton had clearly recognised the need to solve (rather than to manage) problems much earlier, but he seems at this juncture to have found an approach to problem-solving especially important, which he duly acknowledged. He went beyond the academic environment too. He was influenced by events in schools, social work, the world of industrial consultancy – and even got involved in the conflict in Northern Ireland, which was not without consequences.

All this came together in *Deviance, Terrorism and War* (1979). This was not Burton's title: he had chosen the book's subtitle 'the process of solving unsolved social and political problems' as a précis of the content. Note: not insoluble, but unsolved. Note also the emphasis on the social as well as the political. Arguably, with due respect to what was to follow, this was Burton's key work, because it was a redefinition. What follows *Deviance, Terrorism and War* is actually a further articulation of it with some refinements and articulation of the core concepts. In terms of content it is light years away from *World Society* (1972). Of course, there were clear strands of continuity, but the conception of the problems at issue was re-thought, and the programmatic development of the process of addressing these problems radically rewritten.

Four main issues form the central agenda of *Deviance, Terrorism and War*: the core concept was needs; the core problem, conflict; the core process, problem-solving; and the core idea was the issue of paradigm shift. It is to these – and the consequences following from their centrality – that we now turn.

First, needs are central to the new frame of reference, but the biological basis of needs is replaced. They are now referred to as universal needs and have an ontological status. They exist in human beings by virtue of the existence of individual beings. To be is to express needs. A key distinction is made between needs and values, a concept that had played a major role in Burton's earlier work. The difference is also about levels of analysis: needs suggest a focus on individuals, whereas values relate to the socio-cultural level of analysis:

> At the heart of the problem of social and individual values is the notion of values itself. If by values is meant only those superficial attitudes and behavioural patterns that are acquired because they are found to be useful in living within a particular society or civilisation, i.e. cultural values, then it is axiomatic that respect for institutions and the norms of society will take precedence over any merely

idiosyncratic individual values. However, individual values may not be limited to those that are successfully internalised through the socialisation process. There may be values which are held by individuals as individuals – human values. (Burton, 1979, pp. 57–8)

Certain implications associated with conformity, authority, socialisation, power and resistance, and attitudes to deviance, follow from this. Individuals are socialised into conventions that are held to be the norms of the group or society, which may amount to vaguely expressed ideas such as 'respectability' (not so long ago a very powerful norm in society), as well as to more tightly enforced compliance with group values such as identity, conformity and so on. To the extent that these norms create ideas about conformity, there then follows an agenda associated with the construction of compliant identities (be these with regard to fashion, self-expression and the like) or more overtly political considerations. Those who do not comply are defined as being deviant, are perhaps marginalised, sometimes incarcerated, with their activities perhaps being defined as illegal (as homosexual activity between consenting adults was in Britain until relatively recently). Respect for 'authority' and 'those in power' are frequently components of the process of socialisation, as expressed, for example, in terms of cultural festivals, holidays to mark the birth of 'national heroes', or high office holders. In Britain, respect for, and deference to, the monarchy has been a component of the national culture for centuries, a process conspicuous in (though not confined to) Britain even at the time of writing. This allows patterns of power to exist, to be reproduced and to become regarded as the 'natural order of things' so that compliance becomes the central element of socialisation. But this is at the expense of the satisfaction of human needs, because 'classical and conventional thinking does not draw a distinction between (cultural) values and (universal) needs' (Burton, 1979, p. 58).

Needs are more fundamental than wants or values, where the term is used 'in quite a different sense to describe those conditions or opportunities that are essential to the individual if he is to be a functioning and cooperative member of society, conditions that are essential to his development and which, through him, are essential to the organisation and survival of society' (Burton, 1979, p. 59). Note especially the cumulative and diagnostic elements of the analysis suggested here. The primary level of analysis is the individual, not the society or state. Following from this, need fulfilment is essential to the proper functioning of the human individual: human beings exist to function positively, not merely *to be* – subservient, compliant or otherwise. Being is also linked to co-operative development with other individuals and groups. Indeed, throughout Burton's works he assumes that individuals are inclined to association rather than competition. He does not take a view of 'human nature' that suggests it is either malign or intrinsically good. Rather, he suggests that people as they exist are associative, interactive, trusting and co-operative. Most of the time, most of the people in most social circumstances behave in a way that is profoundly social. Yet authorities respond to the problems in society by making wrong assumptions and often making a bad situation worse. The Thatcher Government in Britain, to take just one recent example, took the view that 'ill-behaved' and 'anti-social' young people should be exposed to 'discipline' and 'short, sharp shocks', through exposure to which they would learn the error of their ways and behave 'properly'. At about the same time, the contemporary agenda of British politics was to be informed by the replacement of modern liberal values, associated with the excesses of the permissive 1960s, with values variously described as 'traditional', 'family' or 'Victorian'.

Note, too, Burton's emphasis on the idea of organisation and survival of society. The organisation of society, he is saying, is a means to an end, and not the end in itself. Societies (for which read groups, communities, states, organisation at any level) should serve the needs of the constituent members. To do so there is a requirement that the system be dynamic, aware of the requirements of change, and with the means to implement it as and when necessary. So often organisations do not do this – because they cannot. Yet if they cannot and they do not, then the very survival of the system itself is at risk, since it will be subject to critique, attack and, perhaps, even violence.

Second, therefore, conflict is central to the analysis as a core problem. The existence of conflict is testimony to the fact that needs are going unfulfilled. Here is a direct and observable link. It does not demand the precise specification of what need is, or needs are, prior to any analysis commencing. It is enough to say that human beings will feel needs; that these inhere in the condition of 'being human' and that whereas fulfilment of need will be consequential in one direction – system maintenance, legitimacy and dynamic stability, the lack of need satisfaction will be directly consequential in another and quite different direction – systemic coercion by leaders against led, repressive measures, control mechanisms, violence and costly systemic decay or costly systemic order and rigidity. Legitimacy, change and adaptation are thus part of the dynamic of conflict, the significance of which can be judged by reference to system performance where these key elements are absent.

By the same token, therefore, though there is a recognition of the importance of conflict in human societies – and the need to resolve it – this is
not seen as an end in itself, since the existence of conflict is a sure sign
of the inherently dysfunctional nature of certain social systems. The
problem is compounded when authorities, perhaps in defence of their
roles as the powerful or 'legal' authority (and he draws a clear distinction
between legal and legitimate authorities), respond to symptoms and
not fundamental causes. They get it wrong, in other words. As Burton
asked pointedly of Northedge, do we really need to know 'why it is that
things are the way they are?' This is a key question, and yet so often we
get the wrong answers. We are the prisoners of our own assumptions.

Third, therefore, there is required a change of process. Specifically, we
need to shift to a set of assumptions that will allow us to separate out
symptoms and causes, address problems as opposed to manifestations
of fundamental human problems, and address them appropriately and
sympathetically. Sympathetically here does not means 'soft': it means
understanding the needs of others and being responsive to them – the
needs to identify, participate, be recognised and so on. Existing institutions
are inappropriate to this task, by and large. So many of the existing
institutions of society are based on adversarial procedures: party politics,
the law and dispute settlement among them. They do not solve problems,
indeed they may (and do) make them worse: 'Failure to appreciate the
limitations of control leads to more law and more penalties as law fails,
without necessarily reducing crime' (Burton, 1979, p. 201). This is just
one specific manifestation of a more generalised problem, as Burton is
clear that 'it is the acceptance, as a legitimate and logically defensible
endeavour, of detailed investigation within a given belief system,
detached from a wider philosophical perspective, that is a reason for
our failure to solve problems' (Burton, 1979, p. 29). Especially notable here
is the quest for general perspectives (the need for 'a more philosophical
perspective perhaps', as he argued to Northedge: you must stress the
nature of the whole), which would presumably serve to illuminate the
limitations of the perspectives he here calls belief-systems.

Problem-solving is the preferred process (indeed, Burton refers to
problem-solving as a discipline). It is this which gives a special role to
social scientists, and places greater emphasis on methodological rigour
and self-awareness:

> it is the special role of social scientists, unlike that of reporters of
> events, to determine continuous trends, i.e. the shifts which are
> occurring in the real world, thereby correcting the lag in perceptions

that dominates policy-making and problem-solving. This is done deductively from propositions about behaviour that can be developed and tested in the present. This implies a constant challenging of conventional thinking and theories. (Burton, 1979, p. 29)

This is especially pregnant, as well as critical. Specialists need to be informed as to the requirements of scientific rigour and procedure. This distinguishes them from 'reporters of events', a markedly critical view of the scientific 'frontiersmen' in International Relations, being that those in positions of academic authority were only – because they could only be – reporters of events. Rigorous analysis demands analysis of trends, with an explanation of the pattern and observation of likely consequences of chosen courses of action: there is still an awareness of 'science' as a series of statements of the 'if...then' variety. This demands engagement with the reality as evidenced by events in the 'here and now', not an understanding of their essences, their manifestation as particular instances of historically-evident trends (where often the new is fitted into what can be explained on the basis of what we think we know), or their assumed uniqueness. This is necessary in order that decision-making can be made more effective, appropriate and legitimate – and less error-prone, engaging in wrong 'definitions of the situation' and the like. The consequences are therefore constant critique and self-awareness, with feedback being a key element of this 'reality-testing' of our theories. There is a need for more rigour and methodological sophistication, rather than a priori assertion as to what the nature of the problem amounts to.

It is clear that Burton is here restating a constant theme in his critique of the conventional wisdom: 'It is not possible to say in advance of a solution to a problem what scope is relevant, what disciplines, what literature, what experience, what data' (Burton, 1979, p. 31). This represents a shift away from the eclecticism associated with the discipline of International Relations, where it was (is?) assumed that there was a problem at the centre of the discipline, which could be understood and explained by drawing in other disciplines as required, thus making the mode of analysis rather eclectic. Clearly, for Burton, this is part of the problem, and he spends much time here getting to grips with the nature, demands and implications of a methodological holism.

For Burton, the issue is one of primacy (the establishment of 'first things first') or, if you will, directionality in the construction of the proper frame of reference:

It is necessary to approach social problems on the basis that behaviour of all actors, individual and small and large groups, is that response to the environment which seems to be the most appropriate in all circumstances as perceived and within the limits of the knowledge available of alternative responses, such that satisfactions will be maximised. This justifies analysing all behaviour within one analytical framework: normal and abnormal, deviant and conforming, individual and group, the haves and the have-nots, the advantaged and the disadvantaged. As analysis proceeds, categories may be differentiated; but what they are must be the result of analysis and not the basis of analysis. For this reason we cannot in advance draw any disciplinary or behavioural boundaries. (Burton, 1979, p. 17)

And what starts off the analysis? The existence of social problems, not least war and conflicts. It is problems before essences, problems before the convenience of the academic discipline, and problems that provoke the search for appropriate methodology. The link that unites the particular with the whole is the dynamic of problem-solving. And there is a second meaning of directionality: on the one hand, there is the idea of how the argument may be constructed afresh, to reveal more. Yet in the second sense in which the term is used here, directionality means taking the whole question of analysing social systems into a new phase: the old will not do; we need to go forward in the search for novelty.

Burton has lengthy treatments of these issues in *Deviance, Terrorism and War*. Where they were a key element of his statement *contra* Northedge in 1974 and elements of the shift in thinking evident in *World Society* in 1972, here they receive a much fuller and more sophisticated treatment which is also more confident, more assertive and more grounded in the relevant literature (including Abrab H. Maslow on needs, but not only him). In due course, they would be more fully developed and cohere around the idea of provention, to which we shall turn in due course.

The implications that follow from these are major: from this point onwards, the operation of human systems is re-perceived; there is a different ontology. Systems are perceived in terms of the needs of members, and not the requirements of authority or role-holders. Nor on the basis of presumptions of morality. In other words, there is a recognition that people and groups act as they do in order to fulfil certain needs, which we must recognise. We need not like them as friends or acquaintances, and they may not always do things as we ourselves would wish. Yet in so far as they act and their behaviour is consequential, they must be recognised as being not only part of the problem, as it were, but a necessary component of the solution. The British imprisoned Jomo Kenyatta of Kenya, exiled Archbishop Makarios of Cyprus and refused to negotiate with 'terrorists' in Northern Ireland, only later recognising that, without the participation of these individuals, a recognition of their expressed needs and a change in the process – both to facilitate their participation in a changing system and allow system change – peaceful relations and a cessation of violence would be elusive, if not impossible. It is interesting that Burton takes, by way of example, terrorist actions, such as the taking of hostages, when he argues that 'within a narrow conception it can be defined immediately as an illegal act. This, however, is merely a label. It is not an analytical description or a definition from which some insights into terrorism can be obtained with a view to its handling or prevention. There might be a political motivation, alienation aspects and others: it would be misleading to draw boundaries in advance of a full analysis' (Burton, 1979, p. 31). Doubtless, specialists would argue that they conduct a full analysis of political terrorism. Burton would suggest that the analysis is, and can only be, partial in so far as it is incapable of seeing the pattern of behaviour holistically. And in so far as acts of terrorism may be defined as illegal acts, then there is a significant point in this; not that it is mindless (even though it may be less than discriminate in its effects) or uncivilised (its use going beyond established norms and values). Rather, it is testimony to the idea that the felt need for recognition (as just one example of an expressed need) – by violent means if necessary – outweighs the cost of violence, vilification and the threat of the legal sanction. As a humane and sensitive individual, Burton is certainly not indifferent to questions of pain and human suffering, but it is entirely pertinent to point out that if there is one thing that crops up repeatedly in *Deviance, Terrorism and War* it is on the need for *analysis*. It may be that 'pure' analysis of situations that involve some individuals in explanations of other human beings being blown to pieces or hacked to death or incinerated is beyond most of us, if not all of us. Yet we should not throw out the baby with the bath water: what Burton strives for – and he too might ultimately acknowledge that it is a goal too far – is an analysis that tends to analysis rather than to ideology, towards what used to be called 'value freedom', if, necessarily, short of the goal of value-freedom, but during a distinction between social science and idealogy. If we concede that we cannot ultimately be detached and value-free, then we might also concede that we can be more analytical in a rigorous, specific and self-aware manner. The violence in Northern Ireland began in 1969 as a direct result of demands expressed with regard to participation, fairness and welfare.

That it became something else should not lead us to lose sight of the fact that, even though the parties and the issues changed, needs were a primary consideration. This is an issue rooted in an analysis of the problem, not a moral evaluation of either of the parties to it, or their actions. This is a separate and related issue, and one to which we shall, necessarily, return in the next chapter. For Burton, again, asks the question: Why are things the way they are and how are we to analyse them?

But, at this stage, Burton identifies another – perhaps lesser and more technical – difficulty, by suggesting that the definition of a problem is not a logical antecedent of the desire to solve it. There may be feedback to suggest a relevant course of action, but there are also forces of resistance to suggest that feedback may be disregarded, not in any accidental fashion but as a positive and deliberate stance. There are vested interests involved in the defence of a defined position: 'It cannot be assumed that those dealing with a problem necessarily wish to solve it. It might seem expedient not to solve a problem or to argue that a holding position is the sought-after "solution". What appear to be difficulties in defining and solving a problem may well be an absence of any desire to define it or solve it' (Burton, 1979, p. 32). Denial of the existence of a problem would also represent a denial of the need for systems to change, or leaders to be removed.

Nor is Burton entirely unsympathetic to the problems associated with the role-holders in complex circumstances: they are prisoners of assumptions, fragmentation of knowledge and the requirements of separate discipline status: 'Part-solutions are rarely helpful and are frequently self-defeating. It is at this point that policy-makers are in greatest difficulty; how to define a problem realistically, yet within a political context' (Burton, 1979, p. 34). However difficult this stance may appear to be at first glance, it tries to get to grips with the perennial problem that has been at the centre of so many debates about the nature of social and political thought over the centuries. It has constantly been asserted – and counter-asserted – that an approach, method, conceptual scheme or theory dealt with the 'realities of the problem'. 'Real-Worldism' has a powerful effect on the status of thought. It also establishes a vantage point from which other approaches can be assessed, and their failure to engage with 'the real world' dismissed. Hence the stance in relation to ideas deemed 'Utopian', where the adherents to this Utopian view are convinced that they are dealing with a reality too. There are constantly repeated assertions, dismissals and debates. Practitioners have their world view too, and it is a perennial observation on the part of practitioners that they envy the luxury of the academic, who can take a long view, detached from the demands of the immediate policy choice. Both practitioners and academics deal with 'reality' of course, though they differ as to what this is.

The plea from Burton is for 'behavioural realism'. We need to look at the way that people behave, in a positive way. This means that we need to be sensitive about labels and language. Recall, when our team performs an act it is to us a 'daring deed'; but when performed by the other side against us, it is a 'sneak raid'. When we score a last-minute goal to save the game, it is a heroic last ditch effort; but when the opposition do so, they have stolen the match. We need to be analytical, not judgemental. This is the first point. The second follows from it, and relates to consequences:

> there will be few 'solutions' to problems of behavioural relationships that do not directly or indirectly relate to altered perceptions and attitudes, altered belief systems, consideration of options not previously considered, altered structures and roles. No 'solution' is complete, no test is adequate, unless accompanied by exploration of the processes by which the solution can be rendered acceptable. The instructions for application must accompany the packet. (Burton, 1979, p. 36)

A lesson learned in the experiences of the CAC now follows, as a necessary part of the solution to the problems identified. Traditionally, problems in the social sciences have been associated with the perception of the (analytical) observer, as well as the participant in the processes being observed:

> The situation is perceived by the observer in terms of his normative standards, his interpretation of behaviour, his knowledge of various pieces of history, sociology, politics and other aspects of the total situation. However, it is the common patterns of behaviour of the actors which are the subject of study, not the common patterns of their overt behaviour as perceived by different observers. The only reality that is relevant is that of the actors, not the reality of the observer. (Burton, 1979, p. 36)

Here is the key to the engagement with reality – it is the reality at the heart of the problem *as experienced*, and Burton is unambiguous: this is the only reality that is relevant. This is the principal concern at the centre of the search for holistic systems of explanation. This was one of the major issues that came out of the experience of the problem-solving workshops associated with the CAC. It represented a major innovation, going beyond what had previously been associated with conflict and 'third party' roles.

The emphasis on the 'behaviour of the actors' as opposed to 'their overt behaviour as perceived' is also telling. It draws our attention to the focus on the causes of problems, not what appear to be symptoms, necessitating a search for the fundamental issues at stake, not the manner of their expression. In other words, individuals do not break the law because they are born 'law-breakers' or 'bad-types', born to a life of crime. That they do so is a symptom of something else. Palestinians, armed with stones and catapults, do not confront Israeli tanks because they see this as some theatrical re-enactment of David and Goliath in reverse. Nor do they do so as an expression of light relief or waywardness, nor because they are born that way or predetermined on that path. They do so – seriously, and at great risk to themselves – in the light of their perception of a real, experienced and felt sense of something, a something that leads them to express themselves. The solution to the problem that expression represents is not a tank; tanks do not solve problems, though they may, on occasion, deal with the symptoms in the short term:

> The solution is not a final end-product. It is itself another set of rela-tionships that contains its own sets of problems. The solution to a conflict problem or an authority problem does not eliminate a party to the conflict and, therefore, creates a new set of relationships and problems. However, this new set of problems will be the sought-for outcome and not merely an unexpected one, as is frequently the case in cybernetic decision-making. (Burton, 1979, p. 5)

This is why conflict resolution is so important, and indeed at the core of Burton's work. Resolution is the key issue in conflict. Management, judicial settlement, arbitration, bargaining and so on are all likely to fail, for one very simple reason: they deal with formal structures – as embedded in legal status, state-centricity or contractual obligation – and not with the behavioural realities of conflict, as experienced. Often they represent an imposed solution that is, in fact, an oxymoron: there cannot be a solution which is imposed – it is 'sought-for' by the people involved, and only those actually involved can construct the process legitimately and successfully. Only when these are engaged appropriately can there be any fundamental resolution, system change and legitimate 'peace' (and where there is a real recognition that there will be conflicts in such a system, but where these will be dealt with by legitimate and consensual means, in a dynamic process of societal adaptation).

Such observation will lead us to the view that we need to change the very basic assumptions we make about men, women and the conditions in which we live. This leads us to Burton's discussion of the need for a paradigm shift, the need for which has again been a constantly expressed theme in his work. He has referred to it as 'power politics', the 'power frame' and in similar terms. We have referred to the old paradigm as the conventional approach, traditional approaches, the conventional wisdom and the like. These are attempts to get to grips with what we tend to treat as the 'given' that underpins our understanding. What is rather difficult to understand is why – especially in the realm of socio-political analysis – there has been such a staunch resistance to change in the 'given', the conventional wisdom. In other areas of human endeavour, we have made measurable progress. In modern medicine, we assume that the blood circulates through the human body: once we did not. It was once thought that 'phlogiston' was the substance that allowed the combustion of air, so that when it was burnt it was 'dephlogisticated'. We once assumed that the Earth was flat, and were we to go far enough, we would fall off the edge. We made discoveries and moved on, established views were altered, and with them social arrangements and social cosmologies. This was not always easy and was often resisted: there was, after all, a natural order of things. Even in social systems, it was assumed that slavery was the natural order of things, and that men were naturally superior to women: so much was self-evident, until it was not. What changed was not only practices but also ideas.

So the natural order of things changes and it is important to see here the significant effects of Burton's pleas for a paradigm shift, which we have encapsulated here as the key breakthrough, the ontological break. From here on, the 'given' is not given. After this, there is a process of redefinition, no acceptance of any pre-existing ideas of what is the given, the real, or the enduring and inescapable condition. At the same time, for Burton, the ontological break is not simply a question of a new theory of reality, as it were. It is also a new approach to the idea of what is possible within the realm of human behaviour and interactions. It is also, therefore, a new ontology of political choice. There is a clear and consistent challenge to the conventional wisdom, however much it is rooted in – and claims authority for the articulation, representation and reproduction of – 'Realism'. Burton clearly draws on the work of Thomas Kuhn on the nature and significance of paradigms (Kuhn, 1962). Fields of study work within a shared set of assumptions – givens – that set up a research agenda and within which scientists solve puzzles, provide explanations and contribute to a development and accumulation of knowledge. However, there comes a time (rare rather than routine) when what is discovered cannot be fitted easily into the existing paradigm, because it is a new kind of discovery, or new knowledge for which no place can be found. At first these may be explained away as aberrations, but as they accumulate in number and multiply in significance, then there is a consequent pressure to develop a new paradigm, which is capable of explaining not only what is 'known' but also these accumulated and consequential novelties. Once this paradigm shift has been effected, then scientists get back to the business of what Kuhn calls 'normal science': the grand problem (which the emergent novelties represent) having been solved, then science and scientists get on with the rather more mundane tasks of 'doing normal science', recognising that most science is of this nature, solving puzzles and not aiming to create revolutions is science, where the solution to the puzzle is assumed to be knowable according to the familiar rules of science as they are taught.

Kuhn argues that the adoption of the new paradigm represents – at one and the same time – the collapse of the old. In the case of social science (and in particular with respect to International Relations and the allied questions of conflict and war), this has not quite been the case, and the persistence of the old paradigm – deemed to be partially or wholly inadequate to the task of explanation in the light of emergent novelties – is significant. Yet it is contended here that the work of Burton – even if it does not represent a free-standing new paradigm in and of itself, is symptomatic of the inadequacies of the old, the elements of the new *and* the nature of the transitionary process not explained by Kuhn (though it has to be recognised that Kuhn wrote of the natural sciences, where there has been a longer-established consensus on the nature of unambiguous concepts, wedded to a consensus with regard to appropriate methodologies: these are far less conspicuous in the realms of social discourse).

Interestingly, Burton seeks an answer to this. He recognises the nature of the Kuhnian frame of reference, and the nature of the scientific consensus, but argues that 'simultaneously there are likely to be events which are unobserved, at least by most people; also observations made to which no significance is attached, merely because they do not happen to fit into pre-conceived ideas' (Burton, 1979, p. 26). In other words, one explanation of why the strict Kuhnian mode of analysis regarding paradigms and paradigm change is different as between the natural and social sciences may be because of the different criteria of 'fit', as it were. In the natural sciences there are clear, precise and demonstrable concepts and procedures to establish fit, and evidence which, within the rules of science, cannot be disregarded. In social analysis, there are disputes about the nature of this reality, its explanations and the methodological process associated with dealing with it. The relevant concepts are contested, elastic and sometimes a mix of reductionist and all-encompassing. Frequently there is a conflation of all of these, and there is surely no better example to be cited than the idea of 'power' in the explanation of politics, domestic and international. The idea of 'balance of power' compounds the point. (It is worth reiterating that this problem of the power frame was a key determinant of Burton's career and intellectual agenda.)

For Burton, the treatment of deviance is a case in point, where 'deviant behaviour was widely accepted as being due to demoralisation or deficiency: today there is a growing acceptance of the general proposition that behaviour, deviant or not, is that response to the perceived environment which is best calculated, in the view of the actor, to achieve his objectives or values', the consequence of this change in perspective representing nothing less than 'a tremendous shift in the definition of a particular social problem' (Burton, 1979, p. 28).

If this – and much of the preceding account – leads us to the view that the dynamic of change is consequently simple, Burton disabuses us of this notion, since

> finding the solution to a problem is a more complex process than envisaged within a power framework. It involves an accurate analysis of the total situation, knowledge of the reasons for social behaviour, probably altered attitudes and, perhaps, changed environmental conditions. The processes are not those adversary ones that characterise traditional institutions ... [but those which] exclude fault, "norms", precedents ... and other techniques associated with zero-sum relationships and rest upon processes relevant to the search for positive sum outcomes. (Burton, 1979, p. 207)

In other words, the process is one where all can win from changed attitudes and behaviour, structures and attitudes. A key issue in all of this is the associated costs (monetary and social) of resistance and conservatism, where the incentives to change far outweigh the benefits of resistance. Change is therefore not a consequence of scales falling from the eyes of those who see the 'wrong things', but rather the result of a process of change perceived to be a rational way to move forward, producing social 'goods' and not social 'bads': 'The application of problem-solving processes assumes rational behaviour; but problem-solving processes themselves avoid bargaining and power confrontations and contribute to rational behaviour' (Burton, 1979, p. 209). In other words, change, and especially co-operation to fulfil needs, will be a central dynamic in all this. There is some validity, therefore, to the view that Burton's works show some influences from the approach to international co-operation, associated with David Mitrany and known as functionalism, but Burton has been rather more generalised in his application of the idea, incorporating it into a wider conceptual scheme.

In summary, (a) the process of open-ended adaptation; (b) resolving (newly-created) conflicts as a matter of course – rather as questions of social pathology; (c) having as its central purpose the creation of legitimated socio-political systems; that (d) have the articulated goal of solving authentically expressed and felt human needs; and where (e) all are capable of benefiting from the new arrangements, are the central components of 'provention'. This, above all, represented a break with the conventional wisdom.

6
Towards Provention

After *Deviance, Terrorism and War* (1979) Burton's work takes on a different character. The process became more of refinement and addressing some of the implied questions. By this stage the material had been chosen, the form rough-hewn: the task ahead was to form the finished creation. He now had the big picture that he had so long sought. He produced a significant literature, with the four volume Conflict Series appearing in 1990 (Burton, 1990a, 1990b; Burton and Dukes, 1990a, 1990b); this was 'provention'. Before we encounter it, however, there are other works to assess, and a key transition needs attention.

In 1982, Burton left the University of Kent at Canterbury for the United States, where he was associated successively with the University of South Carolina (where he was the International Studies Association visiting scholar), the University of Maryland, George Mason University (in Virginia) and the United States Institute of Peace. He was now well into his sixties, had left behind International Relations and was in an environment more receptive to – and more supportive of – work in conflict resolution. The United States, as a social system and an academic environment, has always put a premium on pioneers, 'frontiersmen' (Rosenau used this description of thinkers in International Relations in the early 1960s as a mark of recognition and status, and not as a sign that they were a nuisance) and the engagement with change. Critics (European?) have seen this as a mark of a society still early on the road to 'mature development', and unaware that there really is nothing new under the sun, still finding itself and, in so doing, finding new words for older realities. Yet Burton found this to be a fertile environment. His work was valued, it was supported, and it formed the basis for curriculum development and innovation not only in thought but also in training programmes, and not only in conflict resolution but also in peace and justice studies.

The transformation in the United States society that saw it change from the essential conformities of the Cold War to the innovations of the 1980s – which Burton both stimulated and benefited from (as did Kenneth Boulding) – was due in no small measure to the effects of the Vietnam War on American society. Peace as a social aim undoubtedly grew in status as a desirable goal in the years after 1975. The external conflict in Indo-China had grown out of established perceptions of a hostile Communism, an established 'domino theory' that predicted a process of collapse to hostile forces were they not stopped, and a search for allies. And costly conflicts developed within American society. A period of introspection followed, and peace became a part of the established discourse, certainly in academia and in the wider society. Of course, there were those who adhered to the notion of peace through strength and military power, but the debate was now more pluralist and tolerant of alternatives. After a long struggle to establish it, the United States Institute of Peace, in Washington DC, is an embodiment of that change in social values. In these circumstances, Burton was to find a ready audience for his ideas and a receptive environment in terms of innovation. In Europe, and in particular in the United Kingdom, the environment was rather less conducive and the study of war was still preferred to the study of peace (though the University of Bradford was the site of the first Department of Peace Studies in the United Kingdom), and by the early 1980s, the nature of peace studies was to be a topic of (rare) public debate and controversy, where there were accusations that centred around tendentiousness, lack of 'real' academic status and the like. It can only be a matter of speculation as to the way in which circumstances might have been different had Burton remained in the United Kingdom: the point is that he did not.

But before he went to the United States he produced the idiosyncratic *Dear Survivors* in 1982. It was cast in the form of a personal epistle to the survivors of a nuclear Third World War, especially those officials charged with the task of social reconstruction, written from the perspective of an individual involved in the planning and execution of post-war reconstruction after 1945. In constructing the argument as he does in this fashion, he makes a major point by way of comment on the development of conflict analysis since 1945. In the aftermath of the Second World War, it seemed to many that the task was a case of resuming as before. There was no idea of a different universe evolving, no presumption in respect of the likely changes in the structures and processes of society, both domestic and international. It was assumed, by and large, that the conventional wisdom that had lasted for a long time would still be valuable; indeed, that there was little need to replace it – and nothing to replace it with.

But, argues Burton, there were major perceptual failures, despite the development of institutions like the United Nations and its agencies. Principal among these were growing devolutionary pressures within states; the failure of entrenched economic policies to deal with questions of welfare and employment, and the rapid development of interdependence in the international system. These errors of interpretation were compounded by the appearance of problems on the policy agenda, especially the advent of the Cold War, the development of divisive tendencies in a significant number of states, the growing gap between rich and poor, the skewing of resources associated with large defence budgets thought to be necessary in the Cold War conditions, and the requirements of nuclear deterrence:

> In retrospect, the inadequate framework in which we operated and which prevented us from anticipating these developments and problems is clear: it was the classical one that had gone unchallenged for centuries. We assumed that every nation-state was independent, that international problems could be separated from national, that there was a reserved area of national jurisdiction. (Burton, 1982, p. 11)

In the light of the changes identified by Burton, it became clear that this existing set of assumptions – a conceptual map that underpinned policy-making – was woefully inadequate; there was, for Burton, the absence of a 'knowledge base'. So that

> little wonder, then, that post World War II reconstruction included an acceptance of coercion politics as the basis of the all pervasive theoretical framework: judicial settlement, power bargaining and negotiation as the appropriate decision making process; and adversary parliamentary, industrial and law and order systems as the institutional foundations. It was within this classical conception of social organisation that we operated, focusing on the immediate goals of a welfare state – which were unattainable in such a world. (Burton, 1982, p. 12)

A central fault was the emphasis on institutional structures as the key unit of analysis, so that 'it is not surprising therefore that the individual – as a participant in society – received little analytical attention. On the contrary, a special type of "man" was invented to fit in with the theories and models of social and economic organisation that had developed' (Burton, 1982, p. 13). The problem, again, in conceptual terms, was the directionality in the reasoning and the consequent distortions in the relevant frame of analysis. The problem, in political terms, was that the requirements of organisations tended to be the key policy goal, so that coherence, authority and maintenance of existing power structures came to be the organising goals and processes relating to them as performance criteria of decision-makers. If people did not fit the system, then they would be made to fit it, for this was what the system required. To risk a persistent and widespread lack of conformity with the demands of the system was to risk its very survival, which, of course, could not be tolerated, as the survival of the institutional structure was the goal of policy.

In due course, and in the light of events, things began to change. There had been the major changes in the international system associated with decolonisation, and successful challenges to European policies, which had been based on long-established foundations of control, coercion and 'good government'. There had also been major changes in domestic societies. Whereas, in many states, the late 1940s and 1950s were periods of austerity followed by recovery from the war, this was also associated with a re-imposition of existing social values (now that the war was over and 'normality' was desirable), associated with conformity, respectability and 'discipline'. Often, the requirements of Cold War policies or conscription assisted in this process, often resulting is an essential social stasis, allied to policies aimed at economic growth. Against that background, therefore, the 1960s was indeed a radical decade, and 'by the late 1960s . . . failure in almost every social and political field prompted reconsideration of many previously accepted assumptions', so that, in due course, existing categories of analysis gave way to newer approaches that put the individual human being at the centre, but this 'was not the malleable and invented individual – economic man, legal man or ideological man – that so conveniently fitted whatever theory was being used'. Instead, 'it was that individual who did not fit into serfdom, slavery, colonialism, capitalism, or socialism. It was that real individual who was being discovered who found positive law and elite societies unacceptable – a very difficult and objectionable individual in any society that was not constructed by and for it' (Burton, 1982, pp. 15–16).

In due course, ideas and knowledge changed: this much is clear. But there was an associated problem that related to the extent to which policy was based on older assumptions that were not consonant with the new realms of behaviour: 'there was an increasing knowledge gap between what was known and the actual knowledge of administrators and politicians' (Burton, 1982, p. 18) and there were major delays in incorporating what was known into a framework of beliefs that informed policy. For the survivors, therefore, Burton suggested that they needed, as a matter of urgency, to find ways to bridge the knowledge gap, which he saw as being measurable – and measured – within decades. It is against this backdrop that his comment to Northedge – to the effect that international politics has nothing to do with the real world, it is a game – carries added weight.

In addressing the question of policy-making, Burton makes a comment that helps to explain his engagement with need, not in terms of what it means to the evolving framework, but what it portends in terms of any future analysis, and especially his search for a concept devoid of 'taint', bias or ideology. He asks whether there can be a scientific – that is, 'objective' – basis on which authoritative decisions can be made (Burton, 1982, p. 20). This is revealing, as it equates science with objectivity, which is a well-established notion in terms of the conventional approaches to an explanation of the natural world. But applying the methods of this 'naturalism' to the field of social analysis has proved to be fraught with difficulty and spawned a massive literature associated with value-freedom in social science. In the 1960s, Burton, convinced of the failures of the conventional wisdom to distinguish adequately between description and analysis, on the one hand, and knowledge and ideology on the other, encountered much of this literature. This is reflected in his earlier work. He sought something that would allow him to be 'objective' – in the sense that the tasks of analysis and policy-making could be separated. The classical position was that there could not be a science of policy-making, since the social and political scientist could present goal options, could point out what was not possible, could recommend alternative means to goals; but there was no basis on which priorities could be ordered other than on the basis of value preferences. On this matter, Burton is more than forthright; and wholly rejects this view.

The source of the problem, for Burton, is that the conventional wisdom stressed states and societies as the primary focus of analysis. In contrast, he argues that

if people within political organisations were taken as the unit of analysis, then there would be certain facts or rules, which as in physics would always be true and would provide a basis for assessing policies;

that there could, therefore, be a science of political theory and a philosophy of public policy (natural and social sciences have the same methods of approach). (Burton, 1982, p. 20)

In other words, shifting the level of analysis to the individual, and more particularly to individual need – which must be satisfied to enable people to feel themselves to be appropriately human – allows us to focus on individuals in much the same way that natural scientists can focus on their own related problems, analyse them and make policy recommend-ations. We can do likewise in the social sciences, if we have appropriate concepts that are not elastic or influenced by social factors (where values or norms are so influenced). This is Burton attempting to be positivist, without the problems of strict positivism, but opting for the term 'behavioural realism': 'Public policy could be concerned with subjective values, while also being concerned with over-riding behavioural traits that are constant and scientifically determined. That subjective values must be the basis of authoritative decision making is itself a subjective judgment that may be false' (Burton, 1982, p. 22).

The book concludes with a statement of the new political realism:

> political reality in a nuclear age is not the relative power of states and people, but the obligation to satisfy human needs by solving human problems without resort to a coercive political system...Participation, recognition, identity, development for all are not the constituent parts of an ideology. They are the politically realistic constituents of any ongoing society. (Burton, 1982, p. 134)

Note the emphases here: the promise of political realism devoid of ideology; the reinterpretation of obligation, not what humankind is obliged to do or be, but what societies, states and systems are obliged to do in the light of the 'human-beingness' of their constituent parts; a belief in politics of participation, not coercion. Nothing is 'given', nothing is stasis.

The main body of the book retraces much of the ground with which we are now more than familiar, with the qualification that Burton grounds the discussions in a wider, relevant literature and with examples taken from different areas of human interaction. International Relations has now become part of a more inclusive, generalised form of reference, and we are approaching the synthesis of the analysis into provention. Yet there is one section of the book that is both forthright and revealing, and it is pertinent in so far as it relates not only to the period referred to as the ontological break, but also to Burton's involvement with the conflict in Ireland.

Prefaced by the remark that he and his colleagues at the CAC in London were not ivory-tower academics, but used to getting their hands ('and reputations') dirty by getting involved in ongoing conflicts, Burton recounts his involvement with Ireland from 1969 to 1976 'initially at the invitation of the Northern Ireland Community Relations Commission – a most useful and important organisation that the British Government abolished' (Burton, 1982, p. 75). He was, he recounts, in direct contact with the para-militarys on both sides, as well as other interested parties, and continues,

> I made notes of every interview. I wish I could share these with you. They are too long and personal for publication. They are also shocking. They reveal in stark detail how the British Ministry of Defence took control of Northern Ireland primarily in order to ensure there was no settlement. The typical worst-case analysis mentality of defence officials feared the emergence of an independent Northern Ireland, which would put British and NATO defence strategies in jeopardy. (Burton, 1982, p. 75)

Indeed, he went so far as to submit a lengthy memorandum to an official committee established by the British government to address the Irish situation, pointing out the requirements of a problem-solving approach as opposed to a power approach: the whole is reproduced here at some length (Burton, 1982, pp. 76–84), with the concomitant explanation that Ireland is included by way of example to illustrate the failures of established traditional power explanations:

> The lesson is that we have to be prepared to innovate, to rethink, to move away from the traditional, to explore – and the exploration of the behavioural seems to be the most exciting and the most rewarding. After all, the problems we are talking about here are, in the last analysis, the problems of satisfying the needs of the unit members of society, people. (Burton, 1982, p. 84)

Global Conflict: The Domestic Sources of International Crisis (Burton, 1984) appeared when Burton was between Kent and North America. There are discussions of public policy, deviance and the problems of change, together with discussions of – among other things – Soviet – American relations. But it is notable for several innovations, representing an incremental articulation of the argument. Most notable are the discussions of positive outcomes ('win–win' situations), second-track diplomacy, and the concluding section on issues associated with problem and process.

With respect to the idea of win–win approaches to the study of conflict, Burton is the first to recognise that this is a view usually thought to be Utopian: in the traditional view, conflicts are about objective clashes of interest, where the gain of one party is the loss of the other. With regard to the international system, Burton suggests that contemporary events are leading us to the view that traditional perspectives on security are faulty, in so far as they are based on the presumption that security is a scarce commodity. These are the assumptions that hold parties to the conflict captive while they are in bargaining mode, unable to see the limitations of the frame of reference. (Yet it is also part of the set of ideas into which many have been socialised in the long term, the frame of reference in International Relations associated with the notion of the security dilemma.) Second, argues Burton, we are prisoners of assumptions that lead us to the practice of settling conflicts through the imposition of legal norms on parties to conflict, to control. The shift required, in the light of these cautionary remarks, is to see that these may be false, and that conflict is in fact rooted in fundamental concerns about human needs:

> We are faced with the proposition that conflict at all levels may not be over scarce resources, such as territory, but over social goods that are not in short supply and, in fact, increase with consumption. The more security one party experiences the more, and not the less, does another party experience. The tactics of security . . . raise problems of scarcity. In thinking about conflict we have tended to confuse tactics and goals. Similarly, territory may be the means by which to achieve identity. (Burton, 1984, p. 140)

The passage above, discussing the nature of win–win situations, is particularly illustrative of the Burton style. It is quick to challenge the existing sets of assumptions. In his discussion he mentions authors whose works seem to be relevant. He pithily makes an alternative, indeed at times radically subversive, point that challenges the very fundamentals of the established mode, and then leaves it, almost as if having made the point, then the implications are self-evident, the point made and the case can proceed. The discussion of win–win, so hugely significant in its implications, is here dealt with in fewer than five pages!

He is correct to draw the distinction, to which we have drawn attention before, between symptoms and causes, but the discussion surely (on this as on other occasions) needs filling out. Yet if this observation leads to the view that Burton's style is merely blandly assertive, it is misleading, for he is careful in following through some parts of the agenda:

> There is, however, one aspect of this alternative approach to the handling of conflict which is not as yet fully understood. A theory of behaviour that argues that certain needs will be pursued regardless of any force that might be used by authorities, suggests to anyone accustomed to traditional notions of law and order a kind of anarchy. (Burton, 1984, pp. 140–1)

Therefore Burton is keen to engage the question of order, as follows:

> in order to achieve human needs, in order to have identity and recognition in a social group, it is obviously necessary to have good relationships with those whose recognition is sought. There is a value attached to relationships. It is this value, not the process of socialisation, that explains what order there is in society. If there is an absence of valued relationships...then there are no constraints on behaviour, except to the degree that there is a value attached to the relationship with a deviant social group. (Burton, 1984, p. 141)

In other words, why should a community/group/individual have respect for a society where it is itself not accorded recognition or respect? The answer to the problem is not punishment, discipline, alienation or distance, but an engagement with the process of establishing relationships out of which come recognition, identity and respect. On that basis, relationships are established and – because they are valued – are likely to be self-sustaining. This does not exhaust the point, but opens up an agenda for future research. Perhaps this is a strength of Burton's economical style: he indicates that we need to know more.

Second-track diplomacy is similarly innovative, based on the notion that conventional diplomacy proceeds on the assumption that parties probably do not like each other, though they feel the need to interact, and indeed view each other in less than favourable terms. The assumption is of malign intent. The second-track approach is the diplomacy of non-diplomats and is based on the assumption of benign intent with regard to motives and intentions. It is particularly important to note that Burton got this idea not from the unadulterated mind of a benign Utopian scholar, but from a practising American diplomat. Central to the second-track approach is the focus less on the system and more on the individual as the unit of analysis, and the approach itself, for Burton, comes out of trends in behavioural research, which, of course, he has sought to synthesise himself:

> The transition that we are now experiencing from social policies based on allocation of values as determined by ideological elites, to social policies that are influenced by the ontological needs of persons and communities is a dramatic and revolutionary one. It is this transition, and the inevitable defences that are made against it, that best explain the high levels of domestic violence and communal and interstate conflict that are universal in contemporary world society. (Burton, 1984, p. 153)

This passage sums up so much of what Burton has to say, in so many thousands of words. The role of the second track of diplomacy is to act as an instrument of transition, recognising the existence of traditional frames of reference, centres of loyalty and adherence to belief systems that underpin conflict, while also recognising the importance of individual and human needs as fundamental and primary issues at the centre of the conflict or problem.

Thus Burton outlines four possible roles for the second-track approach, not in opposition to established first-track approaches (this is a usual, though erroneous, view) but proceeding in the same direction. The first task is to continue unofficial communication between the protagonists, without prior commitment, to address issues that create tension in the relationships. Second, is the establishment of a service/institution – official or semi-official – to provide services for those engaged in conflict. Third, this could be allied to a centre devoted to training and this related in turn to a research institute. And why might this be required? Because 'there is at present no credible institution within the international system to which participants in a major internal dispute can turn should they wish to seek assistance in resolving the dispute' (Burton, 1984, p. 156). Why not? Often they are not within the jurisdiction of the United Nations, and the United Nations has become too politicised to take on the tasks. Also, the ordinary processes of diplomacy have failed, in the face of problems associated with seeming to be weak in recognising the demands of others, the apparent need for preconditions, concessions and gestures, and so on. What is required, for Burton, is a system analogous to that of the Red Cross, where legitimacy is based on a perception of their competence to act in a given sphere, within the realm of conflict resolution, but also with an eye to the needs of research as well as action. Interestingly, the semi-academic meetings that took place within the context of the Pugwash meetings prior to the 1963 Partial Test Ban Treaty are recalled here by Burton. He is always aware of the need for organisations as instruments to effect practical changes emanating from the changes in thought. Nor, it should be remarked, does he neglect the potential roles and significance of scholars and the potential of academic seminars.

Two chapters towards the end of the book span discussions of problem and process in fewer than fifteen pages, yet they are especially important. Not least because Burton seeks to go beyond what is apparently the problem to assess the fundamentals of the problem. For example, regarding the East–West conflict, he suggested that it was not ideological, but rather a result of transitions and dynamics associated with the development of great powers. The major powers are thus locked into a situation that is beyond their capabilities to control, where they are the prisoners of dysfunctional policies and where they cannot concede in face of policies based on deterrence and confrontation. The problem is that they have to see what the problem is – and Burton suggests that it is not about ideologies – it is about selective perception on the part of decision-makers and consequent defensive foreign policies:

> Many countries in the contemporary world society are members of alliances and have large military forces at their disposal only because they are faced with internal opposition, because they are not legitimised authorities that can stand on their own feet through popular support. Internal instability and international tensions and conflicts are not separate problems; the one leads to the other. (Burton, 1984, p. 174)

The Soviet experience is cited by Burton by way of example, as is the American response to challenges in Latin America, where the performance of the market system is leading to underdevelopment, but where the United States sees this as a threat to its underlying capitalist market system (Burton, 1984, p. 174). This does not say all there is to say, since it is a characteristic of Burton that he does not explain all. But what he does do is to challenge sufficiently to dent the established mind-set and prompt a reaction: what, after all, really is 'the problem'? It may not be what we think it is. And if the problem is not quite what it seems, then the processes thought relevant to dealing with it are probably not appropriate either. Tools for the task are required, but they will follow on only when we have defined the task. Evidence leads Burton to the view that unofficial diplomacy along a second track can be significant in itself and a tool of transition.

There is also an innovation in respect to methodology, particularly his engagement with American social thought that led him to an encounter (limited at this stage) with the relatively little-known (especially outside the USA?) American philosopher, Charles Sanders Peirce. In 1975 – in the short essay on the nature of universal values – Burton stated that the problem to be addressed should be the key to the study, and that it should precede the methodology; the former would define the form and relevance of the latter. In Peirce he found a legitimate – if distinctly unconventional – philosophical foundation for that stance. At this stage, his engagement with Peirce is by way of contrast, again, with the power of established approaches to reasoning, as this informs policy-making, defining the problem.

The problem with much policy-making is that it is based on inductive reasoning, with decision-makers selecting evidence to suit, and countering arguments with selected evidence as well. Working within their framework of beliefs, they are fed information ('intelligence' for example), 'but the total data are never available and ideological selections are made from whatever data are available' (Burton, 1984, p. 21). Yet gathering information that fits is clearly a deception. How, we want to know, can we be sure that deterrence works, for example? 'The way out [for Peirce] is "abduction", or a searching analysis and examination of our original hypotheses, our conceptual notions and assumptions and prejudices' (Burton, 1984, p. 23). At this stage this is pretty much all there is by way of encounter with Peirce, but he was to say more in his discussions associated with 'provention'.

In 1987, now firmly ensconced in Virginia, Burton produced *Resolving Deep-Rooted Conflict: A Handbook*. As the title suggests, the work was designed less as a study of the philosophical-behavioural aspects of conflicts and more of a practical orientation to inform actual processes of conflict resolution. Fifty-six rules are the theme of the book, allied to a preliminary discussion that sets out the context for a consideration of them. But they are of interest more for what they represent than in what they say in detail. The existence of the work itself is symptomatic of the maturity of the field of conflict resolution. Whereas *Conflict and Communication* (1969) was a pioneer work in the field, of necessity, this later work is a work based on accumulated evidence: it gives advice and instruction about what should be done, and by whom. It is policy-orientated and the foundation upon which those so inclined can acquire the skills of the conflict resolution specialist. The preliminary hypotheses so carefully developed in London at the CAC are replaced by a much more confidently articulated set of rules for action.

The four-volume Conflict Series appeared in 1990. Burton edited *Conflict: Human Needs Theory* (1990a), the product of a conference held in 1989 to discuss the nature and significance of human needs. In introducing this work, Burton recognised explicitly the influential role of an earlier work on human needs, itself a product of a conference held a decade earlier. Katrin Lederer's *Human Needs* (Lederer, 1980) (also on the question of needs, see Braybrooke (1987) and Ignatieff (1994)) was a discussion of needs as a theory of development, but it stimulated Burton to the effect that, in relation to his long-term studies of conflict,

> it became clear to me that conflicts of this kind were not generated primarily – or even at all – by shortages of goods or even by claims to territory. There were fundamental issues in all cases, issues touching on individual and group security, identity and recognition. The power of human needs was greater than military might. The conditions that explained conflict and therefore suggested means towards its resolution, were frustrated human needs, not human lawlessness or character deformities. Needs theory moved the focus away from the individual as miscreant and aimed it at the absence of legitimisation of structures, institutions and policies as the primary source of conflict. (Burton, 1990a, p. xv)

Such a statement demands our attention for what it signifies. The affirmation that the power of human needs is greater than the power of military might, and the recognition that territoriality is less important than is usually supposed finally breaks the long links between Burton and the discipline of International Relations. The problem of social order, as defined in International Relations, is that associated with a particular *problematique*, where there is no central authority. States in interaction are the starting point. That defines much of the consensus defining and uniting the discipline. For Burton, the question is more fundamental, not always or necessarily involving states, the existence of discipline-based perspectives being positive hindrances to appropriately holistic and a-disciplinary requirements of analyses of human behaviour.

In sixteen chapters, the questions associated with needs are addressed. There is a variety of interpretations and no clear demand for a consensus on the use of terms or an agreed agenda of research. The collection is evidence that the issue of need is being engaged seriously and consistently, across a range of areas. There are discussions by Sites, Kelman, Mitchell, Galtung and Sandole, among others. A second set of essays is that edited by Burton and Frank Dukes, *Conflict: Readings in Management and Resolution* (Burton and Dukes, 1990a). This might be seen as an indication of where we are and how we got here with regard to approaches to understanding conflict from an alternative perspective. The editors describe it, appropriately, as a 'start-up' library for the general reader, the student and practitioner on the subject of conflict and its resolution. There are established contributions from pioneers such as Quincy Wright and Kenneth Boulding, as well as long-established and valued colleagues of Burton, including Banks, Groom, de Reuck and more recent colleagues at George Mason University. In part, therefore, this collection might be seen not only as a collection of writings that have value, but also a recognition, by Burton, of the value of the contribution of colleagues on the way to prevention. Not only are these contributions significant in their own right, they are also significant for Burton's own intellectual odyssey.

Conflict: Practices in Management, Settlement and Resolution (Burton and Dukes, 1990b) is a survey and development of practice, in twenty-two short chapters. Some are well-established but others are less well-known. Some are familiar from earlier works of Burton, and some are more conventional, if not entirely mainstream. Especially notable, however, are the further discussions of two-track diplomacy and alternative dispute resolution, and there is a short treatment of provention.

The most important of the works – because it is a remarkable synthesis of all that has gone before – is *Conflict: Resolution and Provention* (Burton, 1990b), where provention is defined (as it is in the title pages of each of the three other works) in these terms: 'prevention has the connotation of containment. The term provention has been introduced to signify taking steps to remove sources of conflict, and more positively to promote conditions in which collaborative and valued relationships control behaviours' (Burton, 1990b). In effect, provention is a general theory of positive social change, where conflict is a central problem area, where the goal is the dynamic of a peaceful society (constituted at all levels of human behaviour), where the relationships are sustained by legitimate mechanisms of reciprocated support and not by coercive measures or by elites, by virtue of their own authority.

Burton sets great store by the works of the long-forgotten American pragmaticist philosopher, Charles Sanders Peirce, finding in them a methodological stance of some significance. Of Peirce he says 'whose writings have only recently been analysed is most useful to students of problem-solving conflict resolution. He stressed the need, first, for hypothesis projection – that is, postulating in an imaginative way possible explanatory hypotheses. These are not guesswork or trial and error, but imaginative hypotheses based on available knowledge, intuitions and insights that he called an "abductive process"' (Burton, 1990b, p. 19). The dynamic element of the process was not to be found in empirical testing in 'the real world', since

> he attached importance to the questioning and elimination of hypotheses not just on empirical grounds, for testing is sometimes impossible, but on analytical, common-sense, intuitive grounds. This he called "retroduction". He did not attach a great deal of value to trial and error and testing, for testing may suggest a fault, but it cannot provide a better theory. (Burton, 1990b, pp. 19–20)

Given attitudes to the nature of social science prevalent for decades as Burton's work developed, it is not hard to see why Peirce was not taken much notice of: the watchwords then were rigour, testing and empiricism. Yet Peirce is now receiving serious attention in the context of dis-cussions pertaining to contemporary thought, science and postmodern debates. Brent has written a biography (Brent, 1993), Lechte identifies him as one of fifty key contemporary thinkers (remarkable for a man who wrote thousands of pages of work but never saw a book of his published in his own lifetime) and sees him as 'the father of a non-positive semiotics' (Lechte, 1994, p. 148), and a recent discussion of the founders of constructive postmodern philosophy sees a particularly significant engagement with his work (Griffin *et al.*, 1993). Earlier discussions of Peirce are to be found in Magee (1987), Honderich (1995) and Gallie (1952). A. Flew suggests that Peirce 'points out the practical difference between belief and doubt: the former is action guiding, the latter stimu-lates enquiry in the struggle to attain belief. Disagreement over the definition of "truth" in William James' work led Peirce to name his own theory "pragmaticism"' (Flew, 1979, p. 245).

Of Peirce, Burton has this to say – at greater length – and clearly allies his own position with that of Peirce, most usually identified (when he is labelled) as a pioneer of American pragmatist philosophy:

> Being analytical, questioning assumptions, seeking clarity of language and concepts, implies the possibility of breaking away from established patterns of thought. For many this is uncomfortable and even dangerous in political affairs, yet the crucial task of preserving and

promoting human values and appropriate institutions cannot be achieved by thought systems and policies that do not take into account all the variable that are relevant. A simplistic or reductionist approach to politics is necessarily destructive of the basic goals of persons and societies.

It was for these reasons that...interest in the posthumous works of Peirce...exploded. He had advocated 'abduction' which means, essentially, to make sure that the original hypothesis reflects all knowledge and experience available. He called it 'critical common sensism'. This contradicted prevailing beliefs that the original hypothesis was a matter merely of personal choice, and that the testing or falsifying process was the essence of science. (Burton, 1990b, p. 256)

Burton's discovery and critical engagement with Peirce is hardly accidental. There is a remarkable conjunction of interest here. Incidentally, it was interesting that W. B. Gallie involved himself in the study of Peirce, even more interesting that he could say of Peirce, more than fifty years ago, 'none of the [foregoing] suffices to explain why Peirce, almost alone among the philosopher-scientists of his age, was able to break away so completely from the restricting influences of the classic Newtonian world picture. And part of the explanation of this fact would seem to be that Peirce possessed an alternative picture of his own' (Gallie, 1952, p. 233). Is it really too presumptuous to assume that, in the light of this observation (almost certainly unknown to him), Burton might, had he encountered Peirce, have found a kindred spirit in him, whom he described as 'a self-employed intellectual, son of a Harvard mathematics professor' (Burton, 1984, p. 22)? In one sense, Burton pre-dated the postmodernists and distanced himself from the enlightenment tradition. These statements need a fuller examination.

By suggesting that he pre-dated the postmodernists, what is being argued is that he found fault with the conventional wisdom as embodied in the traditions of disciplines and established frameworks of explanation. But he did not then detach himself, to the extent that nothing seemed to make sense and that it was, at worst, all about words, meaning, signs and language, with all that this heralded in terms of a descent into endless relativism. To be imprecise and unsure about some things did not mean that we were unable to understand *anything*. In pursuit of an appropriate methodological foundation, Burton never lost sight of the problem – the social pathology of human societies that produced conflict. In that, he was at one with Peirce in being located within the traditions of pragmatism, and a survey of his work shows that, when it came to questions of method, he was pragmatic – he used what he saw when he thought that it was useful, and discarded it when it was not. He was always methodologically self-aware, but did not truly engage the logic of detachment associated with the idea of Enlightenment science.

J. Dryzek has a relevant observation to make here in terms of a discussion of what he calls discursive democracy, which resonates with what Burton has to say with regard to changes in institutions and structures in relation to felt needs. Dryzek suggests that the legacy of the Enlightenment is a problem in so far as intellectual debates and the nature of modern democracy are discussed in terms of rationality and objectivity, where, since the Enlightenment, rationality has come to demand two things:

> the first is effective instrumental action; instrumental rationality may be defined in terms of the capacity to devise, select and effect good means to clarified ends. The second is the idea that rational choices concerning theories and beliefs about matters of fact, and even about values and morals, should be made through reference to a set of objective standards equally applicable – and accessible – to all individuals. This second aspect of post-Enlightenment rationality is generally referred to as objectivism. (Dryzek, 1990, pp. 3–4)

For Burton, this is surely a sign of the emergence of a critical literature, directed explicitly at established modes of thought, and limitations that inhere in them. In this sense, then, the idea of 'provention' is less an individualist creation of an iconoclast and more a symptom of a developing critique, part of which is the articulation of new concepts and terms designed to take debates forward and engage new ideas of social interactions and 'realities'. Alongside Burton's 'provention' we might also set Kenneth Boulding's 'ecodynamics' and 'human betterment', E. O. Wilson's 'consilience' and Galtung's 'structural violence'. In relation to this last term, when first introduced by Galtung, this seemed like an unnecessary neologism, but it is now a standard part of the lexicon used to explain conflict and societies.

Undoubtedly, provention is the summation and encapsulation of the elements of Burton's schlolarly agenda, which has been shown to last. Some things he abandoned along the way, but the search was not 'for' provention: this in itself was not the holy grail, and there never was a 'Burtonian project'. What he sought was an alternative, motivated by an inability and unwillingness to live within and by reference to the dominant modes of conventional thought, and associated practices.

There was something out there to be found which was capable of explaining what was wrong, and how it could be put right. He did not know what it was, where it was, nor how to get at it. That he did get it is the thread that runs, one hopes at any rate, through much of the preceding account.

In the next chapter, the argument for a consideration of provention is made in the light of the nature of contemporary problems. But, at this point, what does provention amount to?

At its centre is the idea of needs. They are presumed to exist, by reference to the existence of human beings in interaction. We cannot prove what they are, in terms of a definitive list, but we can surmise that they amount to some things that are important constituents of being human, rather than a mere object or inert, insensate thing, and we can do this by inference. The existence of human needs that are not being satisfied may be evidenced by reference to the existence, persistence and apparent insolubility of human conflicts, which seem to get worse rather than better, apparent examples of 'progress' notwithstanding. Conflict is not being resolved because it is not understood when viewed from the perspective of the requirements of systems of power and authority, which should exist to serve the needs and aspirations of human beings. Much political philosophy and practice reverses this line of argument, putting system requirements first. Thus there are pressures on structures and systems, and where control mechanisms are inadequate, or indeed adequate in only one perspective, conflict results, and it is frequently violent conflict. The root of conflict is the human being, not structures of power, authority or obedience.

In this sense, therefore, provention is at one and the same time a theory of general social systems and a reconstruction of political philosophy, constructed not in terms of contestable rights, 'oughts', obligations and the like, but rather in the ontologically rooted requirements of human beings, expressed positively in terms of what it is they need – and what price they are prepared to pay to ensure that they are noticed, heeded, recognised and so on. The philosophy rests on the indirectly-verifiable idea that the existence of unfulfilled needs can be measured by reference to the presence of what can be observed – war, conflict and dissent – which behaviours are deemed to have causes rather than occurring randomly. In this sense, provention rooted in the observation of behaviour – construed in the manner of Burton – is a promise of improvement on the limitations of established discourse and practice, established political philosophy and the pitfalls of postmodernist discourse. These are removed from actually experienced life-conditions and there is no promise of an engagement with those conditions. Provention is thus aimed at a direct engagement with actually experienced problems, and their solutions. There is no desired end-state, only open-ended adaptation as needs are expressed and systems change, as they must. The history of human development is the history of change, yet our understanding of the nature, meaning and significance of change is relatively poor, given our other claims to knowledge. That much, and much of the foregoing, is pretty much self-evident from a Burtonian perspective. Yet it is not so straightforward.

Rather fittingly, perhaps, Burton concludes *Resolution and Provention* with a quotation from Michael Banks:

> the slow and weak progress of conflict resolution is due mainly to the obstruction of the status quo ideology. That ideology has produced a theory that explains politics 'scientifically' and justifies them empirically. We call for a paradigm shift. The difficulty is that while the forces of the status quo *do* have a paradigm, and it must be removed before we can progress, we do not have what appears to them to be a satisfactory alternative. I suspect that the new paradigm will not be seen until *after* the old one has gone, or at least has been discredited. That could be too late! The challenge is to produce an acceptable alternative even while the status quo ideology still exists. (Burton, 1990b, p. 277)

The costs associated with adherence to the status quo ideologies are identified as a possible means to effect change and receive attention in two subsequent short works, though the discussion here is brief, even cryptic, and hints at more than is delivered.

Conflict Resolution: Its Languages and Processes appeared in 1996 and *Violence Explained* in 1997 (Burton, 1996a, 1997). By the time the second of these was published, Burton was eighty-two years old, still writing, still driven, still articulating an alternative. *Conflict Resolution* was written as an introductory text and the first part is written in the form of an A to Z, the language component. It can be read as the skeleton of the work we have subsumed here under the label of provention. The first entry is 'abduction' and there are, for example, entries on 'alternative dispute resolution', 'behaviour', 'holism' (which 'is not necessarily less "scientific" or reliable. On the contrary . . . its analysis of a total situation can be more reliable. This is because it is deductive, relying on adequate theories of behaviour rather than relying only on empirical data for its explanations and analyses') (Burton, 1996a, p. 30), and 'right/wrong' (conceptions of which prevail within a power or legal frame: 'The concepts relate to morality. Therefore they must be treated as cultural') (p. 40); 'rights' (which 'implies treatment consistent with justice or orderly arrangements. It is therefore a cultural term') (p. 40); 'security' (whose 'general political use is in reference to military security. In conflict resolution the term is intended to signify the guarantee of satisfaction of human needs, now and in the future') (p. 41).

The second part of the book sets in context rules relating to the processes of conflict resolution, with a set of rules after the form of those set out in the *Handbook* of 1987 and the resumé of them presented in *Conflict: Practices in Management, Settlement and Resolution* (Burton and Dukes, 1990b). The importance of these rules is specified; they 'must be deduced from, and be in accord with the theoretical framework of conflict resolution. Their precise nature also emerges out of experience. Although the evolution of theory and experience with the process will lead to changes in the rules, departing from them for reasons of temporary expediency is risky and cannot be justified' (Burton, 1996a, p. 46).

The second of these works is rather symptomatic of the shift in Burton's perspective over the years; violence is to be explained, at all levels: 'There is an international system, but it is one of many' he argued to Northedge in 1974: as if to make the point again, he does it with more facility, because among the book's eighteen chapters, the 'international system' attracts explicit attention in only one. In the Introduction to the work, Vivienne Jabri describes it as an updated version of *Deviance, Terrorism and War* (Burton, 1979). It is and it is not. It is in the sense that *Deviance, Terrorism and War* marked the ontological break in Burton's work, so that the period since then has been one of refinement and articulation rather than re-discovery; after that point, Burton always seemed to be writing with more confidence and authority; he knew what he was about and, more to the point, what the problem was about too. Yet this later work is not simply an update of *Deviance, Terrorism and War* if, by that term, we were to mean a mere restatement. It is an appropriate restatement in a more confident form of much of what was being addressed in the earlier work, though restated here for a wider audience and with more general application. In that sense it is a more confident distillation, rather than an update – not entirely novel, to be sure, but certainly not dated or apologetic. It takes the issues out to a wider public, to a rather less esoteric debate, and a closer involvement with the processes of education and a new consensus. Yet the real problems with these works is that they display all the allied strengths and faults that inhere in Burton's work: they relate to the question not of substance but of style. There really is a need for the argument to be spelt out, with a view to a further enunciation of the more subtle nuances involved, not merely with the statement of an issue, theme or point, but some – at least – of the implications that follow from it and how Burton sees them. At the very least, taking a constructive view here, this sets out the agenda for a fuller explication of the detailed construction, implications and implementation of provention. In other words, where we are now, where Burton has brought us, is to the end of the beginning. That is not to belittle the nature and meaning of provention: it is consistent with the path of Rosenau's 'frontiersman': he sets out a path to how to get from where we are to where we want to be: an appreciation of the details and subtleties of the landscape can await those who follow. Those who are driven, are driven by the compulsion to find a goal, and are seeking a path where none previously existed. A new path can turn into a well-trodden new direction, where there is a mix of promise and new direction out of a problem-ridden landscape.

In *Conflict: Resolution and Provention* Burton states:

> protest against the present, which is a virtually universal and continuing phenomenon, does not necessarily include a recipe for the future. All systems, authoritarian and democratic, are facing insurmountable problems and are, as a consequence, being challenged... Ultimately, however, the problem of conflict, its resolution and provention, comes down to the need for a paradigm shift from a power to a problem-solving framework and this means that it is a problem of education...finally education leading to a popular consensus. (Burton, 1990b, p. 260)

This desired state of affairs is still a long way off, though there have been significant strides made in peace thinking, peace education and the acquisition of conflict resolution skills. Yet a survey of the present, to which we now turn, reveals that the accumulated practical consequences of acting within a traditional and 'conventional' frame of reference are far from benign, perhaps leading to an evaluation of current practice which could reveal not only the limitation of those practices but also the attractiveness of a shift towards alternative frameworks, such as 'provention'. In due course, provention could become just another word in the language of a new politics. Peirce needed to invent 'pragmaticism' because no other word would suffice, and Burton, with 'provention', followed suit.

7
On the Need for – and Relevance of – Provention

The manifest persistence of deep-seated social problems would seem, even on a cursory reading, to make the case for a new political philosophy, provention. After all, if we knew enough (on the basis of several thousand years of accumulated experience, wisdom and 'knowledge'), why are there so many problems that we seem to be able to manage, at best? The best defence we seem to be able to muster is that we are doing the best we can in the times we face and that, like Tom Paine, we can find solace only in the notion that 'these are the times that try men's souls' (*Oxford Dictionary of Quotations*, 1971, p. 160).

There can be little doubt that the world after the end of the Cold War has hardly turned out to be the much-anticipated New World Order. Why is this? It may be a strange concatenation of circumstances – or the result of poor leadership. Or, more fundamentally, it may be because the underlying assumptions – rooted in past history, system performance and structures, and relevant performance criteria, are now rendered erroneous. It may be that, according to these entrenched assumptions, the perceptions of the problems are such that they cannot be solved according to current operating principles. This is worthy of further discussion before we move to a consideration of what Burton sees as a new political philosophy. We should be in no doubt: what Burton suggests in the light of provention is that the very foundations of politics be reconstructed. As he has argued consistently over decades, we have got it wrong, and we make wrong definitions of the situation. He challenges the very notion of what politics is all about. An entrenched view is that politics is the art of the possible. But this in itself confuses the issue, for what is possible is a political assumption. In this logic, we do our best 'in the circumstances' as we find them, and manage the problem. Deals are done, negotiations concluded, differences are split (or recognised) and systems of order enforced – or resisted. But the problems are not solved, and conflicts are not resolved. And, often, the harder we try, the worse things seems to get. The record, to which we now turn, is in fact the accumulation (and, at best, limited amelioration) of social 'bads'. It may be that what is required is a politics appropriate to the twenty-first century, not a politics rooted in traditional assumptions about the nature of humankind, society and politics.

The Westphalian system was a response to the chaos and disorder that was typical of the Thirty Years' War in Europe. During the three decades after 1618, Europe was marked by instability and conflict, centred principally around the notions of order and authority. Religious and secular claims to authority were contested and gave rise to much bloody conflict, and in the course of those three decades Europeans were killed in their millions. People, and even whole towns and villages, disappeared from the map of Europe. Among many other issues on the agenda of the assembly in Westphalia, one major question confronted those who sought to establish order after 1648: How was it to be restored and, once restored, made to last? Two major considerations emanated from the Westphalian settlement, with a necessary corollary. First, it was accepted – and recognised (the principle of recognition being acknowledged as central to the operation of a states system) – that the authorities had an established right to rule within a given territory. Thus was the principle of sovereignty established. Authority was established in a given territory. Second, the idea was established that the recognition of the right to rule also established the recognition of the authority inhering in territoriality: the right to rule in a given place. And the necessary corollary was the recognition of the idea of non-intervention. Essentially, what it amounted to was a code of conduct: I recognise your right to rule in your territory; you recognise my right to rule in mine and, consequently, we do not contest the right to rule in the territory of the other – hence the rule of non-intervention, which obtained in the operation of the system of states. Above all it was a system of states which helped themselves. Beyond the state there was no authority: thus it was a self-help system, devoid of central authority, where the members of the system took it upon themselves to pursue their own interests as they saw fit. War was not outlawed, but was deemed to be a legitimate and legally-defined right of states. In response to the excesses of the Thirty Years' War, there were certain restraints on war (with respect to an emergent set of 'rules of the game' as understood and applied by the European states), so that, though wars were not bloodless, they were more likely to be wars of position, often limited by weather or season.

That Napoleon took his French troops to the gates of Moscow in 1812 is ample testimony to the aims of the French: they sought to overturn the old order, domestically and internationally. That they did not prevail is only part of the story, for what also happened in the period 1770–1820 was that, in effect, the very bases of social and political life were challenged; the basis of the system persisted in principle, but the fundamentals were challenged in practice. Principally, political systems became more subject to ideological, as opposed to dynastic, limits; the will of the king gave way to the will of the people. Nationalism, the will of the people and the essence of nationalism replaced established notions of elitist politics. Restraint and common interest gave way to political will and contested grounds of political authority. Wars were subject more to the limits of technology than to the restraints of law and ethics. Politics seemed more to determine the limits of war rather than the reverse. In short, events outran assumptions; and dynamics challenged control.

This was the age of steam and manufactures; the shift to cities from towns, wherein were sown the seeds of mass and urban society. It was the age of Byron, the Shelleys, Wordsworth, Godwin and Wollstonecraft, Goethe, Tom Paine, Jefferson, Beethoven and Marx. The nature of man, woman, time, space and society were at issue, and the debates and processes that they assisted in starting, or which they sought to influence, gave rise to the major debates of the nineteenth century, the century of the great 'isms' – capitalism, socialism, liberalism, anarchism, and Communism among them – that so dominated the development of political, social and intellectual debate for a century or more. (It is worth saying, again – and at the risk of repetition, that so much of the traditional agenda of International Relations scholarship misses the implications of the wider agenda.) In short, the wider context within which the Westphalian system was to operate was altering radically, with consequences for the conduct of that system, not least with regard to the nature and function of war as an instrument of policy. As the centuries moved on, what was the continued utility and validity of 'Westphalia'? Not just as a reference point in the historical development of the states-system, but as an indication of guiding principles and foundational assumptions of the very system itself? By reference to which we can turn to two or three major indicators: namely, war, peace and welfare.

Curiously, the century that separated 1815 from 1914 came to be known, in the conventional wisdom of international politics, as the 'century of peace', not because it was free from conflict, but because a war between the great powers of the day was avoided. Of course, there were wars and there were tensions, often associated with the development of empires in Asia, Africa and elsewhere. Agadir and Fashoda stand as useful examples. There were also major changes in technology that served to effect large changes in the conduct of war, though many of them were ignored. There were lessons to be learned from the American Civil War, but many went unheeded, especially in Europe.

But how was it that an assassination in Sarajevo precipitated the unfolding of events such that, within weeks, the major powers of the day were locked in full-scale war? What happened was that interlocking alliances, tied together by express or implied security guarantees, did not work in so far as threats to use force were insufficient to prevent war. Security guarantees, once called into effect, were at the heart of the process of turning an incident into a war of colossal dimensions and impact. And when the states did resort to war, there was a fundamental mismatch between assumptions about the nature of warfare and its actual conduct. Men marched to war, many optimistically viewing the war as an adventure, soon to be over.

The First World War represents a defining moment in modern world history. It changed many countries and it changed attitudes: to society, to leadership, to fate and fatalism, to life and to death. On the first day of the Battle of the Somme, 1 July 1916, the British sustained 60,000 casualties, 20,000 of them losing their lives. By the time the 'battle' ended in November, more than a million casualties had been sustained by the British, French and German forces, and the front had moved approximately five miles. The war gave rise to war memorials in towns, cities and hamlets across the globe, but especially in Europe . Beyond this, it influenced art, literature, cinema and much else besides. Arguably, it was a prelude to the literary, philosophical and cultural movement widely known as 'modernism', in so far as it redefined the nature of the relationship between society and the individual, loyalty and the state. Yet the war also changed the nature of war itself, for now (with the advent of the airship, aeroplane and the tank) societies themselves were vulnerable, not just the clearly-defined combatants. Furthermore, what was the nature of the moral distinction between men at the front and women at the rear when the women made shells for the men to fire at the enemy; were not they also legitimate targets in war?

But it did not prove to be the war to end all wars. Arguably, the causes of the Second World War are to be found in the settlement of the First. This much is well-known. But the more important, lasting, point is that war within a system of Westphalian assumptions is one thing, given certain assumptions about society and politics. But war within a

Westphalian system where ideologically committed and opposed societies (and industrial societies at that) are pitted against each other in wars of attrition, is quite another. Warfare becomes less decisive, more destructive, less discriminate, longer in duration and acts as an instrument of social change. Principles and practice do not fit easily. It is said that there were those in the First World War who argued that, given the relative casualty rates, by the time all the Germans were dead, some British would be left, thus the British would have won. The mismatch between Westphalian principles and practice was to be thrown into even more stark relief.

The Second World War was, similarly, a total war, only more so. Millions were killed, many in their own homes, by bombs dropped from aircraft, in firestorm raids and, at the last, by atomic bombs . And so was ushered in the nuclear age, allowing a single bomber to effect destruction more efficiently than a thousand bombers just months before. The atomic bomb represented a technical threshold, but it is as well to remember the destruction of Berlin, Dresden and Tokyo that preceded it. The evidence as to the utility of strategic bombing was inconclusive (though proponents of bombing argued that it would be decisive). Attitudes were also sometimes rather odd. Winston Churchill argued that the bombing of the Germans would weaken their will to fight, while also arguing that the bombing of Britain by Germany would stiffen British resolve. A strange, but significant, approach to 'otherness'.

But the atomic bomb paved the way for nuclear deterrence, and that in itself saw a change of assumptions of immense proportions and consequences. There are many books on the development of the Cold War and nuclear deterrence, and no synopsis will be attempted here. However, we need to confront one of the major features of the nuclear age; namely, the proliferation of something in the region of 50,000 nuclear devices, sufficient to kill every person on the planet ten times over, all in pursuit of what some called 'strategic stability' and others called 'peace'. What we do not know is whether nuclear threats in fact deterred; many assumed that the existence of nuclear weapons, and an apparent American willingness to use them in defence of its European allies, had deterred the Soviet Union from attacking western Europe. That the Japanese surrendered as they did seemed to validate the logic of bombing. That the Soviet Union stayed put and then collapsed seemed to validate the assumptions of many strategists, that deterrence deters.

Yet many of the strategies developed as a means to an end seemed to assume a curious logic, but one that seemed to contravene common sense. City swapping, mutual assured destruction and the like seemed to take politics into a surreal realm, with 'acceptable' levels of casualties reckoned in millions, and the deaths of civilians reckoned as 'collateral damage'. Pilots approaching an area with a view to bombing 'ingressed into the target area', in hopes of effecting a 'surgical air strike'. Now the very language of war and conflict was removed from common parlance. By the 1980s, in the United States, schemes were piloted to test the feasibility of underground tunnels, missiles on sleds, breakout technology and the like, as well as a rather sophisticated version of the shell-game, where the Soviet Union would almost be invited to guess which silo was filled with a missile and take a chance on targeting the right one. Millions of dollars were spent on such schemes. And as the numbers of nuclear weapons proliferated, so did the chances of accidental nuclear war increase. With the demise of the Cold War come revelations that the world came closer to nuclear catastrophe than was ever reported at the time, with weapons ready to be armed on runways, exercises seeming to be preludes to nuclear attack, flocks of geese seeming to be, on a radar screen, missiles. All of this was to prevent nuclear war, ensure stability and enhance the prospects of 'peace'. Yet it was a peace that rested, by its very nature, on the very edge of destruction and demanded of rational leaders that they make clear that they would be prepared to act irrationally if need be, risking the destruction of much of the population to whom they were constitutionally responsible. The aim was deterrence, and if weapons were used, then it was argued that the military had failed in their primary role, that of maintaining deterrence.

One of the most persistent of assumptions has related to the nature of security. Presumably, at some stage in the development of human societies, there was ample justification for the notion that politics was about the struggle for scarce resources, whether this be land, water, animals and, later, other resources. Above all, groups and societies sought to be secure from the threat of disruption – by weather, climate or neighbours. The assumption developed that security was a scarce commodity, to be achieved at great cost and, having been achieved, to be safeguarded. It was a scarce commodity. This also led on to the notion that saw security in 'less and more' terms: more for my neighbour meant less for me. Hence the idea of what came to be known as 'zero-sum' approaches to security, and the related assumption that politics was about struggle between parties for the issues or resources that separated them. Ownership and property were also important.

In turn, as these assumptions became entrenched, means to the greater end of security were developed. Warrior classes led on to the development of armed forces, sometimes as a professional class and then, as we proceeded into the age of mass society and industrialisation, mass citizen armies armed and equipped by industries by then devoted to the purpose. Nationalism was a marked force in modern politics and it was assumed that nations were in competition. Empires were acquired by the major European states as their knowledge of, and control over, the rest of the world proceeded. Battle fleets were a consequent symbol, giving credence to world power and influence. By the time of the First World War, millions had been killed, and there were those who argued that if some Britons were left alive when all the Germans were dead, then victory would be Britain's: a curious manifestation of an essentially competitive view of security.

Nuclear war has been avoided, but 'hot wars' abounded during the period of the Cold War, and they persist despite the Cold War's end (a prime example being that involving Russia and Chechnya, as well as the conflict in the former Yugoslavia). As decolonisation proceeded apace, opportunities for Cold War interventions and proxy wars presented themselves. If the Soviet Union sought influence in a place, then, by an almost inexorable logic, the United States sought to establish a presence to match it. Often there were major arms transfers as well, thus fuelling conflicts.

Not all conflicts involved the United States and the Soviet Union, of course, as the end of colonialism spawned its own instabilities. When, in the nineteenth century, the Europeans drew their lines on maps of Africa, they created territories and separated tribes and groups. When, in the 1960s and after, these territories became independent, many were unstable, unable or incapable of making multi-tribal or multi-ethnic democracy work. Conflicts developed, then worsened, then persisted, with huge implications for the domestic populations (the distinction between combatants and non-combatants seemed to matter less and less; weapons seemed to be less discriminating, more inhumane – and lasting, so that, in Vietnam and Cambodia, there are thousands of people without limbs as a consequence of stepping on uncleared land-mines left from the war of the 1970s), famine and, in the longer term, debt.

The incidence of conflicts in poorer areas of the world helps to explain why development has been so difficult to achieve. But only partly so. Poorer countries have been locked into a system of dominance and dependence, and their official status of independence notwithstanding, they have been essentially 'unfree'. They have sought to exist in a world not of their own making, but one in which they must survive. Many have found this difficult. Subsistence agriculture has often been replaced with cash-crop strategies of development, but where this has failed, there have been major problems in terms of food supplies and appropriate strategies. A persistent image on television screens since the 1980s has been the image of stark poverty. These images have been similar, though varied, and persistent rather than isolated, indicating that poverty is endemic in the contemporary system of states. In order to develop, many states have adopted measures that appear to help in the short run, but which are questionable in the longer term. For example, many in India have resorted to cutting down trees for fuel, serving in the longer term to speed the run-off of rainwater, causing flooding and silting of rivers. Clearing of forests in South America has been pursued as a goal, but with measurably deleterious effects on the stability of the ecosphere. All are measures that seem rational and reasonable in the short term, but which have accumulated costs.

Of course, questions relating to the environment are not confined to poorer countries. Far from it, as many of the poor argue that pollution has been the product of the economic developments they seek, and which the industrialised states have achieved. There are problems related to acid rain, as a consequence of burning fossil fuels; waste disposal associated with the harnessing of nuclear energy; the environmental impact of oil exploration, extraction and transport; pollution associated with the development of large cities based on car transport; and the like. Mass tourism has changed the nature of tourist destinations, and the demand for more airports and runways often provokes opposition on the grounds of environmental impact and noise pollution. In the Gulf War of 1991, environmental damage was used as a weapon of war when oil wells were set alight.

All these activities have been part of modernisation, political and social development, arguably of the liberation of men and women from toil. But they are now consequential, and measurably so. We can measure the size, shape and location of the holes in the ozone layer. We can locate oil slicks from space, and we can measure the impact of species damage, by reference to the impact of pollution on the extended food chain. We can readily assess the impact of accumulated heavy metals that have flowed into the oceans of the world as states have used rivers as outlets for waste. And fish are at risk from chemicals where they are not at risk from overfishing. These activities represent the accumulated long-term consequences of industrial activity since about 1760. Which is to make the point that, in little over 200 years, we have accumulated serious environmental problems, sometimes by accident, but principally by simply being industrial and exploitative of resources, consistent with the goals of industry and economic development. The accumulated consequences are system-wide and there are serious questions as to whether inter-governmental procedures alone can solve the problems of environment. The controversial Hague Summit of 2000 showed in the starkest of detail the nature of the limitations of a state-centric approach to problem management. Manifestly, US negotiators sought to shift the burden of change on to others, preferring this to seeking to change American national norms and values. Presumably, acting within the logic of the traditional domestic–international dichotomy, part of the process of diplomacy is to defend 'national interests' (in this particular case the defence of the 'American way' as this relates to the automobile) and resist the imposition of change. A state cannot be compelled to accede to a convention, and it may withdraw at a time it, and it alone, thinks is appropriate. As his presidency proceeded, George W. Bush made it clear that the United States would defend its own interests first and foremost, and in the context of discussions and debates about National Missile Defence, Kyoto and energy development, the stance was described as one of 'US unilateralism' especially by those who found this a worrying development in a world said to be globalised and 'getting smaller'.

What is clear, however, is that the logic of Westphalia, whereby states can do as they wish in their own territory and also use the high seas as they see fit (to dispose of waste, test weapons, sink ships or oil platforms), cannot long persist if the oceans are to continue in reasonable condition over the longer term. There has emerged the notion that the oceans are the common heritage of mankind, but even despite this view, the dumping of a redundant oil-storage platform in the Atlantic was still a preferred option, backed by the British government, in 1995, until political pressure prompted a re-assessment. In Europe, British and Spanish fishermen stand opposed about rights of access to fish. And where fish are caught, many are thrown back into the sea – dead – because quotas do not permit them to be landed.

Industrial activity and underdevelopment, set side by side, reveal a situation where utilisation of global resources is massively skewed. The United States is a huge consumer of world energy, set beside the consumption of, for the sake of comparison, South America and Africa. The gap between rich and poor in global terms is widening, and the poor are becoming ever poorer not only in relative terms but also in absolute ones. The life chances of many in the Third World are poor.

Nor is this all. In fact, the logic of the Westphalian system, which acknowledges the general rule of non-intervention in the internal affairs of a state, effectively leaves many populations open to abuse by their own governments, in terms of imprisonment, torture and systematic abuse of human rights. In the 1970s, the Soviet authorities imprisoned dissidents or classified them as insane and locked them in hospitals, instructing others not to interfere in the affairs of the Soviet Union when questions were raised about the Soviet record on human rights. The government of Iraq has in recent years altered the environment systematically in order to effect the enforced shift of the Marsh Arabs from their traditional habitat. Kurds have also been mistreated. The government of China, in the period leading up to the international women's conference of September 1995, executed criminals in order to 'clean up' ahead of the conference and to warn others to behave when the conference was under way.

In summary, a wider and more significant peace has not prevailed, and the agenda of international politics has widened and deepened. Many of the older approaches to politics and diplomacy are questionable in terms of their basis in logic and their efficacy in public policy. Indeed, the pursuit of peace through military victory has led to achievements that are almost surreal in their implications; indeed, costly and counter-productive in the longer term. The Americans bombed Vietnam repeatedly on the assumption that the Vietnamese would yield and then negotiate if they were not defeated. When this did not occur, they increased the bombing, again and again. When it became clear that they could not effect a jungle strategy, they sought to rid much of the country of jungle through a strategy of defoliation – then to discover the effects on human beings of the toxic chemicals used. The Americans left Vietnam having achieved 'peace with honour'; but all knew it to be defeat with dishonour, with lasting consequences for American society and the future conduct of American foreign policy.

To prevent the secession of Chechnya, in 1995, Russian troops fought Chechen forces and many were killed on both sides. The city of Grozny, along with other towns, was systematically destroyed in the process, as a conscious policy. In so doing, both sides expended resources they could scarcely afford, caused enormous damage and destruction that will need to be rebuilt, and created even more animosity than existed prior to the violence. The Chechens were 'defeated', though mindful of the sacrifices made in the struggle, restored to the place deemed appropriate for them by the Russians but hardly restored to a state of peace and harmony. And then there followed the Second Chechen War in October 1999. Whether this is an appropriate approach to the resolution of conflict is questionable in the extreme. Compliance in the face of coercion is notoriously inefficient as an approach to dealing with others. Which, in turn, highlights the fundamental differences between conflict settlement based on 'hard bargaining' and deep-seated conflict resolution, which seeks not to settle apparent differences but rather to address fundamental issues at the centre of conflict.

Where many people argue that the supreme achievement of international conduct during the twentieth century was the achievement of peace, it has proven to be a curious peace; one that rested on the threat to devastate others, and where the risks of accidental nuclear war were significant. Moreover, it has been a partial peace, in so far as some have 'enjoyed' peace through deterrence, while others have experienced wars. Peace has been at best partial and at worst illusory. Millions have been involved and killed in wars despite a systemic characteristic, according to the conventional wisdom, of peace. The utility of threats is questionable, and the achievements of resorting to violence equally so. European powers sought to retain power in colonies through force in many cases and, as costs accumulated, they ceded power to those with whom they said they would never negotiate – until they did. On the presumption that deterrence deters, vast nuclear arsenals were developed. On the basis that 'my enemy's enemy is my friend', states were armed, only to later use the arms against their suppliers, as was the case in Iraq. When Iran was the enemy, Iraq was armed as a friend of the West, with well-known consequences.

In sum, the achievements of international political conduct in the twentieth century were uneven and, in the case of many of them, open to question. Hugely significant wars designed and fought to prevent the rise of Germany and Japan need to be set against the political agenda of the 1990s, where Germany and Japan are, in economic terms, great powers, arguably with great political potential, possibly looking to seats on a restructured United Nations Security Council. Mistrust and misperception played a role in the development and perpetuation of the Cold War. A structure of nuclear deterrence aimed at peace was a peace that rested on the edge of destruction of the human race, if deterrence failed; where armed forces often argued that, as in the case of the US Strategic Air Command, 'peace is our profession'; and where a test of their utility was their ability to maintain a nuclear peace while being prepared (and willing, if necessary) to fight a nuclear war. By the 1990s, it became clear that both the United States and the Soviet Union had raced to develop nuclear weapons, often without regard to the accumulated costs. The collapse of the Soviet Union revealed the accumulation of nuclear waste problems, catalogues of nuclear accidents, no procedures for the safe dismantling of nuclear weapons and so on. In the United States, decommissioning of military bases must wait until their rehabilitation to a safe condition, which will take decades, and, where this is not possible, for the foreseeable future certain areas have been designated as 'national sacrifice zones'.

It may be, of course, that many of these accumulated consequences might have been avoided with better leadership, vision and planning. Arguably, there is some merit in this view. But so too is there merit in the view that the question is not primarily a question of leadership but of logic, the logical framework underlying the conduct of international politics. The problem, at base, is in the nature of the assumptions that are brought to bear in a world of states, devoid of central authority, dating from the seventeenth century. The assumptions are 'me first' in the time span of the 'here and now'. It is a self-help system. There is no higher authority. States do reserve the right to go to war, often regardless of its changing nature and ignorant of how, having got into a war, they might extricate themselves when it becomes clear that they cannot 'win'. Governments owe their primary obligations to their own citizens, and it is not clear that they are aware of any obligation to those beyond their own frontiers; even when they are, it is only when their interests coincide. Governments, in the nature of politics, are subject to sanction, electoral or otherwise, and work in a short-run time perspective. It is an oft-repeated, but valid, observation that practitioners envy academics the luxury of the long-term perspective. In the logic of international politics that is Westphalia, states are concerned with the attainment of order and, having attained it, seeking its continuation. As the logic would have it, given order or disorder, the goal is order. If the order is just, so much the better, but first there must be order. And in so far as there is a concern for order, it must be stable. Yet the very context of inter-state activity is that it is a context marked by constant change – in technology, values, communication, language and so on.

What is at issue, therefore, is the appropriateness of essentially seventeenth-century assumptions as we enter the twenty-first century. It is a matter of striking contrast that in so many areas of human activity we have made enormous progress not only in knowledge but also in conduct since the seventeenth century, yet we have made so little progress in international politics. Of course, we have survived as the human race and have, thus far, saved ourselves from nuclear disaster. But we are now aware of the accumulation of social disbenefits. These are not accidental accumulations: they are the direct and consequential products of our conduct of inter-state activity within a given frame of reference. If states are free to dump waste at sea, or put smoke into the environment, they will. If nobody wants to go in and solve the problems in Bosnia, nobody does. There is no state-logic imperative that any other state should, or must, though there may be a moral frame of reference. If a state wants to do only one particular thing and not what others want of it, then that is all that it does. It may bow to pressure – or not.

Mention has already been made with regard to problems of domestic systems by reference to Iraq, China and Russia. Yet the problems of domestic political systems go beyond these spectacular cases. Indeed, there are deep-seated problems in democracies that deemed to be, on one reading, secure and stable. On closer inspection, there are systemic faults in countries such as the United States and the United Kingdom. In both, crime is a real and widespread social problem. Many states in the United States have reintroduced capital punishment in recent years as a response to the perceived problem of violent crime. In the United Kingdom, there are repeated calls for 'stiffer sentences', 'short, sharp shocks', 'boot camp' for young offenders, and more prisons. It is argued frequently that if people will not willingly do as they are told, they must be made to do so. Discipline is an issue, car theft increasing, and crimes against persons and property increasing. In Britain, the theft of mobile telephones has increased five-fold in two years. Yet there is also evidence that offenders are not deterred by the threat of incarceration. Very many (the majority?) of those who receive custodial sentences and probation go on to re-offend. Prison is deemed to be not so much a deterrent as an occupational hazard. From some statistics, the United States has the largest prison population in the world, a disproportionate number of whom are from ethnic minorities.

Why, it might be asked, should criminals and the dispossessed respect a society that does not respect *them*, which relegates them to the status of the marginalised – that statistic, the 'long-term unemployed', many of whom after a time cease to be employable, often because they have turned to drugs? What is the relevance of societal norms? In the context of a 'me-first' society, why look to the interests of others? The unemployed and unemployable have looked for work and found none, exhausted available training schemes and still not found work, and thus experienced a loss of status and self-esteem, indeed often social marginalisation. The short-term route to status, esteem and wealth may then be car theft and petty crime, mugging, bullying and the like. In many areas of advanced industrial society, sections of that society have opted out. They cease to register to vote, they do not vote and they live within their own defined sub-system – with their own norms, language and code of conduct. More to the point, these norms may relate to theft, crime, killing and the crossing of sub-cultural norms of violence. Many black people in the United States have effectively detached themselves from the political system – which means that they have different norms, values and ethics, and language – as well as important and violent systems of rites of passage and belonging. And this is not a problem confined to the United States. We need also to look at the experiences of ethnic communities in, for example, France, the Netherlands and the United Kingdom, to see the problems of latent and overt racism and violence.

In the face of these problems, politics often tends to take a backward turn. When the country was in economic difficulties, Ronald Reagan reminded Americans of the days when they 'rode tall in the saddle', when nobody 'pushed them around', and Americans were proud. This mood stimulated a defence-led boom, which was at the heart of the deficit problem that preoccupied much of the Clinton presidency – and the cutting back of which hit welfare and social development programmes. In Britain, Margaret Thatcher (who argued that there was no such thing as society, only people and their families) and her successor, John Major, yearned for a return to 'traditional values', when family mattered and England was typified by having a beer on the village green, to the sound of leather on willow. Most people never knew these values, and they are beyond the comprehension of many now.

More widespread is a disaffection with economic and political systems. Leaders are often not trusted, and even where they are trusted they are often not respected, seeming to be self-serving rather than serving the community at large: 'Britain's democratic system needs to be re-established. Popular disenchantment with the political process, particularly amongst the young, is at an all-time high. Politicians are seen as untrustworthy and venal, while the system is viewed as remote and irrelevant' (*New Statesman*, 18 August 1995, p. 5). Much was made of the controversial presidential election in the United States in November 2000. The nation, it was said, was split, represented by the closeness of the presidential race, the 50–50 split in the Senate and almost a similar split in the House of Representatives. This would be a significant problem in itself. More significant is the fact that only marginally more than half of the electorate in fact voted: just 51 per cent. The candidate, George W. Bush, found this, without irony, to be impressive. This was not entirely a question of ethnic minorities, but was a part of it. The significance lies in the observation that a huge proportion of the population manifestly felt ill-served by the political system.

Undoubtedly, television has changed the form as well as the content of politics. In the era of television, politics is reduced to the sound-bite rather than extended political debate and discourse; and it is political theatre in some cases. In Britain, the political meeting has given way to the photo-opportunity, with sites selected well before elections are called. Presentation is all-important, the 'spin-doctor' a new player in the political game. A simple statement often repeated is, for many, what politics has come to symbolise. Why? Because more and more people feel that political systems do not serve them. Nor is this the view only of the deprived underclasses. In the United Kingdom, many people – very clearly middle-class – are disaffected, are uncomfortable, indeed insecure. They cope with fear of crime and the burden of debt, and seem to be more sceptical about the political realm; perhaps, indeed, mistrustful of politicians. Membership of political parties is falling. In short, there is a disaffection with politics, which is a problem in itself. In many states, where people are disaffected with party politics they are involved to the extent that they can themselves participate in single-issue politics, such as welfare, environment and development issues. (In Britain, the membership of the Royal Society for the Protection of Birds is now approaching a million – greater than the combined membership of the Conservative, Labour and Liberal Democratic parties.) Most significantly, these are deemed to be more relevant as approaches to politics, where people feel involved and capable of doing something.

But in the longer term and the wider perspective there is a significant process of detachment from the extended civil society, in practice or in prospect. This is especially true where there are divisions along ethnic lines, where identifiable groups feel that the system that serves the majority does not, because it cannot, serve them as an identifiable minority, and even where it does so, it does not seem as if it serves them fairly. There are many instances of these circumstances – whether in Northern Ireland, Cyprus, Turkey, Sri Lanka, Canada or Spain. If this is the case, then we need to re-examine the basis of democracy to ensure that it can cope with currently-divided or segmented societies and ensure long-term participation of all, rather than some. How appropriate is democracy where ethnicity and cultural differences are evident and motive forces?

Another problem in much of the developed world is a increasing sense of insecurity within affluence. Conspicuous by their proliferation are security mechanisms, alarms (on cars and houses), fences and guard-dogs. Communities feeling insecure are retreating to fenced-off areas. There are advertisements for 'secure' retirement communities. There is a flight from cities to secure suburbs. There is a sense of security through privacy, shutting-off 'out there'. There are security guards in supermarkets and shopping centres. Closed-circuit television cameras are commonplace in streets, car-parks, schools and campuses. Along with 'private affluence and public squalor' (in Galbraith's famous phrase) come, now, private security and communal insecurity. Many do not go out at night, some have set limits on where they go, when and with whom. People engage with the world via television, and when this gets difficult, they switch off, or escape into fantasy via games or films. For many (the average American watches television for 28 hours per week), television is the route to vicarious engagement with 'otherness', with all that implies for the power of stereotyping of difference.

There is a widespread assumption that children are 'at risk' when they venture outside their homes, though there is much evidence also that they are at greater risk from those they know than from strangers. In Britain in 2000, concern about the placing of known paedophiles in the community led to demonstrations, violence and fears of groups taking their own punitive action. One response to this fear is that people now deliver their children to school by car, even over short distances, prompting concern not only with regard to the environmental impact of such practices, but also with regard to the impact of this on the processes of social interaction (or the lack of it) and the effects on child health.

In summary, it is clear that many of the structures and processes of domestic economics and politics have become more problematic. It is widely held that there is a crisis of faith, institutions and faith in institutions. Fundamentally, there is a sense that there is a crisis of legitimacy. More and more people seem to feel that politics is for others and not for them; that they must take to themselves the means to welfare and security, even where this involves them in breaking the law and turning to crime as an efficacious short-cut that, for many (it seems), is a new norm. The encounter with otherness is often perceived as a threat.

One of the fundamental changes in the world since 1945 has been the restructuring of the world economy. Old industries in traditional centres of affluence and wealth have gone, with the rise of new economies variously scattered across the globe. What is particularly evident is the extent to which this process of structural adjustment was unplanned, unpredicted and handled with great difficulty and at enormous social cost. Unemployment has become an international issue of immense proportions, widening definitions of security and raising questions about the relationships that link together citizens, states, welfare, jobs, training and society. Market forces are deemed to be important in this cumulative dynamic. But there are very clear accumulated costs in terms of social dislocation, and loss of identity and community. Often, scapegoating is a convenient, perhaps predictable, response. It may be an inappropriate response but it can give rise to conflict within and between societies. In such circumstances, for many, the traditional approaches to and patterns of politics seem to be confused and inappropriate. (Or, perversely, as in the case of Russia, the old order that was problematic now seems reassuring.) After a while, nobody cares, nobody seems in control, and nobody seems responsible for much. Decisions taken seem to run in the face of local common-sense experiences; where, for example, in Britain mines with significant reserves of coal have been closed down, ostensibly because there is no market, yet they later reopen and sell coal at a profit. There is a sense of accumulated problems, lack of identity and worth, loss of self and identity, and there is clear evidence that these responses are widespread and deeply felt in numerous areas.

And one of the traditional distinctions that has become increasingly hazy is the traditional one that separates international and domestic politics. Formerly, domestic politics were clearly territorial in nature, bounded by law and sovereignty. Foreign policy began at the country's edge, dealing with those 'out there', unlike ourselves by reason of identity, history, culture, language and experience. Where, now, is 'out there', as perceived from a former mining village in northern England, a former steel town in Pennsylvania, a rundown farm in Saskatchewan, a poor village in India, on an indigenous community in Africa? For many, the traditional relationships that bound community and society are long gone. The road from town or city hall to state or regional capital, via elected representatives and responsive electoral mechanisms exists no more. Employers may, ultimately, take decisions from thousands of miles away; profits may be repatriated to corporate headquarters in another country; and, where jobs do come, they may be accompanied by profoundly different cultural practices.

James Rosenau has much to say about this evident 'turbulence in world politics', arguing the case for the inclusion of individuals into the analysis, suggesting that

> most theories of world politics tend to underestimate, even ignore, the interplay of micro and macro dynamics and the many ways in which the coherence of national collectivities, the stability of inter-national structures and the composition of systemic agendas are linked to the activities of officials and citizens. To a very great extent, the prevailing approaches to the subject treat the micro level as a

constant, as if the skills and orientations of individuals somehow remained fixed and peripheral relative to the great changes wrought by technology and the requirements of interdependence in the nuclear age. (Rosenau, 1990, p. 25)

He continues with the observation that 'students of global politics have not begun to take account of the transformation at work within societies ... the dynamics of the post-industrial society tend to be taken for granted' (Rosenau, 1990, p. 17), while at the same time 'the prevailing orientation seems, rather, to presume that the basic structures and processes of international politics remain intact even as change swirls through the component parts' (Rosenau, 1990, p. 18). Can we be sure that this situation has improved in more than a decade since this was written?

In other words, there is a real need to shift the foundations of our knowing into a more appropriate mind-set, one that fits the world the way it is, however messy that may be, and however difficult the task. The problem we have is that the concepts, increasingly, do not fit. We need to innovate in order to improve.

Of Burton's *Conflict: Resolution and Provention* it was said that 'this is one of the early books of the twenty-first century ... Tackling the deep-rooted causes of conflict, as Burton insists we do, rather than treating its symptoms opens the door to a wide array of peaceful instruments humankind badly needs as we approach the third millennium' (Saunders, 1990). In the light of this cursory survey of the agenda of political concerns, it is clear that there are real problems related not only to questions of political performance but also with respect to the assumptions that underpin them. Burton seeks to innovate in order to improve. That there is a need to improve system performance is demonstrated in the discussion in this chapter. If this sounds over-pessimistic, Burton's judgement is even more severe because, as we shall see in the next chapter, the case for Burton's framework of provention to be taken seriously is evident, given what he calls 'civilisation in crisis'.

8
Conclusion

Martin Griffiths is surely right when he observes that 'Burton's works cannot be easily classified within the conventional frameworks of analysis in the study of international relations' and stresses that 'Burton has been a trenchant critic of the view that international relations can stand apart from other disciplines in the social sciences.' At the same time, Griffiths recognises that Burton has produced 'a unique corpus of work that continues to inspire students of world society today' (Griffiths, 1999 p. 109). That it cannot easily be classified – in a survey of fifty contemporary thinkers in International Relations, Griffiths places Burton at the head of the queue of 'Radical/Critical' thinkers, with Johan Galtung and Richard Falk, though there is no place for Kenneth Boulding – may help to explain the relative lack of engagement with much of Burton's work in some quarters. Yet it may be that Burton is being engaged in the light of the mounting problems of comprehension, taking on greater relevance in view of the problems besetting International Relations.

As International Relations moved forward from the 1960s, the period of positivism and empiricism receded, with some lasting influences, but it is also fair to say that much work was of an ephemeral nature, and often the 'debates' about theory and method generated more heat than light. What was changing was that the underlying state-centric paradigm was collapsing. Indeed, we can go so far as to say that International Relations is, even now, searching for a new paradigm to replace state-centricity. In saying as much, it seems that many of the discussions about the so-called 'inter-paradigm debate' in International Relations are misplaced, even missing the point: there is a significant proliferation of approaches, models and explanatory frameworks to explain the new concerns of the discipline. But at the same time there is clear evidence that work being done beyond the boundary of the discipline, as it were, is necessarily encroaching on to the traditional turf of International Relations. There is, therefore, trouble at the centre allied to trouble at the boundary, and there is, in fact, a search for a paradigm, not a debate about the merits of extant and proliferating paradigms: these proliferating schemes and interpretations, approaches even, are not paradigms but rather symptoms of the problems besetting International Relations as a discipline. States are still part of the subject. But the issue can be stated succinctly – 'states plus what other actors?' In other words, which other actors affect outcomes in order to shape and contribute to the dynamics of a subject that is searching not only for a new paradigm but also a newly constituted name that can embody its concerns accurately? World politics? World society? Global society? Global village? A planet 'getting smaller'? What we are seeking is a new paradigm that will inform the study of global social dynamics in the twenty-first century: the limitations of the paradigm associated with the seventeenth-century vintage paradigm of state-centricity are manifest, and concepts that were developed to explain it are now no longer capable of being stretched.

By the 1960s it had become clear that states were not the only actors in the drama of international relationships, as there had been a proliferation of new actors affecting outcomes. They may or may not have had legal status, but they were frequently legitimate manifestations of belief and/ or concerns. Thus they may be expressions of identity (such as ETA, the Palestinian Liberation Organisation, or the Irish Republican Army); they may reflect changes in values – such as Greenpeace; problems, such as the proliferation of land mines; and so on. By the end of the twentieth century, to cut a long agenda short, there were now thousands of actors in world politics, across a range of issues. And many of these actors have raised questions about the nature, significance, authority and autonomy of the state, long regarded as the actor at the centre of the discipline of International Relations.

International Relations has responded by trying to address these issues as they have emerged – hence the emergence of specialist approaches and issue areas such as Global Political Economy, International Relations of the Environment, the International Politics of Sport, the Growth of International Organisations, to mention but a few. International Relations has also been much influenced by the wider cultural and political concerns that have affected much of our social debate, such as Feminism, Cultural Studies, the social construction of 'reality', and the like. In a significant way, the claims of International Relations as a discrete discipline are *de facto* challenged by the emergent overlaps and convergent concerns of these new areas of concern and attention.

Now all this raises the central question as to the autonomy of International Relations as an academic discipline. After 1919, it appeared with a very central and pressing *problematique*: order and war in a system of states. In contemporary circumstances, order is not the sole preserve of states: it also relates partly to the activities of 'markets' (as in currency and commodities), which can (and do) have profound effects on states and governments, often rendering them vulnerable to destabilisation, deflection from declared policies, and unpredicted costs of adjustment – with important effects on other aspects of the policy agenda, not least the welfare of the citizens for whom they are legally responsible. Second, many states are essentially unviable, and part of the problem associated with conflict is the attempt to force those who feel that a state is not legitimate to accept rules and authority enforced from the centre. Often state authorities militate against the need fulfilment of many citizens for whom they are ostensibly responsible. And even in advanced states, where there is no open revolt, there are pressures for devolution of authority, as in the United Kingdom in recent years. In other words, the problem is more than one of poor government although there are examples of this, at the time of writting, Burma and Iraq.

Yet the 'old' problem of war has not been displaced on the agenda of International Relations by the arrival of 'new' issues. Nor have all states been marginalised by the proliferation of other actors. The agenda has become more complex, criss-crossing, harder to handle for many in positions of authority. Burton dealt with the emerging issue of complexity in world society in the 1960s. Most of his later work has been devoted to the question of conflict and the need for a new political philosophy. In the light of this assessment of International Relations being in great difficulties at best, and perhaps even in terminal decline, it is to Burton that scholars might turn, with benefit to themselves and their discipline. If people will not fit to states, then what?

It is now a decade and more since Ken Booth observed that, for International Relations, our work is our words, and our words do not work any more. In such circumstances, scholars of International Relations might be well advised to take seriously the claims of radicals who identify the continuing limitations – perhaps even the worsening problems associated with the stretching of concepts that cannot bear the added burdens placed upon them. It may be that innovators and radicals are deemed anachronistic. Nevertheless, we might entertain the notion that there will come a set of circumstances where the work of the radicals is apt, pertinent and even vital in terms of understanding what is going on. Stretching the concept of security may be of some utility, but struggling to make it fit what it was designed to do is probably taking things too far. Why not see what the likes of Burton, Galtung and Boulding have to offer? Sceptics might find more to provention than meets the eye.

Second, what is striking about these three scholars is that they all outgrew the disciplinary limitations they first encountered: Burton, the scholar-civil servant-diplomat; Boulding, the economist turned social theorist; and Galtung, the sociologist turned polymath – all went beyond the bounds of convention. In seeking to assess contemporary social conditions they have all sought to do so by resorting to new words and concepts. In suggesting what is possible, they have suggested what is *not* possible within the patterns of current policies and discourse. They have not been bound by the limits of the old – and in diagnosing the limits of the old they have sought to innovate. (So too has Edward O. Wilson, with his notion of 'consilience' (Wilson, 1998).) Rather than dismiss them as those who have moved on, why not ask: what was the problem that caused them to move on and discuss questions of conflict in radically different terms?

Also of especial note is that neither Burton, Boulding nor Galtung has studied history, to the extent that they are bound by its discourse – and its limitation. Certainly Burton was, and is, always suspicious about the written records of diplomatic history and 'expert knowledge': whenever he encountered it (especially as a practitioner), it was wrong. He was, after all, a diplomat, and knew the truth when and where he was involved. Cynthia Kerman has this to say about Kenneth Boulding's encounter with history: it was reading H. G. Wells' *Outline of History* 'combined with his own encounter with the reinterpretation of English history from the point of view of an Irish school friend – that convinced him that history teachers were liars, that (as he later insisted in *The Image*) the narrow picture of history presented by one country's schools was a source of dissension and war' (Kerman, 1974, p. 91).

Burton *et al.* have freed themselves from the limits not only of words but also of method. Again, Ken Booth is relevant and pertinent: 'Our central myths have internalised conflict as a foundational myth. We have constituted ourselves in conflict, from class struggle to Mutual Assured Destruction. One reason why humanity persists with so dismal a view of its own potentiality is history, the story we tell about our past' (Booth, 1997, p. 86). In not being the prisoners of history, the pioneer peace researchers that Booth now identifies as having much to say to us, despite earlier being marginalised or dismissed, have always been anti-foundationalist, radical and reconstitutive. Morgenthau made much of the notion of human nature. Some philosophers make much of the human condition, the need to struggle, and all of the rest of it. But what of those whose nature is benign, co-operative, caring and nurturing? Are these aspects of behaviour unusual, Utopian – deviant, perhaps? Best to assume that there is no such thing as human nature, and that the human condition is what human beings make of it – when they are at liberty to do so. Never mind what some people say we ought to do (for the moment at least: Burton has not brought philosophical debate to an end with his notion of provention). Ask what it is that people say that they need to be at peace and to be human – and explore the nature of extant peaceful societies. There *are* some!

The work of Burton and others is also relevant in relation to what we can call the 'statist pretence'. This draws attention to the idea that we really ought not to assume that the state is some form of ultimate achievement of political order. Because the state is the institution that 'we' have – we invented it, legitimised it and we live in it – we really should not pretend that there is thus an ultimate limit to political adaptation, and that we have reached that limit, especially when, as suggested earlier, the state is part of the problem in many areas of the planet, and not the means to the solution. We have not reached the highest form of social evolution, manifested in the state as the embodiment of the collective social will. Change and adaptation are constants, and institutions are legitimate only in so far as they serve the people who constitute them: they have no sacred or mythical status, only as far as those who seek to invent it do so. Might it be prudent, therefore, to speculate as to what (legitimate) structures and processes of human interaction might be necessary, desirable – indeed, imperative – in a set of alternative futures? Provention can be instrumental in this.

Moreover, we would be well advised to dismiss another illusion. States do not do anything. People take action in international relationships, as in all others. People act as agents of, or in the name of, states. There is nothing unique about the behaviour of people who act in the name of the state, nor are there questions of 'it's worse because they are acting for millions'. A father acting for a family of two, without means or hope, knows the power of responsibility and obligation; a wife or husband divorcing know the nature of intense conflict. In this, Burton has gone straight through the age-old problem known as 'the level of analysis problem in International Relations'. It does not need re-interpreting; it needs replacement. His focus on relationships stresses the need to unite the individual with the evolving nature of world society – and he did so, to repeat, in the 1960s and 1970s, well before the agenda of globalisation. The need here is to grasp the intellectual nettle of holism.

For some, globalisation is a threat, and for others a promise. The fact of globalisation has had dramatic consequences for many academic disciplines, and nowhere is this more so than in the conjunctions of International Relations, Social Theory and Cultural Studies. Each of these has an agenda that in one way or another encompasses identity, change and the like. Whether or not it is the impact of McDonald's, the Internet, cyberwar and the rest, it is an agenda where identity and being in an era of globalisation are key issues. Confronting the issue of change is vital, but we do not need to re-invent the wheel. Postmodernist approaches neither define the agenda nor do they exhaust it. For those working in this area, Burton's stress on needs is a valuable opening out of the agenda, and Boulding's stress on human betterment is equally important. For both Boulding and Burton, change is the key element in much of their work, and it is by the same token still a conspicuously under-developed concern in International Relations. Traditionally, International Relations has been concerned with the preservation of order and stability in the here and now – the short term: the long term can look after itself, if we can survive into the long term. We need to invest the study of global politics with a temporal dimension: this is not Utopian and it may be vitally creative. Although the 1960s notion of International Relations becoming a predictive science now seems a little passé for many, we would do well to remember that for years many scholars in this field were dumbstruck when the Cold War ended as it did, in circumstances that few predicted, and its ending led to much confusion and uncertainty about where we were heading in the future. The New World Order we got was not the one that was widely forecast.

Finally, a stress on conflict resolution. The primary level of analysis for Burton is the human being, and conflict will be resolved when the issues that separate people disappear. This all sounds so obvious. Yet look at conventional approaches to the management of conflict, and a statement and restatement of the obvious seems to be necessary. The Russians destroy Grozny in order to win the war in Chechnya, on the assumption that in 'winning' they can get the Chechens back on side, and promise to rebuild. But long after the war is over, Chechnya is an insecure place devoid of legitimate authority, and poor. In the Middle East, there is still a persistent dispute between the Israelis and the Palestinians regarding sovereignty, against a backdrop of several wars, insurrections, peace deals and conferences, and the like. At ground level, there is persistent insecurity. New rounds of peace talks regularly begin. The point is that conflict cannot be resolved from the top down, but only from the primary level upwards. Leaders may create the framework, people create the peaceful relationships – and they can be coerced into doing so only at great cost, if at all.

In addressing his own agenda and finding his own articulation of the real (not Realist) agenda, Burton has been equal to the task. He might even have enjoyed his career as a member of 'the awkward squad'. Yet he has never lost sight of what are the primary issues. The key for John Burton is addressing conflict explicitly and solving the problem – and so often we do not do that. It is remarkable that for such a long time conflict in society has not received the attention it deserves, as an issue *in itself* and not merely as an adjunct to questions of order, justice and stability. Given the salience, persistence and cost of human conflict, it is remarkable that it has been the task of recent pioneers of peace research and radical International Relations scholars to try to reorientate the agenda. It is surely no longer justifiable to suggest that order is the immediate goal – a just world order if we can get around to it. The reason why there is so much conflict is because a significant proportion of the human race lives in unpeaceful conditions: this is no mystery, and neither is it a condition to which they – or we – should be condemned, or from which they cannot escape. Basic human needs are going unsatisfied, and this is profoundly consequential.

For John Burton, the system will change when we assess the high costs of resistance and opt for a change in our assumptions and practices. We are unlikely to find this either a comfortable or a comforting process. Yet change we will – and must, for it is clear that we cannot proceed securely into an uncertain future allied to outdated institutions, each with its own justification, history and mythology. For Burton, we face nothing less than a condition of a crisis of civilisation where there are 'poverty and starvation amongst plenty within and between nations, uncontrollable violence at all social levels, ethnic conflict and cleansing, drugs, crime and corruption, personal insecurity – and avoidable environmental pollution and depletion. All increasing at exponential rates' (Burton, 1996c, p. 5). In the light of such an assessment – and Burton was not alone in saying as much, a long time ago – is it at all realistic, sustainable and conducive to civil society to consider that peace, order and security are to be found in fenced and defensible compounds only for those who can afford such 'solutions'? (see Rogers (2000) for a discussion of the development of Heritage Parks in South Africa).

To take another example: a major systemic response to the outbreak of conflicts after the end of the Cold War has been the massive proliferation in the area of peacekeeping. We should not be surprised at this. But we can ask, fruitfully if uncomfortably, where is this process leading, in what time scale, and with what sense of alternative approaches to conflict resolution? For how long can what kind of peace be kept? Who will lead the effort, pay the price, shoulder the burden, and accept the responsibility? The United Nations may take the lead in this, or it may not. And we would do well to recall that we have had a peacekeeping of sorts in Korea, Northern Ireland and Cyprus for many decades. In other words, the cost issues associated with the implementation of current policies may very soon be upon us, and we ought to entertain the notion that confronting long-term unacceptable costs may cause us to reappraise working assumptions and practices. One problem for governments is that their citizens are often acutely aware of the likely costs of involvement in foreign conflicts – and peacekeeping endeavours. John Burton has always sought an alternative to the conventional wisdom, and has outlined the framework of provention that demands further articulation. That process of articulation and implementation is now under way in the United States, Australia and to a lesser extent in the United Kingdom, where conflict resolution issues and aspects of peace research have been placed on the agenda by a new generation of scholars, for undergraduates as well as research students from varied backgrounds.

In the same vein, the response to the process of migration has been the provision of patrol boats, fences, barriers and a tightening of inspection procedures. This is to be expected, but it deals only with the symptoms, and not the causes. Why is it, we might ask, that hundreds of thousands of people put themselves at great risk, and their lives in the hands of the unscrupulous, in order to find a better life. What is it that they are trying to escape, that they should take such great risks? Why have some would-be immigrants to the United States been apprehended sixteen times or more, but still keep trying to enter the country? And when they finally enter successfully, they will exist in a shadow land, without status or entitlements, and still at risk. On a global scale, needs are the problem; and fences are not the long-term solution.

Burton has been sceptical but constructive, he has been impatient and driven, not least by the notion that things are the way they are not the way they have to be. International Relations, struggling to adapt an anachronistic system to the needs and demands of the twenty-first century, might engage usefully with his work – and that of others in Peace Research. There is enough of it – after nearly fifty years of work, this is not surprising – and it deals with a realistic agenda that scholars of International Relations will find helpful in a time of transition.

The issue, after all, is not simply about intellectual neatness or some similar question. It is about the performance of our institutions and practices pertaining to the question of peaceful relations. This was always at the centre of International Relations, from its foundation. It has been a life-long preoccupation of John Burton, who has for many years sought constructive intervention, motivated by social improvement. In constructing his own approach he has developed a conceptual agenda of rich promise, and has avoided many of the pitfalls associated with postmodernism. We do, really, know enough to be able to do better, even acknowledging that there is much still to do.

So what are we to make of Burton?

Of Burton's development of provention we can say that he has developed it, as a framework for the understanding of human behaviour, with some difficulty, informed by a sense that something needed to be done because there was evidently something wrong, indeed fundamentally wrong, with conventional theory and practice. The articulation of provention has been the result of chance meetings, encounters with works that served to add to Burton's conceptual vocabulary, if not always contributing to an eloquence of style. Yet we should beware of assuming that the difficulties of style are symptomatic of some defect or problem. Burton did not set out to be scholar, never mind a literary man or stylist. He was driven by other and different considerations. Clearly, there are difficulties with his written exposition, but these might be seen in a different light. Consider, for example, this comment from the British historian, Edward Thompson: of the Welsh-born writer, critic and pioneer of Cultural Studies, Raymond Williams, he remarked 'There is something in the unruffled stamina of this man which suggests a major thinker. The very awkwardness of his style is that of a mind which must find its own way' (Thompson, 1994, p. 255). This comment could apply to Burton with equal facility. Undoubtedly, Burton has shown great intellectual stamina; he has borne the burden of being a pioneer and an outsider with remarkable fortitude, and has shown no little courage in taking on the accumulated wisdom of 2000 years and more. Moreover, as early as his doctoral dissertation, he flew in the face of the fashionable, showing remarkable intellectual courage in face of the then-prevalent views of Italy, Germany and Japan. He has not been deterred by critics, he has not been deflected from his task by adversity (be it lack of professional acclaim from colleagues, or even the refusal to recognise his work as germane or relevant by many of his so-called colleagues). He has been determined to say what he has to say, in the best way that he can, for more than forty years: he has, in fact, found his own way.

Thompson is again helpful by way of assessing, if somewhat indirectly, how we should view Burton. Of Christopher Caudwell, a leading left-wing intellectual of the 1930s who was killed in the Spanish Civil War, Thompson said, 'He was attempting to offer, not an alternative view in one special area (economics or politics) but to effect a rupture with a whole received view of the world, with its vocabulary and its terms of argument' (Thompson, 1994, p. 125).

So too has Burton sought a decisive rupture with the conventional views he has encountered. Nor has he finished, for he continues to articulate his version, and vision, of an alternative political philosophy rooted not in the realm of normative concerns but in what he has termed 'behavioural realism'. For Burton has resisted involvement with questions of conventional importance to the political philosophers. For him they have threatened an endless and open-endedly relativistic debate akin to the theology he shunned as a young man, which is to say it is resting in faith rather than proof, belief rather than evidence, and the abstract rather than the ontological. He has sought to establish human relations, not in terms of the normative but in the more positive, pressing questions of human needs. In that, he has achieved a major response to the challenge set by a fellow 'frontiersman', David Singer, who argued many years ago that

> My conviction is that we must, in one fashion or another, break away from the normative assumptions which seem to be implicit in so many of the formulations found in contemporary social science... we seem to be in increasing danger of forgetting that the basic unit of any social system is the individual human being and that any scientific formulation must take cognizance of that fact. In my judgment, no theory which ignores the single person is scientifically adequate or morally defensible. In sum, what is proposed here is that we begin some systematic research which can simultaneously 'think big' and 'think small', and which embraces in a rigorous synthesis both the lone individual and all of mankind. (Singer, 1970)

That quotation ends Burton's *Deviance, Terrorism and War* (1979): what came after it was a further articulation of provention, consistent with that goal. Burton has done it in his own fashion, which is 'provention'. Need is at the root of his scheme to effect a rupture, but a rupture aimed not at destruction but rather at a reconstruction of a new frame of reference central to which are not states, but people as living beings, and not as conceptual schemes or as holders of abstract rights, or those in whom inhere certain rights by virtue of their being human. In this, he can find roots in the so-called 'behavioural revolution' of the 1960s, in so far as that mood (its effects were never revolutionary) stimulated a concern for individuals and individual values, people in politics rather than the formal study of political institutions. Burton's concern for needs starts with the proposition that the world is full of certain wrongs (we identified some of these earlier, juxtaposed with Burton's call for a new political philosophy), rather than that there are certain rights. And it is these wrongs that are at the root of destructive conflicts.

Yet we need to go beyond a mere, though sincere, assertion that the Burtonian achievement that is provention is significant in itself. Indeed, the point is not that it should be significant in relation to itself, but rather more significant in terms of its relationship to the major issues that motivated Burton to begin to develop it. Why try to effect a rupture in established ways of thought? To what audience is Burton addressing his framework of provention? At the beginning of a new millennium this is clear enough. As far as International Relations is concerned, we see a discipline in crisis, and as far as the practice of international relations is concerned we see a world that is more rather than less conflictual. There are conflicts going unresolved because the wrong frame of reference is brought to bear.

In economics, there is concern that it too is paralysed by virtue of the inability of economists to understand and explain the pressing issues of poverty, debt, welfare and issues of value. On a global scale, the period of modernity has culminated in debt greater than might have been imagined in the 1950s, allied to poverty and a gap between rich and poor that is widening rather than narrowing.

In political science, the agenda in need of being addressed is the disengagement of people from politics, where they were once engaged, and with building appropriate systems of representation where people have so far not been represented. There is a crisis of confidence in terms of democratic politics: elections become ends in themselves, and politics becomes reduced to nothing more than the image and the sound bite, with the consequence that political practice becomes merely the conjunction of cynicism and opportunism.

In politics, economics and, international relations there is a crisis of relevance, a crisis of meaning. To repeat yet again what Ken Booth has said of International Relations, 'our work is our words and our words do not work any more'. That sentiment might be shared by other fellow social scientists trying to make theories of representative democracy work in varied and various societies; or trying to make theories of value and money cope with selfishness allied to indifference, where welfare means fences and guards rather than shared values and a shared feeling of unity with other human beings.

There is a crisis in thought as well as in practice. Not for nothing does Burton see us as a civilisation in crisis. Hence his call for the development of what amounts to a new political philosophy coming out of the construction of provention. The old will not suffice to minister to our contemporary needs. What we need is something that will suffice, that will effect change, and that will ensure adaptation. There must be innovation.

In summary, Burton's role has been enabling. In so far as his life and works have spanned the twentieth century, he has assisted in the transition of human thought (in a broad way, but especially in relation to issues of war, peace and conflict) out of the nineteenth century tradition of *Machtpolitik*, into a preparation for the necessary task of global problem-solving. In that he has been both instrumental and anticipatory, a man of impatience allied to vision. Arguably, a man ahead of his time. Consider, by way of example, this remarkable passage written by Burton in 1996, describing Herbert Vere Evatt as a man out of his time:

[His] times were ones of unusual philosophical doubt. They were times of extreme ideologies, with no objective reference points by which to assess them. Bigotry was widespread in public political life and also in clandestine private and official agencies which, with the arrogance of ignorance, set out to save democracy from itself. There were indeed 'true believers' but [he] was not one of them. He was caught in a political environment, domestic and international, that intuitively, intellectually and emotionally was unacceptable to him. But there was no clear philosophical option with which he could identify himself, much less articulate...It was precisely because he was concerned with problem-solving conflict resolution, rather than authoritarian dispute settlement, that [he] was misunderstood...to his credit, as a party politician. The adversarial party political system was quite outside his intellectual frame...Many found it hard to work with him. (Burton, 1996b, pp. 1–9).

The comment, and the description, apply with equal facility to John Burton.

There is, of course, much to do, for Burton has prepared the ground for further study rather than exhausted the agenda he has constructed.

In that, his own achievement represents the challenge. He has taken us only so far, and there is much to do. Not least of these is a further analysis of what it is that Burton is saying. One major problem with his work is that of style: his style has tended to leave much implicit; his examples tend to be narrow and over-used; and his evidence is impressionistic, rather than systematic and broad-based. He is – in discussion of a point (and often a key point) – seldom exhaustive and never prone to the accusation that he overdoes the discussion to the point of engaging the detail in all its rococo style. As a relative latecomer to academic life, his work sometimes seems to lack the deepest of roots in 'the literature'. As his academic career developed, he located himself in a wider literature, but frequently his critique is that of assertion, rather than lengthy exposition. This is not a plea that he ought to have been loquacious or long-winded: he had a point to make, he made it and moved on. In so doing, he sometimes made himself an easy target for his critics – and they were many. In their eyes, he did not understand, and for some, no doubt, provention is both new and unnecessary.

But there is more to it than merely questions of style. There are also substantive concerns, and there is the question of objectivity. Burton enhanced the biological bases of needs, only to leave it behind, preferring instead the idea of ontological and universal need. We can see what he is driving at. We can understand his need to escape from the limits of 'loaded' concepts. Is the idea that there are objective needs waiting to be satisfied the same as a stance about value freedom? Perhaps not. Richard Little argued in the mid-1980s that 'no model is free from ideology. Since John Burton wishes to change the world, he has no alternative but to make the argument for change in ideological terms. It is counter-productive to dress one's values in natural science garb. A non-ideological model of social order is a chimera which it is a mistake to claim or pursue' (Little, 1984, p. 95).

But is the situation so clear cut? The pursuit of a chimera may not lead us to a fruitful conclusion, yet it may involve the revelation of other prevalent myths that are deemed to be not mythical by the adherents, but part of the reality. In other words, the pursuit may ultimately not get us to the presumed destination, but it will have not been valueless either. Yet it may be that Little overstates the case. Peace Research (aimed at understanding the causes of war and the conditions of peace, motivated by the desire for socio-political change) is a respectable and now well-established approach to the explanation of social processes and the diagnosis of social ills. It was not always as well established. It has always been – and remains – a value-laden exercise. There has always been a recognition that Peace Research was not value-free: it was problem-centred and research-orientated. The analogy was often drawn between it and the problem of war, and the medical scientist and the problem of cancer. It may be that the wish is the father to the thought, but it need not be the case that what follows is a politics in disguise. To take just one example, the public debate that surrounded the nature and significance of peace studies in Britain in the early 1980s was focused heavily on the idea that it was, according to the critics, tendentious and a kind of Unilateralist politics in disguise (see Dunn, 1985) but despite this the case against was, though repeatedly asserted (as it had been in the early days of peace research in 1950s America), not made conclusively. The attack was more political than the object of it. The values and norms that underpin Peace Research – which Burton did so much to establish – are not a bad foundation upon which to rest provention.

Burton has not been a reckless propagandist: the difference as between *The Alternative* of 1954 and the alternative represented by 'provention' belies comparison in terms of the structure of the argument and the mode of exposition, though this is not to deny elements of continuity, as the previous discussions illustrate. So perhaps to put it in terms of the question of 'ideology' is a wrong emphasis. The distance between the problem and appropriate method is one to be bridged by academic rigour and discipline, but also pragmatically. Burton has done this; he has, perhaps, not been as patient or rigorous as he might have been on occasion – there is too much assertion and often not enough demonstration – but provention, surely, is more than an argument for change in merely ideological terms. And is it the case that the pursuit of a chimera has been counter-productive? Whatever else, it has been instrumental, and surely significant for that.

There is a fundamental requirement that the question of need be addressed further. Burton asserts that needs are ontological and universal (claims to their biological basis having been discarded along the way). So much is clear to him. But this does not exhaust the debate; rather, it opens up an agenda for research. The assertion that these needs are as Burton suggests is useful, and clearly performs a heuristic function. But the point to which Burton takes us is not to the end of the road in the debate about needs: he would be the first to recognise this, and says so repeatedly. The collection of essays brought together as an element of the 1990 Conflict Series is a clear recognition that the ground has only just been cleared. But Burton evidently takes the view that we can make some progress when the underbrush is removed: we do not – and we cannot – wait for the time when we are in the comfort of the forest clearing, and free from risk.

Vivienne Jabri asks us to consider the extent to which the definition – and constitution – of need is itself cultural (Jabri, 1996). Are needs culturally defined, or do they transcend culture? We should not be surprised at this. Burton is clear, but others are still unconvinced. And the implications are significant because, as Mack (1991, p. 95) asserts, if 'need' as an organising concept collapses, then all else goes too. Not necessarily, but this is a cautionary input to the required debate.

Another issue waiting to be addressed is the extent to which needs are gender-specific. One pertinent comment was offered to the effect that there was no evidence of women in Burton's work. In one sense, since he is person-centric, he saw no need for a specific gender division. On the other hand, can gender differences related to need be subsumed, or are they crucially important and different?

And what of power? Burton spoke of the power of communication and the power of human needs. But what of the power of power? What is to be made of it? Dysfunctional – always and in all circumstances? What of the mechanisms of control where control is necessary and desirable, as, for example, in the case of those who are a danger to themselves and a threat to others?

What of the power of resistance? Burton suggests that change will come about when the accumulated costs of adhering to existing practices (of stasis, resistance and control; and of managing the problems rather than solving them) are realised and become insupportable. Change will then be deemed necessary and desirable. There is some logic in this. Ultimately, the Soviet Union collapsed, Ceauşescu fell, apartheid collapsed, the United States' forces left Vietnam, and the European empires collapsed. Yet there were heavy costs involved in all of these: in the case of the former USSR, millions of Soviet citizens were consumed by the system itself, and high costs were allied to policies of denial and deception. It may well be that, ultimately, systems decline and fall – but some will find the cost of resistance worth paying. Might there be a system of cost–benefit analysis allied to provention (and prediction?) which can demonstrate the likely cost implications of both resistance and change?

But this is where Burton unites the general and the specific. Innovation in conflict resolution recognises that there are disutilities inherent in the exercise of power, and that people do not want to start out from where they are: they seek ways of escape. Conflict resolution procedures offer them that. And lest it be overlooked, in the course of his work, Burton has developed an integrated framework that allows us to conjoin the

individual and world society. That they are so conjoined in the framework
of provention shows how Burton developed his holistic perspective.
It is that need for holism that International Relations, Economics,
Sociology and other disciplines are striving to encompass – from within
the boundaries of their own discipline.

Banks, too, has seen the great potential that inheres in Burton's work,
and we have referred to it, particularly his observation that Burton
offers a way out of the contemporary impasse in International Relations. For example, he argues that

> not everyone will agree with Edward Azar's claim in the foreword
> that *Global Conflict* does for international relations what Keynes's
> *General Theory* did for economics, if only because Keynes's statement
> was a complete statement whereas this one mostly reports on theories
> that are fully explained only in previous books. However, the analogy
> does carry weight. Burton is right to argue that the world's problems
> are severe. His vision does rival that of Keynes in its analytic insight,
> its broad scope and its spirit of consistent reformism. (Banks,
> 1985a, p. 230)

Work done by Burton since 1985 can, surely, only have added weight to
the claims that Burton and Keynes should be mentioned together. Even
those unsure as to this juxtaposition might at least contemplate it a little.

Doubtless there will be those who feel that a juxtaposition of Burton
and Keynes is preposterous: they will, in all likelihood, not have read
this far in this book. But there is real substance to the claim made by
Azar: he was an intelligent, articulate individual, and his comment
deserves serious consideration. Burton, like Keynes, both shunned and
went beyond the 'classical' thought in their disciplines, by exposing its
limited explanatory claims. Both went on to address the generalities
that were thought, previously, to be discussible in specific terms: for
Keynes it was not a case of the equilibrium conditions of employment
as dictated by classical assumptions of stability and sound money, but
'the general theory of employment, interest and money'. Old assumptions
tended to make a bad situation worse. Keynes changed them – effected
a synthesis – with profound practical consequences. For Burton, it is
a general theory of (conflictual) behaviour, a new synthesis. Old
assumptions made bad situations worse. It may be that Burton's framework sets out the potential for a synthesis of existing thought that will
allow us to understand properly the world at the start of the twenty-first
century: not as a world of states but as a world of people, with profound

practical consequences. This does not exhaust the comparison: indeed, it ought to stimulate inquiry into the nature of the genesis of 'general theory', but it should not be dismissed out of hand. Of Keynes, incidentally, Stewart said that his 'great contribution to economics was to show that the modern economy did not work in the way that everyone had supposed, and to provide a new and completely convincing explanation of how it did work. This new explanation is the foundation of modern economics' (Stewart, 1972, p. 296). Burton has shown that international relations do not work according to the tenets of the conventional wisdom; some authors (in increasing numbers) seeking to explain the problems of our time are convinced of the power of Burton's conceptual frame of reference, and provention has the potential – at the very least – to underpin a new explanation of a globalised planet.

The meaning and significance of provention

Having given an indication of the nature and orientation of provention at the outset in order to inform what followed, and having surveyed the genealogy of provention in the preceding treatment of Burton's work, leaving several aspects of provention either implied or unamplified, at this point we can discuss the nature and significance explicitly, but not definitively.

We cannot be definitive, since much remains to be done in relation to the development of provention. But, by way of a conclusion to this work – and by way of being an introduction to the work which follows this – we can say something of significance about the several achievements of provention, the significant instrumentalities represented by provention, and the functions that provention has performed and is able still to promise more.

First, provention is rejectionist in so far as it rejects the ontological premises of International Relations as an academic discipline and as an approach to global politics generally, and the issue of conflictual behaviour more specifically. For Burton, the proposition, in relation to Northedge in the 1960s, was that 'international politics has nothing to do with the real world: it is a game'. Following that confrontation, Burton sought, *de facto*, to amplify it over the course of the following four decades. His response was to put people at the centre of the analysis, since they are where politics and social intercourse being, and are thus the primary focus or level of analysis. A focus on states, as a means to understanding war, peace, conflict and order is now partial, and indeed in many circumstances misleading in terms of assumptions, policies and outcomes.

So often, 'conventional wisdom' is incapable of solving problems of human relationships, since it is informed by the wrong ontologies and epistemologies. So often, people are made to fit into norms, structures and processes that are said to serve the goals of good, order, justice, stability, normality, community and conformity. We can understand clearly the goal of order as this is understood in International Relations, where the alternative is assumed to be war and chaos. So much is established in the intellectual tradition. Yet order comes to be almost the dominant goal in itself: challenges to certain conceptions of order are coerced, change is prevented, and certain – but only specific – interests are served. The problem is defined as one of system maintenance rather than system adaptation.

From a provention perspective, people are primary, processes of change are essential and structures are only secondary: structures are the means to an end of human betterment, conflict resolution and societal adaptation. Change is the constant. So often we either fail to acknowledge that this is the case, and misunderstand the consequences when we understand, with uncertainty. The defence of the stance associated with the conventional wisdom is that 'we are living in the real world, doing the best we can to manage the problems in the short run and dealing with the aspects of the agenda that we can deal with'. This is a defensible position in one respect, where it is consistent with a given definition of 'the real world' and a consequent constructivist position in relation to what this 'realism' actually constitutes.

However, Burton, too, is a social and political realist, but without the capital 'R' of traditional Realism and all that attends upon it. Lest we forget, Burton dealt with the real world as he saw it, as a civil servant, diplomat and academic. That it was not a conventional definition of reality was the point, and it was consequential for Burton in career terms and with regard to his relationships with International Relations as an academic discipline. He confronted it, rejected its assumptions and moved on. In this sense, provention is critical and rejectionist, and in this respect there is a perfectly useful and valid comparison between Burton and Keynes. Keynes confronted economic orthodoxy (conventional wisdom if you will) in its premises and its policy implications. At a time of slump, economic orthodoxy made the problems worse, and balanced budgets mitigated against appropriate solutions. What Keynes proposed was widely regarded heresy at best and lunacy at worst. So does the conventional wisdom and orthodoxy treat innovators. In the fullness of time, Keynes came to be treated differently, and his place in the pantheon of economic theory and economic policy-making was assured. This cannot – yet – be said of Burton, but what can be said is that Burton's response to orthodoxy was, and is, no less significant compared to the challenge that Keynes represented. Currently, too, much orthodoxy sees Burton's provention as challenging, but probably not relevant to 'real world issues', since it does not, in these terms, start out from where we are. Yet, current policies just might be wrong in their assumptions, wrong in their implementation and wrong in their accumulated consequences. Reality changes.

Burton moved on to construct an approach that was – is – realist in its assumptions, and programmatic in its implications. It is also relevant to continuing problems within states and societies, and within an evolving globalising realm. In other words, we need to solve problems and resolve conflict, and not control or manage them. We need to address the nature, significance and outcomes of socio-political processes that are confrontational and may serve the interests of those who participate, yet which seem irrelevant to many more. There is a crisis in civil society in so far as citizens are refusing to participate in the political process in large numbers. In the year 2000, the election of the candidate George W. Bush to the presidency of the United States was controversial. The more fundamental problem was why, yet again, only about half of the voters eligible to vote bothered to do so. And in the French election for the National Assembly in June 2002, turnout fell to a record low. In municipal elections in Britain, some inner-city wards see turn-outs as low as 20 per cent. As Burton might suggest, this could be due in no small part to the notion that people see the political system as being (increasingly) irrelevant to the tasks of addressing, never mind fulfilling, the needs of citizens and voters.

Hence the need for structural adaptation and the development of new processes, not of electronic voting – in supermarkets or elsewhere (for these are merely responses that address symptoms and not causes) – but of searching for systems and processes that have about them the key attribute of legitimacy, which allows, fosters and sustains participation, and within which individuals can feel that they have achieved some worth, status and identity. If this were to be the case, the probability of self-sustaining systems would be markedly increased. But adaptation must be allowed as a process: so often, individuals are coerced into conformity. In common parlance, if they will not conform, then they will be forced to do so. This approach is evident in relation to disaffected youth in American and European cities, as well as in relation to the leader of the Palestinian Authority. We might entertain the notion that coercion and violence may be counter-productive.

Moreover, provention is critical of existing socio-political processes which achieve outcomes (that are valued by some) but which do not solve social problems. Among thses are the adversarial processes associated with both the law and politics. In relation to the law, there is an adversarial process that has its own rules, and in which certain outcomes are sought. But the 'solution' to the process of the law 'taking its course' may not solve the underlying problems of justice, and might even see innocent individuals found guilty. In politics, the process is similar. It satisfies the needs of some (whether it is the need for re-election, or the need to appease some groups, or to satisfy others), but so often outcomes fall short of promises and stated goals. As the former British prime minister, Harold Macmillan said, 'events' get in the way. But, over time, there is a loss of faith in politics and the political system. From a Burtonian perspective, like international politics, it is a game and it may have less to do with the real world than proponents, adherents and participants would have us believe.

In relation to approaches to conflict resolution, the idea of resolution itself (rather than settlement, management or control) has been central to the development of provention, not least with regard to the development of techniques and processes of conflict resolution. In this respect, provention is innovative at the level of thought about how systems work and how techniques might be altered, one as a means to the other.

Burton, in so far as he has developed provention as a response to the limits of an academic discipline, has performed the task – hardly incidental, though it may appear so – of revealing the limits of partial perspectives in our approach to complex problems. Of course, the world is complex, and we need to resort to strategies that make the complex comprehensible. How we do so is the problem, not the problem itself. To focus on states, for example, is one thing, and indeed defensible, but only in so far as this focus on states is appropriate, defensible, authentic, productive, accurate and so on. The problem is that, in the first decade of the twenty-first century, a focus on states is decreasingly relevant. International relations has been constructed on a dichotomy – that the state exists and as a consequence separates politics into domestic and international – but this is increasingly in question. We live in a world of states and markets, ethnicity and diversity, identity and community, gender and so on. It is hardly surprising that International Relations as an academic discipline is struggling, at best, to keep pace. And provention is not the only approach that threatens the continuing validity of a focus on states in a world of globalisation.

Provention may thus be seen to be a means to paradigm change, where a paradigm is not an approach, theory or model (so often, the word 'paradigm' has been used as a term interchangeable with every one of these) but a widely shared set of assumptions about how the world is, and how it can be understood. This is the central problem associated with the current status of International Relations. It is not a case of 'states plus' or 'essential concerns and issues plus' in order that we can cope and keep pace. What is required is a new approach to understanding. That is what Keynes said, and that is what Burton says also.

We are dealing with novelties that do not readily fit with our assumptions. We should not try to make them fit, but should change our assumptions about the way the world is: we need a paradigm change. Provention is both a symptom of the crisis in conventional systems of thought (Burton first identified them in the 1950s) and a means of resolving the crises and conflicts within our conventional systems of thought. In summary, provention is centred on the principal level of analysis – the person. Second, if focuses not on what people ought to do (according to an ethical code – which may or may not be relevant, legitimate or otherwise – either imported, imposed or defined as conformist norms), but on their perceived needs, how they feel, where they are, here and now. Clearly, therefore, Burton shows some affinity with the approach that focuses on human behavior, a mood much in evidence when he engaged with the literature of International Relations in the 1960s. But a focus on the questions of needs (what they are, how they develop, how they are articulated and satisfied) is not to render questions of ethics – how ought people to behave in relation to each other, for example – to the periphery. But it is to question the claim to ethics of primacy in the discussions of social relationships, order and identity, and security and conflict.

Only by understanding the key interplay of, first, putting the person at the centre of the analysis, and, second, asking why and how people do what they do, can we understand why our locality, our society and our world are so conflictual, problematical and violent. We start with the problem first, not the presumptions of order and conformity (because that leads us into question of deviance, norms and compliance). Only then can we understand the fears of people who are afraid to leave their homes after dark, the expectations of black children in American cities that they will die a violent death before they reach the age of twenty, and the persistent failures of policy in, for example, the Middle East. At the very least (and there is infinitely more to it than this), an engagement with provention at the various levels of social intercourse and in relation to extant academic disciplines and areas of study might lead us to the view that we just *might* be wrong, in one way or another, and how we might begin to get it right. Scepticism is in itself an instrument of social change. Controversy in the social sciences should be stimulated and not repressed.

Burtonians – believers and proponents of what Burton has had to say over the years – are clearly of one view as to what is represented by the neologism that is 'provention', but even those who are sceptical might be less than dismissive, for they may find within provention an instrumental, pragmatic and promising response to problems of our time. It is not a cure-all, necessarily, but to resolve some of our pressing conflicts would be no little achievement. We might just entertain the notion that it could be a decisive step on the way to human betterment. And it might amount to a more appropriate approach to political and social behaviour, compared to the writings of the long-dead which constitute the Western intellectual tradition, where the key concepts are conflict resolution, participation, legitimacy, recognition of identity, satisfaction of needs, and peaceful change.

So where do we go from here? The pioneers prepare. The critics distil and discard, as the believers assimilate and incorporate. What is good lasts. This is deemed to be too valuable/too important to miss, and endowed with a status such that it demands incorporation into teaching syllabuses – this is the key change. What is taught is the key change in the development of ideas. What is taught also has an implication for what is implemented. What is taught then becomes part of the material that explains what is to be explained – the old will not suffice, and the new is taken on board.

In other words, the process of change is time-bound; sometimes (rarely) it is fast, and mostly it is incremental-incorporationist. Slowly, then, what is important becomes incorporated into what needs to be taught to specialists and undergraduates – if not as the conventional wisdom, then as the grounded underpinnings of the discipline they study. This is crucial, for it is not quite the process of debate and/or competition suggested by the idea of the inter-paradigm debate. It is incremental. This is why what Banks had to say is so significant – what is it that we teach to our students (Banks, 1985a)? What defines and redefines the process of curricular innovation and development? This is why it is important to stress that the biggest revolution is the revolution in ideas. Protest may work, yet the key to innovation and change is *ideas* – hence peace *research*. Hence the need for conceptual innovation and 'frontiersmen'. When it came down to thinking about the frontier, to stretch the analogy, most people stayed put – until they felt it was time to go.

It is incumbent on teachers to ensure that their students are exposed to not only the lasting concerns of their subject, but also to the emergent and significant challenges that are deemed – by nature of salience, assault or novelty – to present significant challenges, with significant here denoting what needs to be brought to the notice of students at an undergraduate level as a matter of course. This is why courses on 'International Theory' or 'Theories of International Behaviour' are necessarily so dynamic and flexible – they need to be, because the world they seek to engage with and explain moves on. The key issue is to understand that new approaches are themselves symptomatic of particular limitations, and there is a need for general developments in order that frames of reference are appropriate to the task.

Thus, for example, peace research and feminist approaches (to name but two) to international relations are symptomatic of limitations as well as suggestions of what is to be included in a novel frame of concepts and concerns. The boundary and the centre are under assault. In time, they will be seen to be what they are – symptoms of transition – to a person-centric (a-gendered) frame of reference that explains the nature of peaceful (and conflictual) relationships, including – but not confined to – relations within and between states.

If the question is raised about the idea of what it is to be taught, the test of a good idea is that it prompts discussion, and it lasts. The ideas of Burton have already been taken up and synthesised to some degree. They are in the literature, not just in their original form, but also informing further analysis. We can cite here the works of Druckman and Mitchell (1995), Dukes (1996), Jabri (1996), Mitchell and Banks (1996), Fisher (1997) and Tidwell (1998). In so far as this sort of literature – is it appropriately described as 'secondary'? – is now spreading, it may indicate that the path identified by the 'frontiersmen' is becoming a more trodden path – indeed, a known route, if not yet a superhighway. And there are institutions within which the discussion, teaching and researching of these ideas is the norm. Burton helped to found some of them, and had some association with others: the International Peace Research Association (IPRA), the United States Institute of Peace, the Institute for Conflict Analysis and Resolution (at George Mason University), the University of Kent, the Institute for Multi-Track Diplomacy (in Washington, DC) among others. It is a point worth reiteration here: for all of his preoccupations with ideas, Burton has also dealt with the development of organisations to a remarkable degree, from the small (such as CAC and the Conflict Research Society in Britain) to the multinational organisations such as IPRA. The way to see these organisations is as instrumentalities, via which the development of ideas can be applied and implemented in the context of the creation of what he once termed 'applied science'.

So, when we speak of provention, what are we to make of it? We do not have to take on board Burton's assumptions root and branch (though some may do so). Provention as a word may not last in a complicated world of change and intellectual dynamism. The argument articulated here is that it is significant, and that it should be of lasting value – and that it will be. But critics need to understand why those innovating feel the need for new concepts and vocabulary. It is not neologism for its own sake, it is not merely trendy, and it is not just psycho-babble, though it must be acknowledged that there are very many neologisms and that there is a periodic engagement with psycho-babble. Burton on provention, Johan Galtung on structural violence, Kenneth Boulding on human betterment (Boulding and Boulding, 1995), and Edward O. Wilson on consilience have sought to innovate in order to say something new and significant about our contemporary socio-political circumstances and the limits of conventional approaches in terms of explaining them. Each of them has also gone beyond the limits of discipline boundaries as conventionally defined by traditional concepts and accepted boundaries. New approaches and new words are both innovative and symptomatic of underlying problems that are incapable of being explained adequately in terms of conventional discourse.

The key question is: what does provention – as a word, a schema, a set of questions, on a set of related ideas – represent; of what is its appearance a symptom? Provention is significant for two fundamental reasons: the limitations it reveals and the possibilities it demonstrates. The strength of the argument may be judged by the fact that the argument cannot be dismissed as mere neologisms – though some may do so on the grounds that the concerns here addressed are unreal, marginal or tangential to essentialist-type concerns. The agenda of suggestion, construction and articulation is what has been taken up in temporal and institutional terms – at the Institute for Conflict Analysis and Resolution, the Centre for the Analysis of Conflict, the United States Institute of Peace, the Institute for Multi-Track Diplomacy and so on – and in the works of Mitchell, Dukes, McDonald, Tidwell and others – and passed on in terms of training skills presented in course constructions – at George Mason University, Fairfox, Virginia, and elsewhere – not radical, and not mainstream, but taught and implemented in a practical and significant way. At inter-state level and all the way 'down' to practical dispute resolution at local levels – in ways that are not publicised (but are known to exist), and which assist with conflict mediation and resolution.

A view about the nature of peace from a rather more conventional – and certainly an un-Burtonian – perspective was proffered in the year 2000 by Sir Michael Howard, for many a (*the*?) leading thinker on matters of war and peace. He observes that 'peace ... is not an order natural to mankind: it is artificial, intricate and highly volatile' (Howard, 2000, p. 104). By way of conclusion, it might be suggested that this is because we have made it so. We have made wrong assumptions about the nature of human beings: we have made wrong assumptions about the natural order of things. We have, moreover, been prisoners of wrong assumptions, and constructed them as the accumulated lessons of history, with the added 'intellectual multiplier', as it were, that if we do not learn them then we are condemned to repeat them. In the operational frame of reference known as 'conventional wisdom', so often we deal with the symptoms and not the causes of problems. Is there a problem with our basic assumptions? For Burton, though not only him, it is time to discard long-established notions of international politics, social structures and political philosophies – such as the notion that deterrence deters, that prison works, that punishment precedes conformity or 'if you seek peace prepare for war'; or 'there are no perpetual friends or enemies, only perpetual interests'; or 'my enemy's enemy is my friend'. These may have been (questionably?) appropriate to their own times, but are less appropriate to ours. Which comments makes the continued re-engagement with, re-discovery of and re-interpretation of 'the classics' seem rather ironic and probably misplaced. There may be virtue and great value – given our own problems – in accepting that the ancient Greeks, for example, are long dead, and their times long gone. We need new assumptions for new times; new tools for the task. Then we may find that peace is realistic and not Utopian; authentic rather than artificial; simple as opposed to intricate; and stable rather than volatile.

It is surely incumbent upon us to explain how and why it was that peace was based on the threat to kill millions and render societies vulnerable to devastation. In hindsight, as Burton might suggest, we should admit that we got it wrong, with wrong assumptions, wrong definitions of the situation and wrong policies: if not all of the time, then at least some of the time. This might be a start. As Sir Peter Medawar once argued, 'we know enough to be able to do better' (*Evening Standard*, 2 April 1986). Doubtless Burton would agree; not least because he has demonstrated both how and why. That is both his achievement – and his challenge. It is intellectually significant, practically challenging and politically relevant.

What matters is not the word 'provention', but rather the faults (in terms of thinking and practical implications) that it illuminates, the alternatives it suggests – and the outcomes it promises. Almost fifty years after *The Alternative* (Burton, 1954), we have an alternative.

Bibliography

Albinski, H. A. (1965) *Australian Attitudes and Policies Towards China* (Princeton, NJ: Princeton University Press).

Banks, M. H. (1984) *Conflict in World Society* (Brighton: Wheatsheaf).

Banks, M. H. (1985a) 'Where We Are Now', *Review of International Studies*, vol. 11, no. 3, pp. 215–33.

Banks, M. H. (1985b) 'The Inter-paradigm Debate' in M. Light and A. J. R. Groom (eds), *International Relations Theory: A Handbook of Current Theory* (London: Pinter), pp. 7–26.

Bay, C. (1970) *The Structure of Freedom* (Stanford, Calif.: Stanford University Press).

Blau, P. M. (1964) *Exchange and Power in Social Life* (New York: Wiley).

Bolton, G. (1990) *The Oxford History of Australia, Vol. 5* (Melbourne: Oxford University Press of Australia).

Booth, K. (1990) 'Security and Emancipation', *Review of International Studies*, vol. 17, pp. 313–26.

Booth, K. (1995) 'Human Wrongs and International Relations', *International Affairs*, vol. 71, no. 1, pp. 103–26.

Booth, K. (1997) 'Security and Self: Confessions of a Fallen Realist' in K. Krause and M. Williams (eds), *Critical Security Studies* (London: UCL Press), pp. 83–119.

Boulding, E. and K. Boulding (1995) *The Future: Images and Processes* (Thousand Oaks, Calif. and London: Sage).

Box, S. (1971) *Deviance, Reality and Society* (New York: Rinehart & Winston).

Braybrooke, D. (1987) *Meeting Needs* (Princeton, NJ: Princeton University Press).

Brent, J. (1993) *Charles Sanders Peirce: A Life* (Bloomington and Indianapolis: Indiana University Press).

Bull, H. and C. Holbraad (1979) 'Introduction' in M. Wight (ed.) *Power Politics* (Harmondsworth: Pelican).

Burton, J. W. (1942) *Restrictive and Constructive Intervention* (Unpublished Ph.D. dissertation, University of London).

Burton, J. W. (1954) *The Alternative* (Sydney: Morgans Publications).

Burton, J. W. (1956) *The Light Grows Brighter* (Sydney: Morgans Publications).

Burton, J. W. (1957) *Labor in Transition* (Privately Published).

Burton, J. W. (1958) *The Nature and Significance of Labor*, The Fifth Chifley Memorial Lecture, University of Melbourne, 11 September.

Burton, J. W. (1962) *Peace Theory* (New York: Knopf).

Burton, J. W. (1965) *International Relations: A General Theory* (London: Cambridge University Press).

Burton, J. W. (ed.) (1966) *Nonalignment* (London: Andre Deutsch).

Burton, J. W. (1968) *Systems, States, Diplomacy and Rules* (London: Cambridge University Press).

Burton, J. W. (1969) *Conflict and Communication* (London: Macmillan).

Burton, J. W. (1972) *World Society* (London: Cambridge University Press).

Burton, J. W., A. J. R. Groom, C. R. Mitchell and A. V. S. deReuck (1974) *The Study of World Society: A London Perspective*, Pittsburgh International Studies Association, Occasional Paper No. 1.

Burton, J. W. (1975) 'Universal Values' in T. Dunn (ed.) *Foundations of Peace and Freedom: The Ecology of a Peaceful World* (Swansea: Davies), pp. 71–82.

Burton, J. W. (1979) *Deviance, Terrorism and War* (Oxford: Martin Robertson).

Burton, J. W. (1982) *Dear Survivors* (London: Pinter).

Burton, J. W. (1984) *Global Conflict: The Domestic Sources of International Crisis* (Brighton: Wheatsheaf).

Burton, J. W. (1987) *Resolving Deep-Rooted Conflicts: A Handbook* (Lanham, Md.: University Press of America).

Burton, J. W. (ed.) (1990a) *Conflict: Human Needs Theory* (London: Macmillan).

Burton, J. W. (1990b) *Conflict: Resolution and Provention* (London: Macmillan).

Burton, J. W. (1996a) *Conflict Resolution: Its Language and Processes* (Lanham, Md./London: Scarecrow Press).

Burton, J. W. (1996b) 'Herbert Vere Evatt: A Man Out of His Time' in D. Day (ed.), *Brave New World: Dr H. V. Evatt and Australian Foreign Policy* (St Lucia: University of Queensland Press).

Burton, J. W. (1996c) 'Civilisations in Crisis: From Adversarial to Problem Solving Processes', *International Journal of Peace Studies*, vol. 1, no. 1 (January), pp. 5–24.

Burton, J. W. (1997) *Violence Explained* (Manchester: Manchester University Press).

Burton, J. W. and F. Dukes (eds) (1990a) *Conflict: Readings in Management and Resolution* (London: Macmillan).

Burton, J. W. and F. Dukes (eds) (1990b) *Conflict: Practices in Management, Settlement and Resolution* (London: Macmillan).

Callinicos, A. (1999) *Social Theory: A Historical Introduction* (Cambridge: Polity Press).

Carr, E. H. (1939) *The Twenty Years' Crisis* (London: Macmillan).

Carthy, J. D. and F. J. Ebling (eds) (1964) *The Natural History of Aggression* (London: Academic Press).

Charlesworth, J. C. (ed.) (1967) *Contemporary Political Analysis* (New York: Free Press).

Clack, P. (1991) 'Theories Amidst Cows and Hills', *Canberra Times*, 8 September.

Coffey, J. (1977) *Political Realism in American Thought* (Lewisburg, Pa.: Bucknell University Press).

Deutsch, K. W. (1957) *Nationalism and Social Communication* (Cambridge, Mass.: MIT Press).

Deutsch, K. W. (1963) *Nerves of Government* (New York: Free Press).

Druckman, D. and C. R. Mitchell (eds) (1995) 'Flexibility in International Negotiation and Mediation', Special Issue of *The Annals of The American Academy of Social and Political Sciences*, vol. 542 (November).

Dryzek, J. (1990) *Discursive Democracy* (Cambridge: Cambridge University Press).

Dukes, E. F. (1996) *Resolving Public Conflict* (Manchester: Manchester University Press).

Dunn, D. J. (1985) 'The Peace Studies Debate', *Political Quarterly*, vol. 56, no. 1 (January–March).

Easton, D. (1953) *The Political System* (New York: Knopf).

Easton, D. (1965) *A Systems Analysis of Political Life* (New York: Wiley).

Easton, D. (1971) *The Political System*, revised edn (New York: Knopf).

Edwards, P. G. (1983) *Prime Ministers and Diplomats: The Making of Australian Foreign Policy 1901–1949* (Melbourne: Oxford University Press).

Fisher, R. J. (1997) *Interactive Conflict Resolution* (Syracuse, NY: Syracuse University Press).

Flew, A. (1979) *A Dictionary of Philosophy* (London: Pan).

Fox, W. T. R. (1968) *The American Study of International Relations* (Columbia, SC: University of South Carolina Press).

Fussell, P. (1975) *The Great War and Modern Memory* (Oxford/New York: Oxford University Press).

Galbraith, J. K. (1981) *A Life in Our Times* (London: Andre Deutsch).

Gallie, W. B. (1952) *Peirce and Pragmatism* (Harmondsworth: Pelican).

Griffin, D. R., J. B. Cobb, M. P. Ford, P. A. Y. Gunter and P. Ochs (1993) *Founders of Constructive Postmodern Philosophy* (Albany, NY: SUNY Press).

Griffiths, M. (1999) *Fifty Key Thinkers in International Relations* (London: Routledge).

Haas, E. B. (1964) *Beyond the Nation-state* (Stanford, Calif.: Stanford University Press).

Haas, E. B. (1968) *The Uniting of Europe* (Stanford, Calif.: Stanford University Press).

Haskill, T. L. (1977) *The Emergence of Professional Social Science* (Urbana, Ill./ Chicago & London, University of Illinois Press).

Hasluck, P. (1980) *Diplomatic Witness* (Melbourne: Melbourne University Press).

Herz, J. H. (1959) *International Politics in the Atomic Age* (New York: Columbia University Press).

Herz, J. H. (1976) *The Nation-state and the Crisis of World Politics* (New York: McKay).

Hinsley, H. F. (1967) *Power and the Pursuit of Peace* (Cambridge: Cambridge University Press).

Hoffmann, S. (ed.) (1960) *Contemporary Theory in International Relations* (Englewood Cliffs, NJ: Prentice-Hall).

Honderich, T. (ed.) (1995) *The Oxford Companion to Philosophy* (Oxford: Oxford University Press).

Howard, M. (2000) *The Invention of Peace* (London: Profile Books).

Ignatieff, M. (1994) *The Needs of Strangers* (London: Vintage Books).

Jabri, V. (1996) *Discourses on Violence* (Manchester: Manchester University Press).

Kaplan, M. A. (1975) *Dissent and the State in Peace and War* (New York: Dunellen).

Kelman, H. C. (1984) 'Foreword' in M. H. Banks (ed.), *Conflict in World Society* (Brighton: Wheatsheaf) pp. xvii–xx.

Kerman, C. (1974) *Creative Tension* (Ann Arbor, Mich.: University of Michigan Press).

Keohane, R. and J. S. Nye (1972) *Transnational Relations and World Politics* (Cambridge, Mass.: Harvard University Press).

Knorr, K. and S. Verba (1961) *Theory and the International System* (Princeton, NJ: Princeton University Press).

Knorr, K. and J. N. Rosenau (1969) *Contending Approaches to International Politics* (Princeton, NJ: Princeton University Press).

Kuhn, T. S. (1962, 1970) *The Structure of Scientific Revolutions*, 1st edn and revd edn (Chicago: University of Chicago Press).

Lawler, P. (1994) *A Question of Values* (Boulder, Col./London: Lynne Rienner).

Lechte, J. (1994) *Fifty Key Contemporary Thinkers* (London: Routledge).

Lederer, K. (ed.) (1980) *Human Needs* (Cambridge, Mass.: Oelgeschlager, Gunn & Hain).

Little, R. (1984) 'The Decision Maker and Social Order: The End of Ideology or Pursuit of a Chimera?' in M. H. Banks (ed.) *Conflict in World Society* (Brighton: Wheatsheaf), pp. 78–95.

Lorenz, K. (1966) *On Aggression* (London: Methuen).

Mack, A. (1985) *Peace Research in the 1980s* (Canberra: Australian National University).

Mack, A. (1991) 'Objectives and Methods of Peace Research' in T. Woodhouse (ed.), *Peace Making in a Troubled World* (Warwick: Berg), pp. 73–106.

Mackenzie, W. J. M. (1968) *Politics and Social Science* (Harmondsworth: Pelican).

Magee, B. (1987) *The Great Philosophers* (Oxford: Oxford University Press).

Manuel, F. E and F. P. Manuel (1979) *Utopian Thought in the Western World* (Oxford: Basil Blackwell).

Meehan, E. J. (1969) *Value Judgement and Social Science* (Homewood, Ill.: Dorsey).

Mitchell, C. R. and M. H. Banks (1996) *Handbook of Conflict Resolution: The Analytical Problem-solving Approach* (London: Pinter).

Morgenthau, H. (1948) *Politics Among Nations* (New York: Knopf).

Morgenthau, H. (1971) *Politics in the Twentieth Century*, revd edn (Chicago/London: University of Chicago Press).

Myrdal, G. (1969) *Objectivity in Social Research* (New York: Pantheon).

Northedge, F. S. (1976) *The International Political System* (London: Faber & Faber).

Olsen, W. C. and A. J. R. Groom (1991) *International Relations Then and Now* (London: HarperCollins).

Pemberton, G. (1991) 'A Matter of Independence', *Canberra Times*, 17 August.

Platig, E. R. (1966) *International Relations Research* (Santa Barbara, Calif.: Clio).

Rogers, P. (2000) *Losing Control: Global Security in the Twenty-first Century* (London: Pluto).

Rosenau, J. N. (1961) *International Politics and Foreign Policy* (New York: Free Press).

Rosenau, J. N. (1969a) *International Politics and Foreign Policy*, rev. edn (New York: Free Press).

Rosenau, J. N. (1969b) *The Scientific Study of Foreign Policy* (New York: Free Press).

Rosenau, J. N. (1990) *Turbulence in World Politics* (Princeton, NJ: Princeton University Press).

Russett, B. M. (1967) *International Regions and the International System* (Chicago: Rand McNally).

Ryan, A. (1991) 'A Society of Nations?', *Times Literary Supplement*, 22 March, pp. 5–6.

Sandole, D. J. (1985) 'Textbooks' in M. Light and A. J. R. Groom (eds), *International Relations: A Handbook of Current Theory* (London: Pinter).

Saunders, H. H. (1990) 'Comment' in Burton, *Conflict: Resolution and Provention*, back cover.

Schulzinger, R. (1984) *The Wise Men of Foreign Affairs: The History of the Council on Foreign Relations* (New York: Columbia University Press).

Schwarzenberger, G. (1964) *Power Politics*, 3rd edn (London: Stevens).

Simon, H. A. (1957) *Administrative Behavior* (New York: Free Press).

Singer, J. D. (1968) *Quantitative International Politics*, (New York: Free Press).

Singer, J. D. (1970) 'International Values, National Interests and Political Development in the International System', *Studies in Comparative International Development*, vol. 6, no. 9.

Singer, J. D. and M. Small (1972) *Wages of War 1815–1965* (New York: Wiley).

Sites, P. M. (1974) *Control: The Basis of Social Order* (New York: Dunellen).

Smith, S. (1987) 'The Development of International Relations as a Social Science', *Millennium*, vol. 16, no. 2 (Summer), pp. 189–206.

Snyder, R., H. W. Bruck and B. Sapin (1962) *Foreign Policy, Decision Making* (New York: Free Press).

Stewart, M. (1972) *Keynes and After*, 2nd edn (Harmondsworth: Pelican).

Strange, S. (1989) 'I Never Meant to Be an Academic' in J. Kruzel and J. N. Rosenau (eds), *Journeys Through World Politics* (Lexington, Mass. & Toronto: D. C. Heath & Co.).

Tanter, R. and R. H. Ullman (eds) (1972) *Theory and Policy in International Relations* (Princeton, NJ: Princeton University Press).

Thompson, E. P. (1994) *Persons and Polemics: Historical Essays* (London: Merlin).

Thornley, A. W. (1979) 'John W. Burton 1875–1970' in *Australian Dictionary of Biography*, vol. 7 (Melbourne: Melbourne University Press).

Tidwell, A. C. (1998) *Conflict Resolved? A Critical Assessment of Conflict Resolution* (London: Pinter).

Vasquez, J. (1983) *The Power of Power Politics* (London: Pinter).

Vernon, R. (1972) *Sovereignty at Bay* (Harmondsworth: Pelican).

Walzer, M. (1977) *Just and Unjust Wars* (New York: Basic Books).

Wight, M. (1979a) *Power Politics* (Harmondsworth: Pelican).

Wight, M. (1979b) *Systems of States* (Leicester: Leicester University Press).

Wilson, E. O. (1973) *Sociobiology: The New Synthesis* (Cambridge, Mass.: Harvard University Press).

Wilson, E. O. (1998) *Consilience: The Unity of Knowledge* (London: Abacus).

Wright, Q. (1955) *The Study of International Relations* (New York: Appleton Century Crofts).

Young, O. R. (1968) *Systems of Political Science* (New York: Prentice-Hall).

Young, O. R. (1969) 'Professor Russett: Industrious Tailor to a Naked Emperor', *World Politics* (April).

Index